EDWARD DOUGLASS WHITE

Southern Biography Series

William J. Cooper, Jr., Editor

Chief Justice Edward Douglass White.

EDWARD DOUGLASS WHITE

Defender of the Conservative Faith

Robert B. Highsaw

Louisiana State University Press
Baton Rouge and London

Designer: Patricia Douglas Crowder
Typeface: VIP Palatino
Typesetter: LSU Press

LIBRARY OF CONGRESS CATALOGING IN PUBLICATION DATA

Highsaw, Robert Baker, 1917–
    Edward Douglass White, defender of the conservative
faith.

    (Southern biography series)
    Bibliography: p.
    Includes index.
    1. White, Edward Douglass, 1845–1921.   2. Judges—
United States—Biography.   I. Title.   II. Series.
KF8745.W5H53   347.73'2634 [B]   80–17874
ISBN 0–8071–0753–0

CONTENTS

ILLUSTRATIONS

Frontispiece
Chief Justice Edward Douglass White

Following page 100
Chief Justice White, 1910
The White family house near Thibodaux, Louisiana
The Fuller Court, 1898
The White Court, *ca.* 1912–1914
White administering the oath of office to Woodrow Wilson
White reviewing a parade
Statue in the plaza of the Louisiana State Supreme Court building

PREFACE

As long ago as the June 12, 1937, issue of *Nation*, Dean Charles E. Clarke of the School of Law at Yale University wrote that there is "the possibility of brilliant promise" in the study of the development of constitutional doctrines of our public law in terms of the personalities of the individual justices. In the intervening decades many judicial biographies have been written which have undertaken to fulfill this promise. Some of these volumes have used the obvious historical and chronological approach, excellent when a large volume of private papers, the correspondence of a lifetime, and perhaps some surviving acquaintances are available. Others, though treating biographical materials in an orderly fashion, have focused largely upon the development of constitutional doctrines and centered around case analysis. A third group of judicial biographies has emphasized methodological techniques, including scaling of opinions, study of the allocation of decision-making within the Supreme Court of the United States, and the relation of public law to contemporary values. Each of these approaches has been valid, and each has offered the reader valuable insights and perceptions.

In general this judicial biography of Chief Justice Edward Douglass White follows the second type of organization and stresses the development and application of his constitutional doctrines, such as dual federalism of the commerce and taxing powers, the Insular Doctrine, and the rule of reason applied in the *Anti-Trust* cases of the first part of this century. The study arranges White's constitutional thought in chronological order within various subject matter categories and pays considerable attention to his approach to the judicial process. It is not intended, however, to be a history of the Fuller and White Courts, nor does it make any attempt to scale White's opinions in relation to those of the twenty other members of the Court who sat with him on the bench between 1894 and 1921. My focus is upon the constitutional thought of Edward White, although opinions delivered by other members of the Court must be considered.

The work of the Supreme Court of the United States has provided a remarkable thread of continuity throughout the history of the American republic. There are few, though some, abrupt departures from the known and accepted, and some of the departures were taken by White, whose respect for *stare decisis* was nonetheless great. The assumption upon which this judicial biography is based is simple: that as an associate justice of the Court and then its ninth chief justice, Edward White's constitutional philosophy and his expression of it in majority, concurring, and dissenting opinions is a useful study in American public law. He was a member of the Court for twenty-seven years and throughout this period demonstrated a consistency of approach to constitutional law that left its imprint upon constitutional interpretation. It is true that some of his views and his doctrines are no longer followed by the Supreme Court and may be classified as legal artifacts, but study of them is essential to an understanding of how the Court developed a large body of constitutional law, following at one time a given line of thought and, as time passed and the membership of the Court changed, pursuing different constitutional thought and doctrines. The judicial revolution of 1937 and the ensuing decades of the Court's history are meaningless unless we know what happened fifty or so years earlier. This statement is not to say that White's judicial career was largely negative, for it was not. It is a fact, however, that he participated in the construction of a system of implied limitations upon express constitutional powers that came to fruition in the early years of Franklin D. Roosevelt's New Deal.

A familiar, even trite, argument contends that the individual justices who comprise the Supreme Court of the United States at any given time are affected by the environment of which they are a part and in which they function. Several chapters of this study, therefore, have been devoted to the early years, legal training, and public career of Edward

Douglass White. The story of these years and later of his tenure on the Court is unfortunately incomplete. With but few exceptions the papers composing his personal files were destroyed shortly after his death because, unlike many other public figures, White did not choose to place his papers with the Library of Congress. Although his opinions are readily available in volumes 154–256 of the *United States Supreme Court Reports*, personal papers which flesh out a man's personality are another matter. I have resorted to scattered letters to and from White in other collections in order to partially fill this gap. Thus, a number of letters were located in the Olney, Taft, Roosevelt, and Wilson collections in the Library of Congress. Additional letters were found in the archives of the Archdiocese of Baltimore, the Special Collections Division of the University Library, Georgetown University, and the Edward Douglass White Memorial, Thibodaux, Louisiana.

I am grateful to the University of Alabama for my current appointment as University Professor, which gave me the free periods of time necessary for sustained research and case analysis. Appreciation is due to many persons who assisted in locating some of the White correspondence and especially to the Reverend John J. Tierney, archivist, Archdiocese of Baltimore, and Jon Reynolds, university archivist, Georgetown University, who gave permission to use letters from their respective collections. I express appreciation to Gail Galloway, curator, and Susanne Owens, assistant curator, Supreme Court of the United States; Jerry L. Kearns, head, Reference Section, Prints and Photographs Division, Library of Congress; Jim Silverberg, director, Publications and Public Relations, Nicholls State University, Thibodaux, Louisiana; and Tony Vidacovich, staff photographer, New Orleans *Times-Picayune*. Each provided me assistance in locating and securing photographs for this volume.

My wife, Mary Wagner Highsaw, read the various drafts of the study and encouraged me in its preparation. I am indebted to my colleagues, Daniel W. Pound and William H. Stewart, Jr., for their critical reading of the manuscript. Eunice Payne reviewed the study and made many helpful suggestions. Kim Ingram, formerly of the staff of the Bureau of Public Administration, gathered some of the information related to White's years in the Senate. Sue Freeman and Paula Franks typed the study in its several revisions. Jean Dee Rosene prepared the manuscript in its final form. I wish also to express gratitude to my editor at the Louisiana State University Press, Judy Bailey, whose queries and comments were both pertinent and constructive. Although I thank them all, errors of fact as well as errors of interpretation are my responsibility.

EDWARD DOUGLASS WHITE

I

White and American Public Law

A recurring problem in western political thought and practice has been the issue of sovereignty. Three centuries ago the French theorist Jean Bodin formulated the concept in his definition of the state and defined it in these terms: "Sovereignty is supreme power over citizens and subjects, unrestrained by the laws." Its characteristic feature is the making of laws, the sovereign's will being the ultimate source of the law of the land. "Sovereignty," as William A. Dunning stated it, "is a political fact, consisting only in the possession and exercise *of supreme power.*" [1] The doctrine may be understood in terms of internal supremacy and external independence.

Because the system of government created by the American Constitution of 1789 was and still is complicated, the issue of sovereignty became one of the more controversial problems of the new Republic, one not completely settled even today. [2] So far as internal supremacy is concerned, the Constitution does extreme violence to sovereignty because it divides and subdivides political power. Our fundamental law thus apportions power, on a territorial basis, between the federal government and the fifty states and, on a functional basis, between the executive, the legislative, and the judicial branches of the central government. It also

1. Jean Bodin, *De Republica Sex*, Lib. I, Ch. 1, quoted in Francis W. Coker, *Readings in Political Philosophy* (Rev. ed.; New York: Macmillan, 1938), 374. William A. Dunning, *A History of Political Theories: From Luther to Montesquieu* (New York: Macmillan, 1905), 100, my italics.
2. See *Nixon v. United States*, 418 U.S. 683 (1974).

precludes some powers so that neither the federal nor the state governments may exercise them. The net result is to create areas of activity in which only the federal government may exercise authority, to provide a broad area of state authority commonly called the police power of the state, and to leave other areas, often undefined, where neither federal nor state governments may act.[3] The effect of the Constitution is to tear the Bodinian concept of internal sovereignty asunder, casting the splintered parts to the four winds. A major problem of American government has always been to reintegrate the fragments of sovereignty and at the same time to provide latitude for individual liberties on which no government may trespass.

If American political leadership in the eighteenth and early nineteenth centuries was strongly affected by social contract theory, it was also practical. This pragmatism was reflected early in the Republic's life by the establishment of judicial review, a doctrine influenced both by concepts of natural law and by the common law tradition that certain fundamental rules of law cannot be altered even by Parliament. Every American university student having no more than a nodding acquaintanceship with American constitutional history has read how Chief Justice John Marshall grafted onto the Constitution the doctrine of judicial review in *Marbury* v. *Madison*.[4] Under the *Marbury* obiter dicta the United States Supreme Court took its first great leap toward establishment of the Court as the umpire of the national government and ultimately of the federal system. Since 1803 many battles have raged around the doctrine, the Court at times extending its power and at other times holding steady, rarely if ever retreating from its basic position. Hardly anyone today questions the legitimacy of the Supreme Court as the final arbiter in the American system of government. Members of the Court come and go, some attaining greater stature than others, but the Court's role in gathering together the scattered strands of sovereignty is firmly established.

American scholarship has produced a voluminous literature in both books and periodicals about members of the Court. Some justices and

3. The first ten amendments and the Fourteenth Amendment, as interpreted, are illustrations.

4. See Edward S. Corwin, "The 'Higher Law' Background of American Constitutional Law," *Harvard Law Review*, XLII (1928–29), 149, 365, and Theodore F. T. Plucknett, "Bonham's Case and Judicial Review," *Harvard Law Review*, XL (1926), 30; *Marbury* v. *Madison*, 1 Cranch 137 (1803).

chief justices are ornaments of American history. John Marshall, Roger B. Taney, Oliver Wendell Holmes, Harlan F. Stone, Louis D. Brandeis, and Benjamin N. Cardozo rank prominently in the pantheon of American public law. A few, such as Chief Justice Morrison R. Waite and Justice Samuel F. Miller, occupy lesser niches. More are virtually unrecognized except for specific cases and have receded into an ever darkening past, appearing occasionally in the footnotes of legal periodicals, constitutional history, or brief sketches of Supreme Court justices.

Among this latter group of Court members is Edward Douglass White, who served as an associate justice from 1894 until 1910 and as chief justice from 1910 until his death in 1921. Causes for his relative obscurity are not hard to find. White was no juristic stylist or felicitous phrasemaker as was Justice Oliver Wendell Holmes. He attracted no attention by using a particular methodology as did the more empirical Justice Brandeis, and he came to the Court with no reputation as a judicial philosopher as did Justice Cardozo. White's prior judicial experience was limited, and his only federal experience before his appointment had been that of United States Senator from Louisiana since 1891. He was not an exponent of free and unlimited currency or silver. He was neither wealthy nor poverty stricken. Edward White was, in short, an unknown quantity in 1894 when he was nominated associate justice.

Yet his tenure as justice and then chief justice was long, stretching over twenty-seven years. These years were important ones for the Republic. The western frontier, so influential in American history, had been virtually closed by 1894. The "farm problem" had already made its first appearance as an issue and a force in American politics. Economic and industrial growth was tremendous, bringing with it monopoly capitalism, the creation of a distinct laboring class, and the consequent emergence of labor unions. The Spanish-American War left the nation with imperialistic holdings in the Caribbean and the Far East. World War I catapulted the nation, more or less unwillingly, into the vortex of world politics. These developments were increasingly the results of what Daniel J. Boorstin has characterized as the "Republic of Technology." Indeed, after 1865 the nation's life was characterized by technological revolutions. Some were small and little noticed. Others were large and significant, such as the widespread use of the reaper, the development of the assembly line in meat packing, or the refinement of the internal combustion engine. Large cities developed where there had been none, and older urban areas doubled and tripled in size. Improved transportation systems carried people and goods, while new technologies in communication transmitted ideas, beliefs, and faiths into the minds of people in cities and on farms. Most of the major industries of the first half of this century were, in fact, based upon the inventions and technologies of the nineteenth century. Technological change was the rule, not the exception. With it came a concept of inevitable progress that touched the lives of countless men and women. The geographical frontier had vanished, but new horizons of human aspiration and experience opened. "A new democratic world," writes Boorstin, "was being created and was being discovered by Americans wherever they lived." [5] In this new world, at the beginning of White's tenure on the Court, rural discontent manifested itself in third parties which in turn coalesced into the Populist Movement. At the end of his service, the First Amendment rights were seriously endangered by Attorney General A. Mitchell Palmer's "red hunt" and legislation aimed at allegedly subversive activities.

Throughout this period the Supreme Court had an essential role as "Keepers of the Covenant," a role in which the Court filled a felt need for human roots and provided "the great fact which changeth not and therefore abideth." [6] Much of the Court's attention, however revered an institution it might have been, was devoted to invalidating new legislation, often legislation enacted by a state legislature. The Court's role began to be seen as that of a body which set limitations on public action regulating economic activity, a trend that would continue until the late 1930s. This role would, however, demand some flexibility in determining the status of overseas possessions.

Edward White, both as associate justice and as chief justice, participated significantly in molding the new sovereignty of the Supreme Court. His influence over the members of the Court was great, but not surprising. More than some members of the Court, White was attuned to the prevailing conservative ideology of the day. Part of his intellectual equip-

5. Daniel J. Boorstin, *The Americans: The Democratic Experience* (New York: Random House, 1973), ix.
6. Max Lerner, *America as a Civilization: Life and Thought in the United States* (New York: Simon & Schuster, 1957), 442.

ment was a deep veneration for precedent and the basic concepts of limited governmental activity or defined spheres of power in which national and state governments went their separate ways. If conservatism demands the preservation of existing traditions and institutions, if it requires that these traditions and institutions operate without change until change is demonstrably better than the present, White was a conservative. This kind of convervatism was reflected in the decisions of both the Fuller Court, of which White was a member, and, later, the White Court itself. It is a matter of historical record that the Court in this period "handed down a good many decisions in key areas that were to be overruled later. . . . All were characteristic of the era when the Court was in tune with the country's mood for progress under the slightly regulated leadership of its enterprising businessmen."[7]

By mirroring so well the conservative world of the first decades of this century, Edward White became a defender of the conservative faith. Ironically, his career on the Court was marked at the beginning by a dissent supporting the "liberal" income tax law of 1894, while his last opinion was a dissent against the validity of a federal statute limiting expenditures in a senatorial campaign as applied to a primary election.[8] He delivered other dissents, but in the twenty-six years between *Pollock* and *Newberry*, White made a significant impact upon American public law.

Writing a generation ago Felix Frankfurter commented that "the history of the Supreme Court is not the history of an abstraction, but the analysis of individuals acting as a Court who make decisions and lay down rules and of other individuals, their successors, who refine, modify, and sometimes even overrule the decisions of their predecessors, reinterpreting and transmuting their doctrines. In law, also, men make a difference. . . . There is no inevitability except as men make it." Two decades later, reviewing a roster of seventy-five members of the Court, Frankfurter found that it would be a "surprising judgment" of history that would exclude "Marshall, William Johnson, Story, Field, Bradley, White

---

7. Morris L. Ernst, *The Great Reversals: Tales of the Supreme Court* (New York: Waybright & Talley, 1973), 83.

8. *Pollock* v. *Farmers' Loan and Trust Company*, 157 U.S. 429, 158 U.S. 601 (1895); *Newberry* v. *United States*, 256 U.S. 232 (1921).

(despite his question-begging verbosities), Holmes, Hughes, Brandeis, and Cardozo in the roster of distinction among our seventy-five."[9]

When Edward White died in 1921, a public career covering almost half a century came to an end. Twenty-seven of those years had been spent upon the bench of the Supreme Court of the United States, sixteen as an associate justice and eleven as chief justice, constituting one of the longer tenures in the history of the Court. The critical period covered by the span of so many years began in the last decade of one century and carried over into the third of the next century, his tenure embracing two wars and a period of social and economic adjustment in our ways of government. White's reputation must largely rest, however, not so much upon his grasp of the problems of the day and the molding of constitutional law to meet those problems as upon a patience and fullness of legal knowledge, an extraordinary ability to weave intricate masses of detail and divergent systems of law into a coherent whole, a true and intense patriotism, and a high sense of judicial responsibility.

Throughout his life Edward White was a member of some social, economic, political, or institutional elite, first in terms of the family into which he was born, then as a Louisiana planter-lawyer-politician, and finally as associate justice and chief justice of the Supreme Court. Any elite socializes its members to its own beliefs and shapes qualities of mind and character as well as predispositions and attitudes. An elite depends for its survival on the continuance of the environment within which it functions, and it conveys to its members the notion that it is theirs to discover and disseminate large and important things. Leadership in government is sometimes as much a duty of the member of an elite as a right.

Although the Civil War destroyed the South's peculiar institution and reduced state and local governments in the region to a shambles for more than a decade, southern elites regained control by 1878 and exerted profound influence even after the advent of populism in the South. Edward White was well-educated in the civil and common law, even though he was never awarded an earned degree, but less knowledgeable on other subjects. With his family, political, and legal background, no evidence suggests, as it did in Holmes's dissents, that he ever seriously

9. Felix Frankfurter, *Mr. Justice Holmes and the Supreme Court* (Cambridge: Harvard University Press, 1938), 8–9; Felix Frankfurter, "The Supreme Court in the Mirror of Justices," *University of Pennsylvania Law Review*, CV (1957), 783.

questioned the economic dogma of the day and its concepts of social Darwinism. No less than Mr. Justice George Sutherland, who would come to the Court in 1922, White lived in what was essentially a conservative world. There is no evidence that this large, bearish, but personable man was less zealous than most of his colleagues, first in the Senate of the United States and then on the Court, to maintain a monopoly capitalism phrased in laissez-faire terms such as liberty of contract. But why should he have questioned them? He was, like all of us, socialized in the prevailing attitudes of his day.

Although he never articulated elitism in so many words, implicit in his opinions was a belief that the masses of people should not decide public policy. His thought also indicates a set of shared beliefs to which he was educated that included limited governmental action under the control of local elites, which resulted from dual federalism; individual freedom of action more in the area of economics than in personal liberties; and the sanctity of private property. The Court existed to protect these values. White had reached the highest office of his profession and, no less than others before and after him, was satisfied to maintain a system which had been so generous to him. Innovation and change rarely find a warm welcome with those who have done well under the old ideology. There would be change, but it would be the change of the law, moving by analogical reasoning in an incremental fashion from one point to another.

As chief justice and administrator of the Court, White was effective until the last few years of his tenure, when the ills and infirmities of his age and the volume of actions arising out of World War I overtook him. White minimized conflict on the Court and kept it under control, aided by his sensitivity to interpersonal relationships. He maintained a satisfactory degree of cohesion in the Court, which, under him, functioned more as a collective body than it did under Chief Justice Melville W. Fuller, but perhaps less so than under his successor, William Howard Taft. He became expert in ruling on procedural points, handling opinions on jurisdictional and procedural issues, and explaining why the Court should not hear a case. Once the Court did hear arguments in a suit, White stated prior to the oral arguments what questions he expected to ask and held counsel responsible for answering them in the oral arguments. Production of opinions, which is one way of measuring the

Court's efforts, was high at the beginning of his chief justiceship, and the backlog of cases declined. Toward the end of his tenure, however, the number of cases began to clog the docket once more, and the frequency of dissents increased, for Brandeis, John H. Clarke, and Holmes were not always wedded to old ideas and concepts.

Few men have attained so high a position in public life with so few obstacles to hurdle or setbacks along the path. His early success and elevation to the Supreme Court probably lay in the fact that, although he was far from a mediocrity, he was not such an outstanding man that he aroused any considerable opposition. His years as a politician and lawyer in Louisiana were not noted for the championing of any markedly controversial causes in the public interest, with the possible exception of the Louisiana lottery. A casual examination might indicate that in the lottery struggle he played the role of a crusader risking his future to destroy a great machine. A closer examination of the facts, however, shows that, although it was not evident on the surface, at the time Edward White entered the fight, the lottery was already on its way out.[10] It had lost much of its leadership and had as its chief foe Francis R. T. Nicholls. The outcome of the fight, of course, may not have been any more apparent to White than to the public at large. The lottery struggle was insignificant as far as any long term social or economic effects were concerned because it was a moral and political issue divorced from the larger problems of the day.

Those persons who knew White have testified to the personal attractiveness of the man. This factor enabled him to influence other members of the Court and was a strong element in his impact upon that tribunal. Few members of the Court have exercised so great a power of judicial persuasion over their colleagues as did White, and on two notable occasions, he translated his minority views into those of the majority: first, with the application of the rule of reason to the Sherman Anti-Trust Act after much difference of opinion among the members of the Court; and second, only four years after he delivered his concurring opinion in *Downes* v. *Bidwell*, when the distinction in applying constitutional guaranties to territories acquired and belonging to the nation and territories subsequently incorporated by Congress into the Union was announced

10. See *Stone* v. *Mississippi*, 101 U.S. 814 (1880).

as the law of the land.[11] Moreover, each of these doctrines became law
without definition of either substantive terms or procedures so that the
position of the Supreme Court in the new sovereignty was enhanced.

With his influence increased by his promotion to the post of chief
justice, White's latter years were marked by continued and perhaps initially greater powers of suasion. Possibly because of his kindly and con-
siderate spirit, his judicial opinions, though strong in advocacy, did not
create the animosity that followed those of some of his colleagues, and
only rarely, however intensely felt his ideas were, did he lash out with
a biting pen to excoriate what seemed to him judicial heresies. Oddly
enough, almost his first opinion on the bench, his dissent in the *Income
Tax* case, formed one of the few exceptions.[12]

As a lawyer, White was greatly influenced by his knowledge of the
civil as well as the common law and by his respect for the traditions of
law. His familiarity with the civil law occasionally made him distinctive,
and his opinions injected into American public law the concept of dual
jurisdiction embodied in medieval political thought, where church and
state held dominance over the same territory. His education, too, may
have left traces in our public law of Jesuit political thought: the "rule of
reason" and the terms *inherent powers* and *inherent limitations*, for example.[13] As applied to the Supreme Court, his respect for legal traditions
resulted in the belief that the Court could discharge its functions free
from the bickerings of factions and the animosities of parties only by the
stability of its teachings and by the aura of permanence surrounding
them.

Moreover, his reverence for *stare decisis* produced a legalistic approach
in which there was an almost total absence of emotional concern for the
results of his decisions. This quality is sometimes praised as admirable
in a judge, indicating a cold and impartial analysis of the issue at hand.
A noted English jurist, famed for his impartiality, once grew tired of
hearing this supposed trait in himself held up for applause and demolished it with the statement that the only impartial person is one who
knows nothing of either side of a question. White's approach may not

11. *Downes* v. *Bidwell*, 182 U.S. 244 (1901).
12. *Pollock* v. *Farmers' Loan and Trust Company*, 157 U.S. 429 (1895), 158 U.S. 601 (1895).
13. Edward S. Corwin, *The Twilight of the Supreme Court* (New Haven: Yale University
Press, 1934), 24.

have been so much the result of a cold and impartial analysis as of his immersion in the dogma of the law and the fact that he had not thought long about other elements involved. His approach could sometimes result in ridiculous situations as it did in *Weems* v. *United States,* where he was willing to permit a man to serve a sentence with almost life-long penalties for a petty crime.[14]

As a judicial statesman, White was moved by an innate conservatism that looked upon the American constitutional system as a model for a well-ordered society that must be preserved. He was desirous of protecting the states from the extension of national power, probably influenced by his experiences during the turbulent years of carpetbag government in Louisiana. He opposed the expansion of national power whenever it appeared to him that such expansion would encroach upon the police power of the states, but if it appeared that there was no such issue involved, White was sympathetic to the exercise of national authority. These views led to the so-called doctrine of dual federalism whereby White envisioned the national government and the states operating each within well-defined spheres of authority. The practical application of this doctrine, however, often resulted in zones within which no government could act.

The chief difficulty with White's concept of dual federalism was that it ran contrary to many of the trends of the time. All the way through, he was fighting a brilliant rearguard action to preserve a construct of the American constitutional system that was static and ultimately doomed. Scarcely a year after his death, in the case of *Stafford* v. *Wallace,* the Court began a movement that culminated in the constitutional revolution of 1937 and ultimately destroyed the doctrine of dual federalism. How well White fought, though, is indicated by the fact that he delayed this development until it was long overdue. The Court had become so thoroughly impregnated with the concept that it formed the basis for striking down the Child Labor Act of 1918, and although Chief Justice White did not write the majority opinion in this case, his doctrine was the influencing factor.[15]

The application of the rule of reason in the interpretation of the Sher-

14. *Weems* v. *United States,* 217 U.S. 349 (1910).
15. *Stafford* v. *Wallace,* 258 U.S. 495, 518–19 (1922); *Hammer* v. *Dagenhart,* 247 U.S. 251 (1918), expressly overruled by *United States* v. *Darby Lumber Co.,* 312 U.S. 100 (1941).

man Anti-Trust Act also reflects a conservative approach, but it has fared better than the doctrine of dual federalism. The rule of reason has taken its place along side other leading constitutional theories. Its effect was to weaken the act as a preventive of monopoly and to remove some of the fear created by passage of the Sherman Act, although this consequence was not due so much to the rule itself as to the attitude of the courts. Whatever the reason for its failure, the judicial application of the act resulted in a reversal of its purpose, turning it into a weapon against labor, something that Congress had never intended. The act was applied to the Danbury Hatters during White's presence on the Court, and in the 1930s it was used by local courts involved in adjudicating sit-down strikes.

Certainly the most politic as well as pragmatic of White's constitutional theories is the Insular Doctrine. The far-reaching effects of this series of cases became apparent only with the growth of international tension and the approach of World War II, because the Insular Doctrine freed Congress from the restrictive provisions of the Constitution unless the acquired territory had been incorporated. At the time of the cases, one of the problems which worried White most was the national government's lack of legal power to dispose of any of these territories if they were held a part of the United States and their peoples were held to be citizens of this country. The wisdom of this view has been demonstrated in American relations with the Philippine Islands, the Insular Doctrine enabling the United States to keep its promise to the people of that territory by granting them the independence they desired. White's formulation of the concept of "incorporated" and "unincorporated" territories owes something to his Jesuit schooling and his civil law background.

Edward White's failure to depart from legalistic habit and come directly to grips with the issues created by monopoly capitalism may have resulted from his lack of training in economics and political science. He remained a lawyer to the end of his days, and the Supreme Court, where questions of constitutional authority are actually issues of political power, is seldom in need of a pure lawyer. Nevertheless, White's tenure on the Court was significant. He was greatly helpful in the development of the Interstate Commerce Act, and his decisions in the area of administrative law began the formulation of those principles that kept the Court from destroying the administrative process by judicial regulation. White also plainly comprehended the responsibility any justice must bear. He saw the danger that arises from constantly resorting to the Constitution to prevent the accomplishment of social objectives that arouse opposition; he feared the resulting impression that the Constitution, with the Supreme Court as its interpreter, is but a barrier to progress. Upon whom, he asked the American bar, "does the duty more clearly rest to modify and correct this evil than upon members of our profession?" [16] White's influence was extensive, and the very consistency of his approach distinguished his theories from the aimless wanderings of the Court in his era. It was his misfortune, and perhaps the nation's as well, that his time had fallen prey to ills that could not be resolved by the dialectic of the law he so admired.

16. "Response of the Late Chief Justice White to Toast at the Annual Banquet of the American Bar Association at Washington, October 22, 1914," *American Bar Association Journal*, VII (1921), 342.

II

The Formative Years

T he White family most probably emigrated to the American colonies in the first half of the eighteenth century, in the person of James White, an Irishman who came to Pennsylvania, where he married, lived, and died. James White's wife was Anne Willcox, the daughter of Thomas Willcox, who appears on the tax lists of Concord Township, Delaware County, Pennsylvania (now the state of Delaware) in 1725. A devout Catholic, White was "one of the founders of the first Catholic church in Philadelphia, St. Mary's, and is buried in that churchyard." Edward White, proud of his Irish ancestry, once remarked, "You can kick a White out of every sod in Ireland."[1]

But James White was more than a simple Irish immigrant. He showed his interest in business and public affairs by being among those who

---

1. A formal biography of Edward Douglass White is as yet unpublished, although a number of published sketches are useful. See "Edward Douglass White Memorial Issue," *Loyola Law Journal*, VII (1926), "Chief Justice White and His Decisions," *Reports of the Louisiana Bar Association*, XXIV (1923), 151–65, Henry P. Dart, Sr., Harry M. Daugherty, William Howard Taft, and others, *Proceedings of the Bar and Officers of the Supreme Court of the United States in Memory of Edward Douglass White*, Washington, December 17, 1921, hereinafter cited as *Proceedings*, Hugh E. Fegin, "Edward Douglass White, Jurist and Statesman," *Georgetown Law Journal*, XIV (1925), 1–21, and XV (1926), 148–68, Ralph H. Jesse, "Chief Justice White," *American Law Review*, XLV (1911), 321–26, Samuel H. Mann, "Chief Justice White," *American Law Review*, LX (1926), 620–37, *An Address* delivered by Henry P. Dart, Sr., October 3, 1921, before the Louisiana Bar Association, New Orleans. These facts were extracted from an address given by Lewis C. Cassidy before the Catholic Alumni Society, Philadelphia, Pa., January 7, 1927; Edward Douglass White speaking to Paul Bakewell, Dean, University of St. Louis School of Law; John W. Davis to Robert B. Highsaw, August 27, 1942.

signed the Non-Importation Agreement of 1765.[2] Although his accumu-
lation of wealth was not large, he was able to bequeath to his son, James
White, Jr., the sum of four hundred pounds and to create a small en-
dowment for a Catholic school.

James White, Jr., born in 1749, was unlike his father. His life reveals
the dissatisfaction and restlessness of a person who is always seeking a
contentment that never materializes. He completed his early education
under the supervision of the Jesuits of Saint Inigoe's in Maryland, and
later his father sent him to Saint Omer's in France. There he was graduated in "the same class with Daniel O'Connell," an outstanding orator
and Irish political leader following the 1801 Acts of Union. In due course
James White returned to Philadelphia and became a "Doctor of Physick."
Although no record of a degree can be found, he studied medicine for a
time at the University of Pennsylvania. This White's improvident habits
and restless soul, however, made it impossible for him to pursue a normal career for long. He soon ran through his inheritance, which, besides
the four hundred pounds, included all his father's law books and his
slave, Cloe.[3] He sold what was left and started on a wandering path. In
succession, he joined his mother's relatives in North Carolina, served
a short enlistment with Nathanael Greene's Continentals, and made
profits from the manufacture of cannons for Washington's army.

The year 1775 found him and his wife Mary at the frontier post of
Nashville, Tennessee, where in the same year the first Edward Douglass
White was born. Here James White again changed professions, this time
to that of lawyer, and embarked upon an occupation later followed by
many Americans of Irish ancestry: in short, he became a politician. He
was "the first delegate to Congress from the new territory and was one
of the active participants in framing the Tennessee Constitution."[4]

This activity did not confine to one spot the wandering grandfather
of a future chief justice. His meandering nature was not yet satisfied,
and Spanish Louisiana beckoned to this doctor, soldier, manufacturer,
lawyer, and politician. The exact reason for his abandonment of a fertile

2. Cassidy, address, 2.
3. "Dr. James White: Pioneer, Politician, and Lawyer (1749–1809)," *Tennessee Historical
Magazine*, I (December, 1915), 282, 284, Knoxville *Sunday Journal*, June 7, 1929; White to
Bakewell.
4. White to Bakewell.

political field in Tennessee is not clear. There were rumors at the time that James White had become an agent in the pay of the Spanish monarch. As far back as August, 1786, White had called on Don Diego Gardoqui, the Spanish minister to the United States, and told him that the western people were disgruntled by Congress's surrender of the navigation of the Mississippi River and that Spain might find these people prepared to declare their independence and to accept Spanish protection in return for the opening of the Mississippi to their trade.[5]

James White may have seen a land of promise in Louisiana, or perhaps his old vague restlessness may have urged him to move. Whatever the reason, he chose an opportune moment for going to Louisiana. At first the advantages were largely economic, the result of sugar planting, but within a few years, the Louisiana Purchase gave rise to a number of political opportunities. White was in a position to exploit these happy circumstances. Although he and his family were not Creoles, that is, not of Spanish or French descent born in the Louisiana region, they were Catholics who had the advantage of having moved to Louisiana before the purchase by President Thomas Jefferson. The first Edward D. White and his son, the future chief justice, were accepted by the wealthy, propertied, and politically important circle of Creoles. In fact, the younger White identified himself strongly with the Creoles and, as long as he was in New Orleans, lived in the French Quarter.

Soon after the purchase, Jefferson recommended to Governor William C. C. Claiborne that the local administration be thoroughly Americanized. One of the results of his recommendation was the appointment in 1803 of James White to a judgeship of the Attakapas District. In this position White materially aided in the development of the territory and quickly gained the confidence of the people.[6]

The fortunate political position of the Whites was enhanced by the approval of the rapidly increasing population of the Louisiana Territory. James's son, Edward White, Sr., made the most of these opportunities. Born in Maury County, Tennessee, in 1775, Edward moved with his family to Saint Martin Parish, Louisiana, in 1799. He attended the common

5. Thomas P. Abernethy, *From Frontier to Plantation in Tennessee: A Study in Frontier Democracy* (Chapel Hill: University of North Carolina Press, 1932), 92–93.
6. Alcée Fortier, *History of Louisiana* (4 vols.; New York: Goupil, 1904), II, 639; Dart in *Proceedings*, 13.

schools in the parish and, taking the inheritance left him by James White, went back to Tennessee, entered college, and graduated from the University of Nashville.[7] Returning to Louisiana, he studied law under Alexander Porter and began practice in Donaldsonville. In 1825, he went to New Orleans, where he became an associate judge of the city court. Four years later he succeeded Edward Livingstone in the United States House of Representatives and served in the Twenty-first, Twenty-second, and Twenty-third Congresses. One noteworthy incident marked his tenure there. The House had instructed its Judiciary Committee to inquire into the desirability of repealing Section 25 of the Judiciary Act. This inquiry was part of an effort to deprive the United States Supreme Court of power to review state laws. William Davis of South Carolina reported for the majority in favor of repeal on January 24, 1831, while James Buchanan of Pennsylvania read a strong minority report in which the senior White concurred, as was to be expected of a Whig.

While in Washington, White met and married Catherine Sidney Lee Ringgold, daughter of Tench Ringgold, onetime marshal of the District of Columbia and a member of one of the more prominent Catholic families of Maryland.[8] One of Mrs. White's brothers was later to handle himself and his battery so well in the Mexican War as to find a responsive recognition in the lines of "My Maryland": "With Ringgold's spirit for the fray." Edward White, Sr., resigned from the House in 1834 and in 1835 returned to his home state to be elected governor.

A kindly man of good humor, he was more noted for his eccentricities than for his executive abilities, his opponents charging that he was so passive a character that he could rouse no enmity. Although a states' rights man, he was also a sugar planter, and sugar, unlike cotton, required tariff protection. In his inaugural address as governor, White attacked Congress's reduction of the sugar tariff as a mere "conciliatory measure" sacrificing the sugar interests to end an "acrimonious conflict which has shaken the Union to its very foundations."[9] As a partial result

7. *Biographical Directory of the American Congress* (1928), 1689, 1691.
8. Hampton L. Carson, "Memorial Tribute to Edward Douglass White," *Reports of the American Bar Association*, XLVI (1921), 25, 26.
9. New Orleans *Bee*, June 6, 1843; quoted in Fortier, *Louisiana*, II, 639. It is clear that the reference is to the political battle among Jackson, Clay, and Calhoun. Since Governor White was a warm friend of Clay, the assault would be expected.

of the defeat of the Second Bank of the United States, which White had opposed in Congress, and the widespread economic chaos of 1837, Louisiana experienced a severe attack of "bankmania" during which the White administration permitted municipalities, business houses, and even individuals to "issue" money. Governor White also negotiated a $500,000 loan to the New Orleans and Nashville Railroad to construct a line connecting the South and the Northeast. This railroad link, which did not materialize in White's time, was based on the same idea that prompted Stephen A. Douglas to back the Illinois Central. In 1839, White was elected again to the House of Representatives and served two terms. He was active in securing construction of the New Orleans Mint and the refunding of monies expended on the Louisiana militia during the Florida Indian wars. Like any House member he sought the relief of private claimants, and he worked for the establishment of new ports in his state and for the improvement of commercial relations with the burgeoning Southwest and with Mexico. Full of honors, if not of years, he retired in 1843 to resume active management of his plantation. There he died, aged fifty-two, in 1847.

Edward Douglass White, Jr., the future chief justice, was born November 3, 1845, the youngest of the five White children.[10] His birthplace, the White plantation, was six miles north of Thibodaux in the district of Attakapas, the most picturesque area of Louisiana. This district stretches between the Teche Bayou and the Mississippi River, not far from the Gulf Coast. It is a flat and fertile land through which many bayous cut their way. The entire region closely conforms to the stereotyped picture of cypress swamps and quiet rivers, fertile bottom lands, and "threats of Spanish bayonets." Within it lay the best of the sugar kingdom.

Although his mother often visited New Orleans with her children, Edward's early years were spent largely on the plantation. These years had emotional significance for White. Indeed, when the time came to sell the family seat, White felt "a certain hesitancy in signing the final word to put the plantation out of my life. I was born there, my father and grandfather lived there and almost everything that is dear to me in

10. After the death of Governor Edward D. White, his widow married A. Brousseau. "Rector's Entrance Book," Georgetown University.

meaning was associated with it." He felt an "impalpable difference" between the country and the city boy.[11]

At the age of six, Ned White, as he was called, and his elder brother, James, were sent to the Preparatory School of the Immaculate Conception in New Orleans. The school was conducted by the Clerks Regular of the Company of Jesus, and Father James Duffo, later the tutor of James Cardinal Gibbons, was one of the eminent Jesuits who taught Ned White. Young White pored over religious principles that became a basic part of his thought, so much so that the moral precepts of Jesuit instruction were later to become apparent and marked in the chief justice.

In the autumn of 1856, Ned and James White left New Orleans for Mount Saint Mary's College, near Emmitsburg, Maryland. Here again Ned was under church influence.[12] The preparatory course of the school lasted for three years. Board and tuition for each boy were $200 a year, including laundry, mending, bed and bedding, and medical care. As a member of the first class, White was assigned courses in grammar, Latin prosody, French, arithmetic, geography, and history. His name was published with the names of other students as having made the grade of *Accesserunt* in English grammar and history, which at Saint Mary's meant a place below first honors.

In 1858 Ned White entered Georgetown University, probably the best Catholic institution of higher learning in the United States. At that time, he would have been a member of the class of 1863, but the Civil War interrupted his studies, and he is listed in the Alumni Directory as "ex-'63, LL.D., 1892." In 1858–1859 he was a member of the second humanities class, but the Georgetown archives do not disclose other subjects. Here again, Ned studied under the Jesuit influence, the President of Georgetown being John Early, Society of Jesus. Nine of the twelve faculty members were brothers of the society. The rigid discipline and religious training made their imprint upon his impressionable mind. As a college student, White laid the foundations of his ethics and learned the spirit and method of scholastic philosophy, which he applied later to the solution of legal problems.

He was a member of the Georgetown cadet corps when, in his third

11. Quoted in *Loyola Law Journal*, VII (1926), 74, 80.
12. Fegin, "Edward Douglass White," 4.

year at the university, the turbulent atmosphere of hatred engendered and nurtured by differing economic systems and social philosophies exploded into the "irrepressible conflict" of the Civil War. With the gathering of the North and South into hostile armies, Ned White hurried home without a degree. Later he was to say, "You know, Mr. Davis, I am not an educated man. . . . No, I went into the army as a boy, and when the war was over there was no further opportunity for education. I attribute to that the fact that I take in information more easily through my ears than my eyes. For instance, if you were arguing a case before me and spoke of the year 1823 and the next time mentioned 1923, it would be as if you had stuck a knife in me." [13] This feeling of White's probably accounts for his habit when a member of the Supreme Court, in preparing himself for the Court's Saturday morning conference, of reviewing aloud the night before the issues that had developed in the case to be decided. Unless he could repeat these questions, White believed that he was not prepared for the conference, and the case was set aside. He took no notes during oral arguments before the Court and admitted that it troubled him to see Justice Oliver Wendell Holmes making abundant notes as counsel pleaded their cases. He never felt a need to refer to notes when he delivered an opinion from the bench.

White did not enlist at once upon leaving Georgetown; after all he was a mere sixteen years of age. Because his family did not approve of his military ambitions, he ran away from home after a year or so and enlisted as a private in the Confederate Army. As other families have sought to do in time of war, his family intervened in his behalf, helping him to receive a lieutenant's commission on the staff of General W. N. R. Beal, the commander in charge of the defense of Port Hudson, Louisiana. His military career was short; White became a prisoner when Port Hudson surrendered to the Union Army on July 8, 1863. After being kept several months as a prisoner of war, he was paroled and ordered to return to Thibodaux and there to surrender himself to the federal officer commanding. Because he was a boy of only eighteen at the time of his capture, he did not frequently refer to his military experience later. When at last, weakened and in poor health, he set out for home, he contracted a

13. Davis to Highsaw, August 27, 1942.

fever and collapsed by the roadside. He thought he would soon die and "made his peace with God." Fortunately friends found him and carried him home.

Half a century later, White told in his own peculiar style a story of his imprisonment that always remained in his mind.

Like everyone else in my environment, as a little boy, I went into the army on the side that didn't win. . . . I was taken prisoner . . . and my mother went to the officer in charge of the prison and asked permission to come to see me. . . . On the next morning I had a prison number, and my number was called out, and I was marched by a corporal of the guard along the deadline, where if a man tries to cross, he is shot. I was taken into a guardroom, and there stood a gentleman. He asked my name, and we passed out into the street—it was a cold February day—there stood a hansom. There was an orderly holding the horse, and the gentleman said, "You have no coat on." I had nothing on but a thin flannel shirt. I said, "Yes, that is so." But he said, "Go back and get your coat." I said, "I cannot go back and get what I have not got." "Oh," he said and putting his hand up to the long heavy blue braided coat . . . he unbuttoned it button by button, took it off his own shoulders and said, "My boy, I am more warmly clothed than you are. Put on my coat." [14]

This kind treatment possibly tinted White's attitude toward the Civil War. He was firmly convinced that the outcome of the war was what it should have been. "My God, Mr. Davis, what if we had succeeded!" He was to show his acceptance of the postwar adjustment, even though it carried with it a period of economic and political reformation. He held that the war had been fought by the North and South to perpetuate constitutional government in the manner in which the people of each of these regions had been taught to believe it should exist. With war cleared from his vision, he could say, "The blue and the gray, thank God, are one." [15]

East of Canal Street is the Vieux Carré, the French Quarter of New Orleans. There was located the office of Edward Bermudez, to whom Edward White went in 1865 to begin his study of law. Bermudez, a lawyer of undoubted ability, was a master of the civil law who had a constant, paternal interest in his young students. His office was a place where the

14. "Address of Chief Justice White," *Princeton Alumni Weekly*, XII (May 15, 1912), 525–26.
15. Davis to Highsaw, August 27, 1942; "Response of the Late Chief Justice White to Toast at the Annual Banquet of the American Bar Association, at Washington, October 22, 1914," *American Bar Association Journal*, VII (1921), 341, 342.

fundamental theories of the civil law were inculcated into the mind of the law student. White studied there among young men with names, like his, well known in the state, fellows full of keen rivalry. It was not long until Edward White was tested with his first case. Bermudez assigned him one of those suits that often go to young lawyers, imposing the greatest amount of labor and responsibility, yet of such a nature that substantial reward would not result. Bermudez no doubt thought that the case was beyond White's ability, and told him that it was probably a forlorn hope, but he added cheerfully, "You may win your spurs with it." [16]

And so White did. The case arose from peculiar local circumstances. It was the defense of an action brought by the Police Jury of Jefferson Parish to recover the cost of constructing a levee to keep the floods of the Mississippi from the defendant planter's adjoining lands. By the early law of Louisiana, the obligation of repairing a levee, and consequently bearing the costs of such repairs, was clearly upon the riparian owner. In short, any person owning land on a river was responsible for keeping that river within its channels. The havoc of the Civil War, however, had been great, and few owners were able to fulfill such a duty. Of necessity the state government had constructed and repaired levees since the war, and the governor had established the Board of Levee Commissioners to organize levee reconstruction. Not only did the legislature endorse this action, but it also provided for the resultant expense by public appropriations and the issuance of bonds.

The validity of the governor's action was attacked on the ground that he had exercised improperly delegated legislative power. At the same time, the military commander, General Philip Sheridan, complicated the issue by removing the governor's commissioners and appointing others. These new commissioners thereupon ordered riparian owners to repair their levees, making a vague promise of recompense from state funds. The suit White was defending arose when his client failed to maintain a levee.

The question presented to the court affected every holder of property along the innumerable streams and bayous of Louisiana. A verdict for the defendant, Tardos, meant profit for every one of them. White was

16. Among White's fellow students, Charles Parlange, Frederic Soniat, and William Spencer became members of the Louisiana Supreme Court; the case was *Police Jury, Parish of Jefferson, Right Bank v. Tardos*, 22 La. Ann. 58 (1870).

aware of this fact—his own family's property in Lafourche Parish would be affected—and knew of the professional recognition that he would receive should he succeed. He studied and prepared for the case with all the energy, zeal, and industry he could muster. He was not in the least discouraged by the lack of legal precedents. White based his case on the contentions that the old private law of Louisiana had been replaced by a new public law and that, the state government having undertaken to repair the levees, the old rule of private obligation had been replaced by a new one of public duty. This argument was accepted by the trial court and affirmed by the Supreme Court of Louisiana. The defendant was relieved of all obligation to pay for levees constructed on his property. This result lifted an enormous burden from all owners of property located on the waterways. *Tardos* paved the way for public policy since followed in Louisiana on the levee issue. "The industry and learning expended in this 'hopeless' case laid the foundation of the future public policy of Louisiana on the levee question, and when the Reconstruction Era was closing, White was drafted into the legislative circle and his earmarks are on many acts passed during his term as State Senator. In the Supreme Court of Louisiana and in the Supreme Court of the United States it was again his duty to discuss and decide questions of similar import, and it may in truth be said that the light of the little candle in his first case has penetrated and illuminated the jurisprudence of our country."[17]

Not all of White's early experiences had happy endings, but his advancement in the legal profession was, nevertheless, unusually rapid.[18] In a short time he had one of the largest practices in New Orleans. His phenomenal rise to leadership in the New Orleans bar may be partly attributed to his temperament toward noncontroversial causes, a tendency which made him acceptable to all classes. In addition, his mastery of French aided his study of the civil law and allowed him to present cases in courts where French was the only spoken language. At an early stage

---

17. Dart in *Proceedings*, 18.
18. A man not without humor, White often told a story of himself which served to dispel illusions as to his first success. Asked to defend a man financially unable to retain counsel, White accepted and made an eloquent plea for his client. Unfortunately the man was found guilty and sentenced to two years at hard labor. Leaving the courtroom, a relative of the unsuccessful defendant asked: "Say, Sam, have you any money?" The answer came promptly: "If I had any money don't you suppose I would have hired a lawyer." Chicago *Legal News*, March 6, 1924.

of his career, White had won distinction among his own people and respect as an emerging legal figure.

No young lawyer of Edward White's social class or family position could neglect the political conditions then existing in Louisiana. The political atmosphere in 1868 and the following decade was clouded.[19] Louisiana's state government typified conditions in the "reconstructed" states of the defeated Confederacy, although Louisiana government was perhaps worse than some and possibly not so bad as a few.

Reconstruction of civil government in Louisiana after the conclusion of the war began with the Louisiana Constitution of 1868, a short document more democratic than earlier constitutions and one upon which much of the state's present governmental structure is based. The first governor elected under this new basic law was Henry Clay Warmoth, a twenty-six year old Republican for whose support the freed blacks in Louisiana were mustered. Warmoth, however, lost favor with the Custom House Republicans as well as with many white citizens for whom he already symbolized the worst in carpetbag government after he gained control of the liberal Republican movement. Following much political maneuvering Warmoth decided not to run for a second term in the 1872 election. His successor in 1873 was William Pitt Kellogg, a Custom House Republican who had President U. S. Grant's support. Kellogg lacked the capacity to run the government, and his administration was characterized by political disunity at a time when violence and economic depression made governance difficult. White, as a young Democratic observer of these events, consistently sided with those leaders determined to unseat the Kellogg government. Although some Louisiana whites supported Warmoth or Kellogg, most of them distrusted their state government. Kellogg's administration was less corrupt than Warmoth's, but a heavy, though reduced, tax burden, falling property values, and the effects of the depression of 1873 contributed to Kellogg's unpopularity. Whatever merits Governor Kellogg's program may have had, he could not deal with the turbulence and political disunity within the state. White later referred to the "anguish, more appalling than the calamity of war, of the period which followed in its wake."[20] These words reflected distress over military rule, corruption in state and local government, heavy

---

19. Ella Lonn, *Reconstruction in Louisiana After 1868* (New York: Putnam, 1918), 158–205.
20. Joe Gray Taylor, *Louisiana Reconstructed, 1863–1877* (Baton Rouge: Louisiana State

public and private indebtedness, and almost a decade of political disorder.

A recent biographer of Warren G. Harding asserted that White reacted to Reconstruction in Louisiana in the same way that many other southerners responded. "A Roman Catholic, White, in the Reconstruction period, had been a local leader of the Ku Klux Klan." It would be begging the question to note that the Klan as such did not operate in Louisiana. Two similar organizations, the Knights of the White Camellia and the White League, had significant membership rolls. White's conservative nature and his scholarly bent of mind, as well as his relative youth, argued against his having had a position of importance or leadership in either of them. Yet, it is possible and even likely that he joined one or the other. No evidence supports such an assertion of membership, but it is a matter of record that White was a member, again only as a private, of a company organized to do battle against the Kellogg administration.[21] Moreover, in one of the first victories against the Reconstruction government, he was elected to the state senate as a candidate pledged to rid Louisiana of the Kellogg government. It is unlikely that he would have been admitted, even as a private, to the company or would have drawn many white votes in the election if he had opposed white resistance to the official state government.

The task of changing control of the state administration was not an easy one. On September 14, 1874, before the election of members of Congress and other officers, a number of supposedly secretly organized and drilled companies of men, one of which included White, threw up barricades while the press urged the partisan leaders "by all that is dear and sacred to the human heart to be true to your company and yourselves." A mixed body of metropolitan police, a few score armed policemen, and approximately three thousand black militia, led by the onetime lieutenant general commanding the First Corps of the Army of Northern Virginia, James Longstreet, faced the attack of larger insurgent forces and fell back to the Mississippi River. Victory over Kellogg was celebrated, but in due course President Grant responded to Kellogg's appeal of Sep-

---

University Press, 1974), 155, 311–12; *Proceedings on the Death of Mr. Justice Lamar*, 241 U.S. xvii (1916).

21. Francis Russell, *The Shadow of Blooming Grove: Warren G. Harding and His Times* (New York: McGraw-Hill, 1968), 12, fn. 3; *In Memoriam*, 149 La. viii (1921).

tember 15 for federal assistance, and three days later the authority of Kellogg was reestablished.[22]

The state senate, to which Edward White had been elected, convened in January 1875, but he declined to take part in the organization of that body. Instead, he cast his lot with certain members of the legislature who had been excluded by the Returning Board. In March, 1875, the Hoar Congressional Committee reached a compromise, and White took his seat with seven other senators. A Republican majority prevailed, however, with Caesar C. Antoine, the black lieutenant governor, as the presiding officer of the Senate.

The Hayes-Tilden controversy of 1876 reached down to influence Louisiana politics. Although Rutherford B. Hayes was given the state's electoral votes in the presidential election, the same election resulted in the triumph of Louisiana's Democratic party movement, headed by Francis R. T. Nicholls.[23] White, as a valued adviser in the complicated negotiations which ended with Nicholls becoming governor, received a reward in the form of an appointment as associate justice of the Supreme Court of Louisiana. The appointment was dated January 10, 1878, when White was just entering his thirty-third year.

Edward White, in a brief term of only fifteen months (until the Constitutional Convention of 1879 created a new court), added strength to a bench that ranked among the best in Louisiana's history. It was fortunate that this court was strong, because when it took up the docket it found many cases left undecided by the outgoing judges. The work assigned to the new court was tremendous, and White assumed office as the justices reached the peak of their effort to decrease the load. In 1914, Chief Justice White said that the total number of cases decided by the Nicholls bench in 1879–1880 would probably show "the heaviest work ever done by a court of last resort in the United States composed of only five judges."[24]

White delivered his first recorded opinion, *Charpaux v. Bellocq*, in February, 1879.[25] As a routine action with no precedents in the common

22. New Orleans *Bulletin*, September 14, 1874; Taylor, *Louisiana Reconstructed*, 292–95.
23. Henry C. Warmoth, *War, Politics and Reconstruction: Stormy Days in Louisiana* (New York: Macmillan, 1930), 258.
24. 31, 32 La. Ann. (1879–1880); quoted by Dart in *Proceedings*, 94.
25. *Charpaux v. Bellocq*, 31 La. Ann. 164 (1879).

law, it had to be decided on the basis of civil law. The question before the court concerned a private transaction in which the plaintiff attempted to void a sale made to him. As such, the case contributed nothing to the constitutional theories White later developed, although it did foreshadow a form or method which he used later as a justice of the United States Supreme Court. This style consisted of a brief statement of the case and its issues, followed by conclusions which were fortified as they were announced and supported by citations drawn from history and the legal writers and jurisprudence of France. White's style was such that he could be beaten only by attacking his premises; otherwise there was no room for debate.

In *Knight* v. *Ragan*, Justice White held that the courts were invested with complete power to review the validity of election returns. A more important case, *New Orleans* v. *Saint Anna's Asylum*, involved a question of the immunity from the ordinary burden of taxation of property held by charitable institutions.[26] White's majority opinion stated a classification defining the immunity of such institutions from taxation: "The fact that the rents and revenues of property owned by a charitable organization are devoted to the charitable purposes for which the corporation was organized will not exempt such property from taxation. It is only when the property itself is actually and directly used for charitable purposes that the law exempts it from taxation."

The last case considered at this point, *Louisiana Levee Company* v. *Louisiana*, involved matters related to levee construction, a subject with which White had become familiar in his preparation for the *Tardos* case.[27] In his opinion White set out his fundamental ideas about the relationship of federal and state courts when dealing with a question concerning the construction of a state statute. He argued that no federal judgment could be admitted if it disregarded "the construction given to a state statute by the highest court in the state, and . . . disregarded the adjudication of the tribunal of last resort within this state as to a question whether the state had attained the constitutional limit." White, however, sidestepped the conclusion that the United States Supreme Court had rendered an

26. *Knight* v. *Ragan*, 31 La. Ann. 289 (1879); *New Orleans* v. *Saint Anna's Asylum*, 31 La. Ann. 292 (1879).

27. *Louisiana Levee Company* v. *Louisiana*, 31 La. Ann 250 (1879).

opinion contrary to the one that he was about to announce by adding that such was not the present case.

Most of the opinions White wrote in his brief tenure on the Louisiana Supreme Court are concerned with civil law and have little relationship to his constitutional theories expressed in later years. Even so, this brief experience on the bench had given White an opportunity to develop a method of thought which he would refine and apply to legal problems arising from constitutional issues.

III
The Louisiana Lottery

N
ewspaper readers in Louisiana were startled in the early days of November, 1888, by an arresting headline, "Over Two Millions Distributed!" So said the Louisiana State Lottery Company, a powerful force in the life of the Creole State for twenty-five years after the Civil War.[1] The notice announced the doubling of stakes. Henceforth, the prize in semiannual drawings would be $600,000, and even in the daily drawings the fortunate ticket holder could win as much as $30,000. Four national banks in New Orleans guaranteed the prompt payment of the winners. "We do hereby certify that we supervise the arrangements for the Monthly and Semi-Annual Drawings of the Louisiana State Lottery Company and in person manage and control the Drawings themselves and that the same are conducted with honesty and fairness and in good faith."[2] This additional promise bore the names of men still honored in the South, former Confederate generals, Pierre Gustave Toutant Beauregard and Jubal A. Early, made famous by many a bitter campaign in the Civil War.

Lotteries had existed in Great Britain before English colonization of North

1. John Samuel Ezell, *Fortune's Merry Wheel: The Lottery in America* (Cambridge: Harvard University Press, 1960) is a thorough examination of the history of lotteries, first in the colonies and then in the United States. For the history of the Louisiana Lottery, see G. W. McGinty, "The Louisiana Lottery Company," *Southwestern Social Science Quarterly*, XX (March, 1940), 330, Berthold C. Alwes, "The History of the Louisiana State Lottery Company," *Louisiana Historical Quarterly*, XXVII (October, 1944), 970, and Edgar H. Farrar, "The Louisiana Lottery: Its History," *Charities Review*, I (1892), 148.

2. Quoted in Marquis James, *They Had Their Hour* (Indianapolis: Bobbs-Merrill, 1934), 265.

America. There they had provided funds for general revenue purposes and also for special projects, including the improvement of London and the purchase of a picture gallery. Since lotteries were an important part of English social and economic history, colonists had a ready precedent at hand when confronted with economic problems. They did not hesitate to import lotteries to a new environment. These lotteries generally fell into two categories, drawings legally sanctioned for public use and those conducted by individuals for personal gain, but not all of them, particularly those conducted for private gain, were honestly operated. Moreover, they diverted limited economic resources from normal business channels, thus disenchanting merchants.[3] As a result opposition developed, and Massachusetts, for example, closed unlicensed lotteries to benefit the poor, whose expectations were often high but whose winnings were equally often low. Nevertheless, some 158 licensed lotteries operated in the colonies, of which 126 were in the New England states.

Between 1790 and 1860, state governments made 130 lottery authorizations.[4] Even so, local governments demanded more lotteries than the various state legislatures were willing to permit. The use of lotteries by cities, towns, and counties for governmental purposes reflected, perhaps, some growing recognition of a slowly emerging urban problem, but more certainly they demonstrated the absence of such usual methods of public funding as bond issues. Since some states had repudiated their bonds in the 1830s, new bonded indebtedness was then, as now, somewhat suspect in several states and cities. In addition, lotteries appeared to be the easiest way to finance the popular internal improvements of the day, partly support education, assist churches in their good works, and provide other benefits. Eventually public opposition to them grew powerful, and many states abolished them, although as late as 1834 campaigns against the lotteries in Maryland and South Carolina were unsuccessful. By 1860, however, almost every state except Delaware prohibited lottery operations.

In the post–Civil War period lotteries revived, mostly in the South and West. Economic depression in the former Confederate states, embittered and impoverished by a war of attrition and ruled by state governments largely imposed and maintained by force, made the region

3. Ezell, *Fortune's Merry Wheel*, 11; Samuel Sewell, "Letter Book," *Massachusetts Historical Society Collections*, 6th Series, II, 102–103, quoted in Ezell, *Fortune's Merry Wheel*, 19.
4. Ezell, *Fortune's Merry Wheel*, 120.

susceptible to this revival. As a matter of history, though, Louisiana had run a drawing for the benefit of its Confederate soldiers as early as 1861, this drawing supplying the soldiers with slightly more than $50,000. The lottery had been held despite explicit constitutional prohibitions in the 1845 and 1852 documents. In Alabama the Tuscaloosa Scientific and Art Association in February, 1866, received a twenty-five-year charter whose purposes were to encourage art, to rebuild and stock with books the University of Alabama Library, which Croxton's Union raiders had reduced to a pile of rubbish, and to establish a scientific museum. Two years later a similar charter was granted, allegedly to benefit the public schools. In 1866 Georgia authorized the Georgia Masonic Home to hold lotteries to fund and construct buildings. A year later the Mississippi Agricultural Society received a twenty-five-year charter for a lottery to benefit the state treasury by $5,000 annually while assisting the state university by a payment of $1,000. At the same time, opposition to lotteries was developing, and in June, 1868, Congress enacted a statute denying the use of the mails to letters concerning lotteries, a grievous blow because many lottery tickets were sold beyond the borders of the state in which the lottery was held.[5]

The Louisiana Lottery, which came to be the best known of the nineteenth century lotteries, began in April, 1864, when the constitutional convention of that year, with disregard of constitutional prohibitions, conferred powers on the legislature to license lotteries and gambling. In Louisiana soon after the end of the Civil War, the local agent for the Alabama and Kentucky lotteries was Charles T. Howard, an ex–Confederate soldier. Howard was an associate of John A. Morris of New York, whose syndicate advanced $100,000 to finance Louisiana lottery operations in 1868. Howard's ambitious scheme envisaged an understanding with the "reconstructed" state administration of Governor Henry Clay Warmoth, a Republican and the current leader of the blacks. Warmoth, fond of ambitious plans, had already promised his credulous black cohorts a machine which would pump white blood into their veins. He now fell into step with Howard, and in the same year, 1868, the Louisiana State Lottery Company was chartered by the legislature as a privately owned

---

5. Thomas Ewing Dabney, *One Hundred Great Years: The Story of the Times-Picayune from Its Founding to 1940* (Baton Rouge: Louisiana State University Press, 1944), 133–35; *Congressional Globe*, 40th Cong., 2nd Sess., 4112, Appendix, 552.

monopoly for twenty-five years, beginning January 1, 1869. The birth of
the lottery was troubled; it came into being only with the solid support
of the black legislative delegation dominated by Pinckney Benton Stuart
Pinchback, the son of a black mother and a Georgia planter and farmer.
The granting of the charter was undoubtedly accompanied by bribery
and fraud, practices which were made explicit in court when a disaffected
member of the company brought action to obtain a larger share of the
profits.[6]

Despite these shenanigans the new Louisiana State Lottery Company came perilously close to failure because graft, inexperience, and
aggressive competition from established companies sapped its strength
and brought it near bankruptcy. Then a strange little man, an obscure
employee of the lottery, Dr. Maximilian A. Dauphin, claimed that he
could transform it into a profitable enterprise if given $50,000 in new
capital, a free hand, and a modest share of the profits.[7] Dauphin proved
to be as good as his word, for he soon made the Louisiana Lottery rich
and powerful. In a few years the twelve monthly drawings netted a profit
of $13 million, a clear return of 47 percent above all expenses. Despite
the lottery's attempts to create a favorable response by gifts for charity
and some public enterprises, however, dissenters questioned its social
desirability while it waxed strong as, one by one, its competitors were
driven from the state.

Some 93 percent of the lottery's income came from other states, and
so did a considerable amount of national criticism. Bills to end lotteries
were introduced in the United States Congress, eleven coming in one
session alone. Magazines also arrayed themselves against the lottery,
and A. K. McClure of the Philadelphia *Times* succeeded in banning the
company's advertisements in Pennsylvania. When McClure came to New
Orleans for a visit, he was met by a libel action as he stepped from the
train. From a safer distance the editor of the Chicago *Herald* wrote bitterly, "Nobody has ever inflicted the slightest loss on the Lottery. They
might as well take their money voluntarily to a highwayman and receive
from him a note in return due on the day of judgment."[8]

6. Frank McGloin, "Shall the Lottery's Charter Be Renewed?" *Forum*, XII (January,
1892), 555; *Antoine v. Smith*, 40 La. Ann. 450 (1886).
7. James, *They Had Their Hour*, 273.
8. Chicago *Herald*, January 9, 1892.

In addition to the usual drawings, under the hope of easy profits, the lottery fostered "policy," whose tickets cost only a small portion of the price of a chance in the regular drawings. Estimated total annual income from policy, under which a player bet that certain numbers would be drawn or would come out in a prestated order, approximated $1,165,000. Policy added to the disrepute of the lottery. "The quest for lucky numbers was fantastic. To see a stray dog meant to play 6, a drunken man was 14, a dead woman 59, a dream of fish 13. . . . Office boys embezzled their employers' postage stamps, the Negro population was demoralized." Probably 90 percent of those persons who supported the lottery were already so poor that their loss had no great popular significance, but with the habit of ingrained misfortune, they played on, sure that "the next time, the next time I shall hold the lucky ticket." [9]

The Louisiana State Lottery Company demonstrated the axiom of the reform movement that nothing endangers free government more than "sinister" interests which conflict with the good of the community. In the two decades that followed 1868, the lottery dictated to a series of legislative sessions, its power residing in the great profit which President Dauphin was amassing for the company. The lottery could and did purchase ballots and legislators on the open market, subsidize the local press, and smooth the ruffled backs of moral and religious associations by generous donations, including gifts for a cemetery and a Confederate memorial building. Lottery profits financed the white revolt against carpetbag government, while lottery stock supported ousted black leaders in style. The Louisiana State Lottery Company was a demonstration of the fact that political power does not necessarily reside in an electorate. It occasioned no surprise that, in the disputed election of 1876, when white Democrats won majorities in the state contests, the Republican state board of canvassers proclaimed a Republican victory. The lottery, though, came to the financial aid of Democrat Francis R. T. Nicholls's candidacy for governor. Whatever Nicholls's sentiments might have been on the lottery issue, no antilottery bill was passed in either the 1877 or the 1878 legislative sessions. Apparently the lottery's service to the reform white government was enough to buy a little time, but the respite was short-lived. The attack continued; the lottery bribed legislators; and the New

9. James, *They Had Their Hour*, 277–78, 278.

Orleans press appeared to be effectively gagged. Moreover, a move to call a constitutional convention and also to permit the electorate to vote on a constitutional amendment banning the lottery failed. To blunt the continued attacks against its existence, the lottery in 1877 trotted out Generals Beauregard and Early to attest to its fairness, while the editor of the *Democrat*, who had referred to "Howard and his brother thieves" and hinted at possible violence directed against lottery officials and property, had suits brought against him for a total of $90,000.[10]

All of this frenetic activity was not enough to stave off legislative action. Early in its 1879 session a bill was introduced in the legislature to repeal all prolottery statutes, including the charter of the Louisiana State Lottery Company. The measure, which included heavy penalties for all lottery activities after March 31, 1879, passed the House 64 to 20, eased by in the Senate 19 to 17, and was signed into law by Governor Nicholls on March 27, 1879. With State Supreme Court Justice White assenting, the court upheld the Louisiana Legislature in *State* v. *Judge*.[11]

Act 44 did not signal an early demise of the lottery. The company immediately filed an action in the United States circuit court seeking an injunction against the application of the statute. The lottery's prospects for a successful legal resolution of its problem seemed to be favorable. Although the United States Supreme Court had upheld a state's right of repeal in a similar case in 1877, Judge Edward Billings, whose authority in the case is not yet perfectly clear, nullified Act 44 by an injunction.

The situation changed rapidly, however, before the case could go to a higher court. Onetime United States Supreme Court associate justice and assistant secretary of war in the Confederate government, the brilliant John Archibald Campbell entered the conflict. As attorney to the lottery company, Campbell reported that questions put to counsel by the bench in the Mississippi Lottery case, then pending, suggested an adverse decision for the Mississippi corporation. To guard against the effects of such a judgment, the Louisiana Lottery bent its efforts toward embedding itself in the constitution of the state. Probably the lottery was not the single cause of the movement for constitutional revision in 1879, but the power it could muster was substantial. Thirty-nine of its Recon-

---

10. Ezell, *Fortune's Merry Wheel*, 251; McGinty, "Louisiana Lottery Company," 334; Alwes, "Lottery Company History," 985–88.

11. *Acts of Louisiana*, 1879, No. 44; *State* v. *Judge*, 32 La. Ann. 721 (1879).

struction friends and its chief counsel were members of the Constitutional Convention, and added pressure could be brought to bear upon the press. After eight days of debate, which included virtually all delegates, Article CLXVII was adopted, in effect repealing the Louisiana Lottery's monopoly, but permitting lotteries to operate until January 1, 1894. The amendment thereby conceded the lottery's operation for another fifteen years, or the full period granted by its charter of incorporation.[12] The lottery was to be subjected, however, to a tax of $40,000 annually, dedicated to use by the New Orleans Charity Hospital.

In December, 1879, the new constitution was ratified by referendum. Several consequences flowed from the constitutional embodiment of the lottery. First, the company celebrated its nearly unassailable position by holding a gala drawing December 17, 1879. Generals Beauregard and Early made another appearance, the latter to draw the numbers and the former to announce the prizes, all in the name of the only lottery "in any state ever voted on and endorsed by its people." More significantly, the lottery appeared to have gained control of the state Democratic party, and its lotteries maintained the company's monopoly: "They are the absolute masters of every ward boss and every politician in the State of Louisiana, whether he be judge, constable, treasurer, member of the State Central Committee, member of the parish committee."[13] Finally, not only were measures to charter new lotteries or abolish the Louisiana company defeated repeatedly in the legislature, but the lottery justly received blame for the dismissal from public service of most of the men who had overthrown the Reconstruction government and opposed the lottery. Among those who departed was Associate Justice Edward Douglass White of the state supreme court, who left the bench in April, 1880, under a new constitutional provision that fixed the age for state supreme court justices at thirty-five. He was but thirty-four.

In less than a decade White, mellow and portly but a terror when aroused, would return to combat the lottery again, but meanwhile, he returned to the practice of law, forming a partnership with another former justice of the state supreme court, William B. Spencer. Evidently

12. *Stone* v. *Mississippi*, 101 U.S. 814 (1880). The Court held that the legislature cannot barter away the police power of the state. A contract against the health or morals of the people may be voided; Louisiana Constitution (1879), Art. CLXVII.

13. Farrar, "Louisiana Lottery," 145.

their practice was large and profitable, for cases that were pending at the time of their retirement from the court were brought to them. The firm of Spencer and White did so well that, long before he entered the national scene, White was recognized locally as an authority in Louisiana in both federal and state law.[14] After Spencer's death, White practiced alone for a time and then formed a new firm with Eugene Sanders, later judge of the federal district court in New Orleans, and Sanders' young protégé, Charles Parlange, a vigorous antilottery lawyer.

Throughout this period, White was a scholar who wanted to know what the law was, how it worked, and what its effects were. Still a bachelor and unencumbered with an immediate family of his own, he often studied in his office far into the night. The law was for him, necessarily, a double field: the civil law, which was a requirement for practice in Louisiana, and the common law, which was followed in the federal courts. In civil law he became familiar with the sources: the *Jus Civile*, the *Legislation of Justinian*, the *Custom of Paris*, the *Recopilacion of Castile*, the *Neuva Recopilacion of the Indies*, and the *Code Napoleon*.[15] His fluency in Latin, French, and Spanish made his studies easier than they might have been.

His study of the common law was another matter. Many Louisiana lawyers were acquainted only with the state's civil code and confined themselves to the state courts, calling in an associate to handle any federal case they might have. Unlike these attorneys White wanted to practice in both state and federal courts. Even while studying with Bermudez, he had enrolled in some courses at the University of Louisiana, located in New Orleans. Scholarly White might be, but he was also pragmatic.

Perhaps it was at this time that White acquired a nervous habit that must have affected his style of writing, which was characterized by sentence piled upon sentence, clause upon clause, until his argument swayed under the mere weight of words as he spun out his line of reasoning. He found that he could write only when pressing the first finger of his right hand against the right side of his nose. Holding the pen between the second finger and his thumb, he had to bend until his nose nearly touched the paper, and should the first finger slip from his nose, the pen would

14. Henry P. Dart, "Chief Justice White," *Louisiana Historical Quarterly*, V (April, 1922), 144, 145.
15. Henry P. Dart, Sr., Harry M. Daugherty, William Howard Taft, and others, *Proceedings of the Bar and Officers of the Supreme Court of the United States in Memory of Edward Douglass White*, Washington, December 17, 1921, p. 16, hereinafter cited as *Proceedings*.

drop from his hand.[16] This handicap did not harm him in his legal practice nor, evidently, in the study of law.

Some evidence of White's abilities as a lawyer is reflected in the Paul
Tulane affair. Tulane came to New Orleans in 1822, prospered in real estate, and returned to New Jersey half a century later. He decided to do-
nate some of his wealth to higher education, and to achieve this purpose,
he turned a portion of his holdings over to a board of administrators, of
whom Edward White was one. White argued, and the board accepted
his reasoning by a narrow majority, that the gift should be turned over
to the University of Louisiana in New Orleans, but Mr. Tulane rejected
this proposal, and the board reversed itself. White persisted and proposed that, since Tulane would not endow a state university, Louisiana
should give the university to the Tulane board of administrators. Many
people thought the idea impractical since it could be accomplished only
by an amendment to the state constitution. After five years of hard work
on White's part, however, the necessary amendment was adopted by
popular vote, and the old state university became part of the new Tulane
University.[17] Edward White was an influential attorney.

White kept a close eye on state politics, and eventually the Louisiana
State Lottery Company entered his life again. In the years after its constitutional embodiment, the lottery fared well indeed. In 1887 stock divi-
dends to shareholders were 110 percent; in 1888, 120 percent; in 1889, 170
percent; and in 1890, 125 percent. The lottery, a perennial issue in Louisiana politics after 1868, sought as usual to meet local complaints by good
works and publicized charities. But more than 90 percent of its business
came from out-of-state sales, and the lottery's statewide public opinion
campaign had no real influence on national opinion. The opposition of
newspaper editors like Alexander K. McClure, critical articles in magazines like the *Friend* and the *Nation*, and the prohibition of lotteries elsewhere were portents of a renewed struggle with the Louisiana Lottery.[18]

In 1888 that perennial campaigner, Francis R. T. Nicholls, decided to

16. Kenneth B. Umbreit, *Our Eleven Chief Justices* (New York: Harper, 1938), 376.
17. White, however, attributed this result to Senator Randall Lee Gibson of Louisiana.
Congressional Record, 52nd Cong., 2nd Sess. (1892), 2345. See Appendix A concerning the
current legal status of Tulane University.
18. Clarence C. Buel, "The Degradation of a State; or, The Charitable Career of the
Louisiana Lottery," *Century*, XLIII (new series XXI) (February, 1892), 624. In 1885 Florida
and Utah prohibited lotteries by their respective constitutions. South Dakota, Idaho, Mon-

run again for the governorship of which he had been deprived by the 1879 Constitution. In January he won the Democratic primary and in the following April was elected to replace the prolottery incumbent. The Nicholls campaign had been directed largely against the lottery company, and Edward White had carried a major share of the campaign. As a gesture of political gratitude, Nicholls saw to it that the legislature elected White to the Senate of the United States to succeed James B. Eustis.[19]

The election of 1888, of course, presaged a reexamination of the status of the Louisiana State Lottery Company, but the lottery would not sit complacently and watch. Its profits were too large to surrender without a struggle, for they amounted to well over $8 million annually, exclusive of income derived from daily drawings. Moreover, the constitution of 1879 forbade lotteries after 1894. The lottery's line of action was clear: if the company were to live, it must secure a constitutional amendment extending its charter. This action would have to begin in the first session of 1890 since consent would have to be quickly manufactured.

The press and the company mobilized through the winter and summer of 1890. Early in the year John A. Morris of the lottery announced that he proposed to allocate the state $500,000 annually instead of the paltry $40,000 a year paid since 1879. On May 12 Governor Nicholls' message to the assembling legislature characterized the constitutional amendment benefiting the lottery as a moral wrong, a state partnership in a nefarious enterprise, and poor politics.[20] On May 13 Morris announced his willingness to pay the state $1 million annually in return for a new charter effective beginning January 1, 1893, for twenty-five years.

Three weeks later on June 4, 1890, the battle line was drawn in the legislature by House Bill 214, which was a constitutional amendment authorizing lotteries in Louisiana to continue for twenty-five years; the amendment also proposed an annual payment of $1 million to the state, of which $350,000 was to go to the public schools, $350,000 was to be used for levees, $150,000 was to be allocated for charities, $100,000 was to be assigned to New Orleans drainage, and $50,000 was to be reserved

---

tana, and Washington also forbade lotteries. In the Forty-ninth and Fiftieth Congresses, nineteen bills to close the use of mails or express companies to lotteries were introduced.

19. Under the Louisiana election laws, White could not take office until the Fifty-first Congress convened in 1891.

20. *Louisiana House Journal*, 1890, 7–32.

for Confederate pensions. The shotgun effect of the proposed payment would have obvious appeal in the statewide referendum.

The usual pressure was brought on legislators by the employment of the usual tactics. A contemporary observer, an unrelenting foe of the lottery, classified the tactics: first, subsidization of newspapers, barrooms, restaurants, and even brothels; second, blackmail of legislators by threats to expose their pasts; and third, a "death watch" over converted legislators who were surrounded by lottery people to seal them off from communication. Throughout the campaign the *Times-Democrat* did its best with New Orleans readers. Noting that Jefferson, as a member of the Continental Congress, had drafted a bill authorizing a lottery to raise funds for the embryonic nation, the paper went on to say that "no more voluntary tax than that derived from the Lottery . . . could be devised . . . a purely voluntary one which no one need pay who does not want to pay, which collects itself without a host of officials and does not give rise to tax dodging."[21]

All of the old arguments were pulled out, dusted off, and used, as the lottery sought to enlarge its influence. When the Mississippi burst its levees in 1890, lottery relief boats appeared first on the scene with food, clothing, and even seed to replace ruined crops. Lottery supporters applauded these acts at the same time that its opponents claimed a doubtless selfish motivation.

Many Louisiana leaders with numbers and organization behind them were against the lottery. Edward D. White, who was treasurer of the Anti-Lottery Democratic Committee, took an active part. His law associate, Charles Parlange, organized an antilottery committee, which by March, 1890, had grown into the Anti-Lottery League of Louisiana, whose express purpose was to "oppose by all honorable means" the renewal of the charter. The league held its first meeting at the old Grunewald Opera House in New Orleans, and two years later the New Orleans *New-Delta* recalled that the speeches "aroused tremendous enthusiasm, especially that of Judge White." It "was a masterpiece of oratory completely demolishing the claims of the lottery people." The *New-Delta*, which had been organized by White, Parlange, and W. L. Vincent as an antilottery paper to oppose the established press, continued in a more excited vein.

21. Farrar, "Louisiana Lottery," 146; New Orleans *Times-Democrat*, January 9, 1890.

White's address, it declared, was "a most powerful arraignment of the hireling press of the state, which, Judas like, has sold the state for thirty pieces of silver. Ladies split their gloves applauding him, while staid businessmen . . . shouted back answers to his questions. The scene was never equaled in New Orleans."[22] More than oratory, however, was required.

Before the 1890 legislative session convened and then during its debates on the lottery amendment, the Louisiana State Lottery Company continued its luminous way. By bribing some legislators and influencing others with hardly more honorable means, the lottery acquired strength, moving toward the two-thirds vote required for passage of a constitutional amendment. Legislators, one by one, found that the lottery did not offend their scruples after all.

The Anti-Lottery League met these defections as well as possible by constructing a tightly knit organization. White's services in this respect were constant and important, so essential that H. Dickson Burns, chairman of the Anti-Lottery Democratic Committee of New Orleans, evaluated his position before the people as authoritative. Contemporary press accounts relate that he organized antilottery clubs and committees, instructed chairmen and managers how to direct the campaign to the best advantage, and gave counsel in fund raising. His wide acquaintance throughout Louisiana and his considerable reservoir of political experience helped him in all of these activities, and the respect many Louisianians held for him was not the least important factor.

All the while the 1890 legislative session continued. In late June, Joseph Armand, an official of the lottery, was arrested on a charge of bribery. For a time, however, it seemed that the experience of 1879 might be repeated and the lottery's charter be extended until 1919. An amended version of House Bill 214, raising the lottery's annual payment to the state to $1,250,000 received exactly the necessary two-thirds majority in the senate, was passed by the house, and on July 1 was sent to Governor Nicholls, who promptly vetoed the measure on grounds of fraud. The house just as promptly overrode his veto, but supporters were unable to muster a two-thirds majority in the senate. The senate's judiciary committee reported, however, that gubernatorial approval was not required

22. New Orleans *New-Delta*, May 12, 1892.

for a constitutional amendment. The house agreed and sent the measure to the secretary of state, who refused to certify it. John A. Morris of the lottery then filed suit to compel a referendum by the people on the amendment and in April, 1891, the state supreme court, divided three-to-two, sustained the lottery's suit and issued a writ of mandamus ordering submission of the amendment for ratification in the 1892 election.[23]

The lottery struggle became an issue of national significance when Congress took action to destroy the lottery's interstate business by prohibiting the use of the mails for lottery tickets after September, 1890. With the Democratic party split into pro and antilottery factions, the election of 1892 was held. The work of White and the antilottery forces in translating the power of political reform was evidenced when Murphy J. Foster and Charles Parlange defeated prolottery candidates Samuel D. McEnery and R. C. Wickliffe for the offices of governor and lieutenant governor, respectively. The lottery amendment was beaten by a vote of 157,422 to 4,225, but the final blow to the lottery was passage by the 1892 legislature of a statute forbidding the sale of lottery tickets after December 31, 1893, and setting penalties for soliciting, advertising, or drawing for any lottery. The lottery thereupon took up residence in Honduras, but it was finished as a political and economic force.[24]

Drawn-out and lengthy political and economic struggles frequently damage the good names of those involved. The *New-Delta*, commenting on Edward White's part in the campaign, claimed that "to him more than any other man in the state is due the credit for the defeat of the Lottery," but White emerged from the battle with some scars. In the midst of the campaign the rabidly partisan *Times-Democrat* had raised the question: "Is Senator-elect White an honest man? Is he a pure man? Will the Senator-elect tell the people of New Orleans how much money it took to secure his election to the United States Senate by the Legislature of Louisiana?" In July, 1890, the *Times-Democrat* repeated its charge that White, as treasurer of the Anti-Lottery Democratic Committee, had received $10,000 from the lottery and had used it in the election of Governor Nicholls. On

23. Alcée Fortier, *History of Louisiana* (4 vols.; New York: Goupil, 1904), IV, 220–23; McGinty, "Louisiana Lottery Company," 324–45.

24. *Congressional Record*, 51st Cong., 1st Sess., 8698–8721, 19150, 10085, subsequently upheld in *In Re Rapier*, 143 U.S. 110 (1892); for the history of the lottery election, see Alwes, "Lottery Company History," 1085–97, Dabney, *One Hundred Great Years*, 345–46, and Fortier, *Louisiana*, IV, 224–25.

July 27 White replied, admitting a contribution of that amount, but claiming that it was legitimately spent. The *Times-Democrat* gleefully declaimed "with added emphasis that Senator-elect White did receive from the Lottery's chief large sums of money with which to conduct his personal campaign; and that we can prove that fact in a Court of Justice where we can place the Senator-elect on the stand under oath." [25] White did not file a libel suit, and the matter was dropped. Whether there was substance in the charges cannot be definitely stated, but, given the heat of the lottery struggle, it is likely that the *Times-Democrat* attack was an act of political and personal retaliation.

In any event, the assault could not have worried White much after 1892. His purpose had been accomplished: the lottery was ended in Louisiana. Driven from the state, barred from the federal mails and then interstate commerce, it survived barely twelve more years. The lottery's end was inevitable, and in 1907 the management of the so-called Honduras National Lottery paid fines of more than $280,000 and closed its books.

The fight against the Louisiana State Lottery Company stands out in any summary of Edward White's political life as unique. As a politician he was never again to espouse a public interest cause. Because the outcome of the long and hard lottery struggle may not have been more evident to him than to the public at large, it may be unfair to conclude that even in this fight he was no crusader. Certainly his early training might have led him to revolt against the widespread graft and corruption produced by the lottery. Edward White had demonstrated in this period his individual force as an energizing power while making his only venture into social reform at the same time.

25. New Orleans *New-Delta*, May 12, 1892; New Orleans *Times-Democrat*, July 18, 1890, (paid political advertisement) July 27, 1890, July 31, 1890.

IV
The Road to the Supreme Court

W hen Edward Douglass White went to Washington in 1891 to assume the seat in the United States Senate to which the legislature had elected him in 1888, he found the city larger but not wholly dissimilar from the one he had left when he returned home from Georgetown University at the outbreak of the Civil War. Washington was pleasant, neither wholly southern nor northern in its overtones. The capital still was not a large municipality, its population being more than 230,000 persons, of whom 154,695 were white and 75,572 were black. Although four out of five white citizens had been born in southern states, Washington was less a southern city than it had once been, and in higher society especially, a southern background had diminished in importance. Although not devoid of light industry and supplied by several well-organized commercial enterprises, the city was still first and foremost the capital of the American Republic. It was, moreover, an urbane community which perhaps did little to create artistic genius, but which valued the arts and annually increased its treasure of literature, art, and the sciences. An English visitor noted an "air of comfort, of leisure, of space, of stateliness you hardly expect in America. It looks a sort of place where nobody has to work for a living, or, at any rate, not hard."[1] Washington's growing number of distinguished citizens made its social life stimulating and even exciting. To this city White returned to take his seat in

1. Constance M. Green, *Washington: Capital City, 1879–1950* (Princeton: Princeton University Press, 1963), 89; G. W. Steevens, *The Land of the Dollar*, 92, quoted in Green, *Washington*, 77.

that exclusive national debating society, the Senate. He would live out his life in Washington.

Edward White took the oath of office on March 4, 1891.[2] He was then forty-six years of age, still a bachelor, and had come to Washington as a respected state political leader. Unknown to the nation at large, he began his senatorial and then judicial career amid conflicts of a social and economic nature, which carried down to the New Deal of the 1930s and, in some respects, to the present.

The Senate of which White became a member included many of the most astute politicians ever found in that body. Among the leaders of the dominant Republican majority was the Pennsylvania delegation of dubious fame, Senators Ben Cameron and Matthew Quay; Ebenezer Hoar still represented Massachusetts; John Sherman of Ohio, author of the antitrust legislation presently to occupy a large place in White's constitutional theories, was still a senator. Of some importance were Henry M. Teller of Colorado, champion of free silver, and David Bennett Hill, Democratic senator and currently the boss of the Democratic organization in New York. Although White brought a considerable reputation from Louisiana, no junior senator could very well expect to merit great consideration in committee assignments. His ability in national affairs was untested, and since the Republicans dominated the Senate, he was appointed to five relatively unimportant committees.[3] The Committee on Claims was the most significant of these assignments, followed by the Public Lands Committee.

The principal issues before the Senate when White joined that deliberative body were the Anti-Option Bill, the silver and tariff questions, and the reduction of appropriations. Somewhat less weighty were proposals dealing with national immigration, equipping railroads with automatic couplers, the Bering Sea controversy with Russia, and the Hawaiian annexation issue. On the three essential issues no action was taken because one branch of the Congress succeeded by action or inaction in stalemating the other. While all of these matters were debated, Senator White did not usually participate in the argument and, with a single exception, limited himself to a few pertinent remarks. In the Fifty-second Congress

2. *Congressional Directory*, 52nd Congress, 1st Sess., 50.
3. White's committee membership in the Fifty-second Congress was Claims, Epidemic Diseases, Public Lands, Claims Against Nicaragua (Select), and Pacific Railroads (Select).

he introduced seventeen bills, all of which conferred special benefits either on Louisiana or upon individual residents of that state. Here he was the politician primarily concerned with the welfare of his constituency. Yet his three years in the Senate possess deep significance in any study of White because his speeches, few though they were, reveal a constitutional philosophy that is identical with that later expressed in his opinions on the bench. He demonstrated a mind capable of close constitutional arguments and an understanding of the legal effects of bills, attributes not usually found in a senator. The processes of reasoning so apparent in later years are exemplified in his remarks.

White's single exception to his usual reticence was prompted by the proposed Hatch Anti-Option Bill, which was designed to prevent trading in commodity futures. The first section of this measure defined *options* to include a contract or agreement whereby a party to the agreement acquired the privilege, but not the obligation, of delivering to another or others at some future time any of the following articles: cotton, hops, wheat, corn, rye, pork, lard, and bacon. *Futures* was defined to mean "any contract or agreement whereby a party contracts or agrees to sell and deliver to another or others at a future time" any of the commodities to which the bill applied when, at the time, the contractor was not actually the owner of the goods concerned. As approved by the House the measure was disguised as a revenue bill, with no pretense that its actual intention was to raise revenue. The prohibition of futures trading was to be accompanied by a license of one thousand dollars and a tax of five cents per pound on the raw commodities when handled by a dealer in futures. When this "revenue" measure reached the Senate, it was attacked by White and other Democratic senators who advocated a strict construction of the Constitution with powerful limitations placed upon the national government, restraining it from interfering with the private affairs of the states.[4]

Somewhat in the empirical style of Louis Brandeis a few years later, Senator White opened his argument by a careful analysis of previous

---

4. His address in opposition lasted two days, July 21–22, 1892. Nine Senators interrupted him more than sixty times with questions and counterarguments. *Congressional Record*, 52nd Cong., 1st Sess. (1892), 6513 *et passim*, 6560–582, 6509; two decades later a similar antioption act of a state legislature was reviewed by the Supreme Court, and White delivered the opinion of the Court, sustaining the legislation: *Gatewood* v. *North Carolina*, 203 U.S. 531 (1906).

legislation of the Anti-Option Bill's nature, mustering his documentary support and placing it before his colleagues. He introduced memorials from the Milwaukee Chamber of Commerce, Chicago banks and bankers, New Orleans banks and bankers, Cotton Factors of New Orleans, New Orleans Cotton Exchange, and the Bankers, Millers, and Merchants of Toledo, Ohio—hardly disinterested observers. He also bolstered his argument by frequent citations from a text, *Denslow's Principles of Economics*. In conclusion, White declared that he could find "no more flagrantly unconstitutional legislation, no legislation tending to undermine and destroy the very foundation of our government, and more calculated to do untold and untellable harm to the people of this great country" than the proposed measure.[5] He denounced the bill because it nullified contracts previously held valid by the states and, as a defender of states' rights, he assailed the licensing provision as one granting authority to the federal government that placed it in a position to invade arbitrarily the sovereignty of the states. If futures trading were to be prohibited, the matter should be left to the states, White contending that the constitutional philosophy of the proposal was inconsistent with a national government of limited powers and state governments possessing vast residual powers.

Apart from the constitutional issues he saw in the bill, White charged that it also involved discrimination, favoring the producing classes against the consumers. The futures system was devised, in fact, to prevent a glut upon the market, to keep the producers away from the "vicious claws" of the buyer. Futures contracts were "the necessary result of the struggle between men for equality," and the practice had resulted from the ingenuity of man responding to the inevitable tendencies of business to draw people together and to place every man upon an equal footing with his fellows. Government should not, White declared, upset this mechanism. The entire passage reveals his belief in the rights of individuals coupled with a grasp of the supposed economic behavior of individuals in a laissez-faire system.

Much more important, however, was Senator White's denunciation of the Anti-Option Bill as an illegitimate use of the taxing power. He could not reconcile the measure with the statement of one of his funda-

5. *Congressional Record,* 52nd Cong., 1st Sess., 6561–582, 6513ff.

mental principles, that Congress may not exercise an otherwise legitimate power to reach an end beyond the scope of power permitted by the
Constitution. The sponsors of the bill had declared it to be a revenue
measure, but the senator from Louisiana viewed it merely as a pretext to
allow the national government to interfere with a purely local contract.
"It is," he commented, "a tax that does not tax. Not even a pretext of taxation can be found on the face of the bill." White reduced the fundamental issue to a single question: "Can the federal government by the abuse
of the taxing power abrogate and destroy every limitation found in the
Constitution and every restriction in favor of the states?"[6]

The senator consistently opposed the use of the taxing power to destroy as a usurpation of the power itself. "The power exists in the Supreme Court," he added, "to prevent the usurpation." Even so White
would evaluate the provisions of the bill to determine whether the proposed revenue act was "an honest exercise of the taxing power or a dishonest scheme to raise revenue and accomplish another purpose." If he
judged it to be dishonest, he could not support the bill. So he stated in
reference to the passage of the Oleomargarine Taxing Statute, "The bill
might, on its face, be a revenue measure and might be to me constitutional, but in the exercise of my function here I would not vote for any
bill if it raised a fraudulent revenue, provided I thought it was intended
to prohibit."[7] In the senator's own words, a legislator is competent to
decide whether the statute in question is "subjectively constitutional"
or not.

What, then, is the test of his subjective constitutionality? It is merely
the examination of the particular measure beyond the language of the
statute. Senators may judge individually the motive for an act of taxation, and the bill becomes an object of subjective consideration. Necessarily no fixed standard determines the subjective constitutionality of a
proposed statute. "It is perfectly self-evident when a bill, which is a revenue bill, comes to me for consideration, as to whether I will vote for it
or not, it may be to me,—if I am allowed to use the word,—subjectively
unconstitutional *per se*, and I may vote for it as constitutional, because I
know that although it is a revenue bill, there is a purpose of destruction

6. *Ibid.*, 6516.
7. *Ibid.*, 6518.

and prohibition contained in it." [8] The Anti-Option Bill could not have White's approval because, considered subjectively, it was an abuse of the taxing power.

White, however, would not have the Supreme Court dare to use this test of subjective unconstitutionality so convenient for a legislator. For the Court the fundamental test is one of "objective constitutionality." The Court must not go behind the expressed purpose of the statute to ascertain its constitutionality. While motivations and purposes are within a senator's sphere of consideration, they are not decisive when the Court reviews the act in question. The sole concern of the Court in reviewing a taxing bill, according to Senator White, is whether the act, on its face, is a revenue measure. When the statute's validity is tested by the Court, the act must be examined only from the point of view of its objective constitutionality. "But when it comes before the Court, the Court can only look at it objectively. The Court must look at its provisions, and if on its face it is a revenue bill, if on its face it be for the purpose of raising revenue, the Court will say that it cannot consider its motive, but must decree its enforcement." And answering a question from the floor, he added: "If I were the Executive or a Judge and the bill came to me, then having passed out of this sphere and into another sphere where motives could not enter, I would say that the sole question presented to me was, does it raise revenue on its face, and, if so, I would hold it constitutional." [9]

To White, however, the Anti-Option Bill was not objectively constitutional because on its face it was not a revenue measure; nor was it subjectively constitutional by his own individual bases of interpretation. As an associate justice of the Supreme Court, he restated the doctrine of objective constitutionality in sustaining the Oleomargarine Tax Act, which, as a senator he regarded as "a dishonest scheme to raise revenue and accomplish another purpose." [10] Of course, Senator White was merely formulating in precise terms a doctrine already long used by the Court, a fact he recognized.

It is perfectly true that in two or three cases the Supreme Court of the United States has said that where on the face of a statute there was the exercise of taxa-

8. *Ibid.*, 6513.
9. *Ibid.*, 6518, 6519.
10. *McCray v. United States*, 195 U.S. 27 (1904); *Congressional Record*, 52nd Cong., 1st Sess., 6519.

tion, as the statute was on its face a taxing statute, the Court would not destroy the face of the statute by wiping out the taxing provision of the statute with the sponge of the motives which may have actuated the members who passed it. Is that the case here [with the Anti-Option Bill]. . . . Where the face of the statute shows no tax . . . then I say the mission of jurisdiction is given the Court of this land to brush away the statute for its flagrant and open violation of the Constitution.[11]

Senator White's condemnation forced amendments to the measure, and the Anti-Option Bill was never passed by the Congress. An amendment, formulated and introduced by the Populist senator, James Zachariah George of Mississippi, provided that options and futures should be treated as illegal restraints upon foreign and interstate commerce. Again White took the floor in opposition and stated a conception of the commerce power, which eventually found expression in Justice William R. Day's majority opinion in the *Child Labor* case.[12]

White maintained that the George amendment imposed no limitations upon the exercise of the commerce power by Congress. With some foresight he wondered if Congress might not at some future date, under its power to regulate foreign and interstate commerce, declare that "too much acreage in cotton impedes interstate commerce." State autonomy itself might well be destroyed if Congress should find a state government inefficient so "that the reflex action of that inefficient government was an impediment to commerce and that hence under the interstate commerce clause of the Constitution the state government should be wiped out." However, Senator White failed to set up a standard or degree beyond which Congress might not act to interfere with purely local affairs. Foreseeing only disastrous consequences to state authority should the George amendment be adopted, he stated: "The power delegated to Congress to regulate commerce between the states may well apply directly not only to interstate commerce, but to the instruments of that commerce . . . when, however, it is attempted by a declaration to vest jurisdiction in the United States as to matters not interstate commerce, simply because of the resulting and reflex action of such commerce, such effort throws down every constitutional barrier which has

11. *Congressional Record*, 52nd Cong., 1st Sess., 6513.
12. *Hammer* v. *Dagenhart*, 247 U.S. 251 (1918).

existed from the foundation of our government and makes the Congress . . . more omnipotent than the Parliament of England." His senatorial doctrine limiting the exercise of the commerce power to subjects purely interstate in character underwent a fundamental change in questions presented to him as a justice, although it is essentially the same doctrine used by the Court in *Hammer* v. *Dagenhart*.[13]

The constitutional view of Senator White did not prevail against the George amendment. By a vote of forty to twenty-nine the Senate ignored his objections and adopted the amendment. The House, however, ultimately rejected the Anti-Option Bill, and the measure died. White came out of the debates with acclaim from the press as a "sound constitutional lawyer."

Two bills in the same session revealed his grasp of legal phraseology. One, the Deadly Weapons in the District of Columbia Bill, passed by the House, proposed to punish the carrying or selling of deadly weapons within the District of Columbia. The senator objected to this measure on the grounds that, although its effect was to prevent the carrying of concealed weapons, it left to the judge the discretion of deciding who should or should not carry such weapons: "It is an elementary aphorism . . . that the worst criminal statute in the world is that which allows judicial discretion to take citizens out of the reach of the statute."[14] His clarifying amendment to the measure was carried. The second bill, the Saturday Bank Half Holiday, provided for optional half holidays on Saturdays for banks in Washington. White opposed this act because it left the decision on whether commercial paper would mature on Saturday or carry over to Monday to the discretion of individual banks.

The first session of the Fifty-third Congress opened in response to a special call from President Grover Cleveland. Its main purpose was to review the financial and tariff issues then perplexing his administration. White's committee assignments were now somewhat more important than they had been in the Fifty-second Congress. He was a member of the Commerce, Indian Depredations, and Interstate Commerce committees

13. *Congressional Record*, 52nd Cong., 2nd Sess., 932; compare with the doctrine enunciated in *Houston, E. & W. Texas Ry. Co.* v. *United States*, 234 U.S. 342 (1914), in which White silently concurred.
14. *Congressional Record*, 52nd Cong., 1st Sess., 5788.

and chairman of the Committee to Audit and Control the Contingent Expenses of the Senate. In the new Congress, the senator from Louisiana spoke on nine public bills and introduced seventeen private measures.

In his second inaugural address President Cleveland had urged the repeal of the Silver Purchase Act. White voted for the repeal and explained that fear alone had demolished our credit structure and intensified the panic of 1893. He felt that a restoration of confidence was the primary need. In his own words:

If ninety-five percent of the transactions of the country are credit as compared with currency, the contraction which took place was not in the currency, which represented only five per cent. Fear destroyed the credit of the country and the destruction of the credit of the country engendered the panic. People took their money and hid it away because the credit of the country was gone. All over the country contracts began to be made for gold, because people feared that the country was going on a silver basis and hence silver depreciated. . . . The whole world . . . began to withdraw credit from us. This withdrawal of credit led to a gradual contraction in the ninety-five per cent which is the greatest volume of currency, and whenever you contract that great volume of currency you lead to fear and fear leads to hoarding of money, no matter what kind of money it is.[15]

If this is a fair sample of his financial acumen, it is a better one of his reasoning processes. The style is the same as that he would later use on the bench.

The second session of the Fifty-third Congress met to revise the tariff. Cleveland was pledged to such a revision, yet the Democratic party was not wholeheartedly with him. Despite the party platform, Senator White fought for the protection of sugar in any tariff bill which Congress might pass. He admitted that he thought "the taking off of the revenue duty from sugar and putting it on a bounty was a wasteful and extravagant expenditure of public money . . . it was a wrong against the revenue system and the quicker it was undone the better."[16] He chose to struggle for a tariff and saw his purpose through when the Wilson-Gorman Act of 1894 was passed. This measure restored duties on sugar that were pleasing to planters and the Sugar Trust alike, but one result of Senator White's efforts in its behalf was the charge that he had received aid from the Sugar Trust in winning his seat in the Senate. What

15. Senator Edward D. White's speech on the Silver Purchase Repeal Act, *Congressional Record*, 53rd Cong., 2nd Sess., 1773.
16. *Ibid.*, 2291.

happened was this: the tariff of 1890 gave a bounty of one-eighth of a cent per pound to sugar producers. For some time White, with his brother and half-brother, had managed the family estate, installing at considerable expense more efficient methods than the mule mill and open kettle system. Although the tariff act of 1890 went into effect before he took his seat in the Senate, the estate profited from it by some $37,367.06 in 1892–1893 and approximately two-thirds of that sum the following year. No evidence supports any charge of corruption on White's part. He was considered at the time, however, to belong to the select corps of Louisiana's sugar planters and might reasonably be expected to represent their interests.[17]

On July 7, 1893, Mr. Justice Samuel Blatchford of New York died. On February 19, 1894, President Cleveland sent the name of Senator Edward D. White of Louisiana to the Senate for confirmation of appointment to the vacancy on the Court created by Justice Blatchford's death. On March 4, 1894, White resigned from the Senate and a few days later took the oath of office as associate justice of the Supreme Court. Behind this bare enumeration of dates there lay a bitter and partisan struggle between certain members of the Senate and the president.

The months preceding White's nomination to the Court had witnessed attack and counterattack arising from a feud between Cleveland and Senator David Bennett Hill of New York. Upon Justice Blatchford's demise the president had sent the name of William B. Hornblower to the Senate without consulting Hill, of whose state Hornblower was a resident. Hornblower, a graduate of Princeton University, an eminent attorney, and counsel to Joseph Pulitzer, was generally conceded to be a man of ability. Unfortunately, Senator Hill regarded Hornblower as an enemy. A few years earlier Hornblower had been a member of a committee of nine appointed by the Bar Association of the City of New York to investigate charges that Judge Isaac Maynard, attorney to the State Board of Canvassers, had manipulated election returns in order to retain control of the state senate for the Democratic party in 1891. The committee, among whose members were Elihu Root, Edmond Randolph Carter, and Clifford A. Hand, returned a unanimous report that Maynard, act-

17. *Senate Miscellaneous Documents*, 52nd Cong., 2nd Sess., 40.

ing under the direction of Hill, then governor of New York, had indeed falsified the election returns. The committee consequently recommended Maynard's impeachment. Hill's anger was directed especially toward Hornblower, who had been appointed to the committee at the request of Judge Maynard's attorney. On January 15, 1894, after an unfavorable report by the Senate Judiciary Committee, the Senate rejected Hornblower's nomination by a vote of twenty-four to thirty, the New York *Herald* reporting that "David Bennett Hill walked out of the session with a broad smile on his face." The next day the New York *Tribune* commented that "the defeat of Mr. Hornblower is, of course, a signal, personal triumph for Mr. Hill. . . . It is not likely to be the last set-back which Mr. Hill will administer to his successful rival." Hill had played his trump card of senatorial courtesy, declaring that, since Cleveland had not consulted him on the appointment, the action of the president "was the first step in the direction of the complete overthrow—unless the executive be checked—of the senatorial prerogative." [18]

The senator from New York indicated that a nomination of Rufus Peckham would be confirmed, but by this time Cleveland had decided to fight for a nominee of his choice as a matter of principle. On January 22, 1894, Cleveland proposed Rufus Peckham's brother, Wheeler H. Peckham, who had fought vigorously against Hill's nomination and election as governor and who had been even more prominent than Hornblower in the Maynard investigation. Hill quickly formed a coalition of eastern, southern, and western senators against Wheeler Peckham's nomination. At the time he sent Wheeler Peckham's nomination to the Senate, Cleveland wrote Joseph Choate, requesting him to use his influence in Peckham's cause and adding, "I desire Mr. Peckham's nomination, first, on account of his fitness and merits, and, second, *because I want the appointment to come from the New York Bar and I have no names in reserve which represent it.*" Peckham, however, had angered the Senate by criticizing its action on the Hornblower nomination. Senator Henry Cabot Lodge of Massachusetts spoke against him, stating: "I do not think it wise to put upon the supreme bench men over sixty years of age, and

18. The feud affecting White's appointment to the Supreme Court is discussed at some length in Robert McElroy, *Grover Cleveland: The Man and the Statesman* (2 vols.; New York: Harper, 1923), II, 126 ff., and Allan Nevins, *Grover Cleveland: A Study in Courage* (New York: Dodd, Mead, 1932), 569–72; New York *Herald*, January 16, 1894; New York *Tribune*, January 17, 1894.

the soundness of this policy has been recognized by the judicial pension law and by the practice of the Senate." Lodge went on to add, "In addition, I was disgusted by the efforts of railroad corporations, through letters and telegrams, to secure votes for Mr. Peckham. Some of these corporations have suits pending." [19] Hill termed the nomination a "spite appointment." On February 16, 1894, the Senate rejected Peckham's nomination by a vote of thirty-two to forty-one.

Cleveland, encouraged by political independents to defy Hill, next offered the appointment to Frederic Coudert, who declined on grounds of personal obligations to clients. On February 19, 1894, the president at last nominated White, and the Senate confirmed the nomination without reference to the Judiciary Committee. Senator Hill seconded the motion for White's confirmation, commenting that White "is offensive to no one. He has not been involved in any factious dissensions. He has not antagonized any regular Democratic organizations." He expressed regret at the same time that "among many excellent men on the bench in New York, and with the large number of great lawyers in that state, he [Cleveland] could not select his candidate there." [20]

The historian, Allan Nevins, argues that the nomination of White to the Supreme Court was "a clear surrender." Certainly the immediate circumstances of White's appointment are curious. After Wheeler Peckham had been rejected, Senator William E. Chandler of New Hampshire was heard to exclaim that the president could not name any man whom the Senate would accept. When this comment reached the White House, Cleveland reportedly answered: "Tomorrow I'll name a man whom the Senate will unanimously confirm and for whom that little son of a bitch himself will be compelled to vote." [21]

As a matter of fact Edward White had no idea that he was under consideration. He had been fighting Cleveland's tariff reduction bill, and when Cleveland called him to the White House to tell him of his nomination, White felt that his departure from the party line might be precipitating a final break with the president. It is a common view that White was kicked upstairs to remove him from the tariff struggle, something

19. McElroy, *Cleveland*, II, 136, italics Cleveland's; New York *Tribune*, January 17, 1894.
20. New York *Times*, February 20, 1894.
21. Nevins, *Cleveland*, 571; the authorized biographer of Cleveland softens this statement to read: "I'll name a man tomorrow whom the Senate will unanimously confirm and for whom that pestiferous wasp himself will have to vote." McElroy, *Cleveland*, II, 134.

he himself may have believed. Certainly those senators who had not expected their colleague's appointment were no less surprised than the Louisiana senator.[22]

Despite the view that White's elevation to the Supreme Court was primarily the result of a factional quarrel among the Democrats or the desire to promote him to a position where he would be out of the tariff battle, other factors were also present| He was known as an advocate of the income tax; except for the tariff issue he had supported Cleveland's financial policies; and his legal talents, along with some previous judicial experience, undoubtedly were known to the president.|

White had won Cleveland's respect in other ways. Some time before the nomination, at a house party given by Delaware Senator James A. Bayard, Cleveland overheard White ask Bayard if there were a Catholic church nearby where he could attend early Mass. "I made up my mind," said Cleveland later to Bliss Perry, "that there was a man who was going to do what he thought was right; and when the vacancy came, I put him on the Supreme Court." Edward White had also shown a sympathetic understanding of the president's perennial difficulty with office seekers. At the White House, said White, there were throngs of people from all over the country seeking government jobs. A vacancy had occurred in Louisiana, and Cleveland sent for White. Two decades later White would remember: "I said, 'Mr. President, I think offices are the curse of the public man; I wish there were no offices.' When a man induces the appointment of one incumbent, he makes one friend and twenty enemies, and nine chances out of ten, the man who is appointed believes he was appointed on his merits, and you appointed him because you had to do it."[23]

There are, of course, a good many motives in any political appointment. Cleveland's pique at David Bennett Hill, his desire to get some nomination to the Court confirmed, his wish to end the tariff debate successfully as soon as possible, and an earnest belief that White was the best man who would be confirmed irrespective of political considerations: any combination of these factors might explain the nomination.

22. Nevins, *Cleveland*, 571; see also Matilda Gresham, *Life of Walter Quinton Gresham* (2 vols.; Chicago: Rand-McNally, 1919), II, 812, 816; New York *Times*, February 20, 1894.

23. Bliss Perry, *And Gladly Teach: Reminiscences* (Boston: Houghton Mifflin, 1935), 146–47; "Address of Chief Justice White," *Princeton Alumni Weekly*, XII (May 15, 1912), 525–26.

Surely they made it desirable. The fact remains, however, that Senator White was not the president's first choice to replace Justice Blatchford, nor even his second or third choice. White's name came to the president's mind because Cleveland was politically embroiled with Senator Hill, but this does not mean that it dictated the appointment to the exclusion of other considerations.

Had Cleveland, in fact, expected White's immediate resignation from the Senate and his exit from the tariff struggle, he was to be disappointed. White did not assume his new position until several weeks after his confirmation, despite criticism. The New York *Times* commented: "The procedure is regarded as extraordinary in the extreme. . . . Both factions feel outraged by it. The sugar men believe that Mr. White is injuring their cause, and the friends of the Wilson bill in the Senate declare that the resignation now in order from Mr. White is that of his judgeship. Some of the criticism of Mr. White by Senators who have recently voted for his transfer to the bench is as strong as has ever been heard here of any public man." In a letter to Father Havens Richards, S.J., of Georgetown University, he explained the delay. "The people of Louisiana were in the throes of almost a struggle for existence before the Senate Finance Committee, and I became haunted with fear that by abandoning them in a moment of emergency I was doing wrong to my conscience. This caused me to resolve to say nothing as to my acceptance of the office until the struggle before the Committee had culminated, and if that culmination was unfavorable to decline the office and to continue in the Senate. I wish I deserved your kind words of commendation." [24]

White's accession to the bench did not provoke any great reaction. Outside of his own state and among governmental officials, he was not well known. No more than two legal periodicals, *Case and Comment* and the Chicago *Legal News*, commented at all. The nation's press was less reticent, but such opposition as existed rested on White's war record and the fact that he filled a vacancy that by rights should have gone to a New Yorker. The New York *Tribune* suggested that the appointment may have been "largely due to a feeling on the part of the friends of the Wilson bill that its chances of passage might be improved if the Senator were gotten out of the way and some less active and influential advocate

24. New York *Times*, March 6, 1894; Edward D. White to Father J. Havens Richards, March 9, 1894, in Georgetown University Archives.

of the sugar interest should replace him in the Louisiana delegation in Congress." The Democratic Brooklyn *Eagle* complained bitterly that "never before has a New Yorker's successor among the associate justices been other than a New Yorker . . . never before has one who was a rebel soldier been chosen for an exclusively Northern circuit. . . . The appointment should never have been made. Personally the man is unobjectionable. By reason of the disloyal record of the man in the past his appointment is outrageous and offensive." The Chattanooga *Times* replied acidly that this notion was "supremely ridiculous." Another newspaper found wry humor in the fact that the same senators who nervously considered the awful dangers of the nomination of the excellent Wheeler Peckham "have now awakened to the fact that their extraordinary zeal had led them to confirm the nomination of an able Southern ex-Confederate soldier." Not unexpectedly, the Populist press scorned White's appointment as that of "a thorough plutocrat and representative of the money power. The people have no friend in Judge White of Louisiana." Through all this dispute, the *Catholic Review* rejoiced that "in these days of religious revival of Know-Nothingism . . . Mr. White's religious belief was no bar to his advancement to the exalted office to which he has just been appointed."[25]

The nomination having been confirmed and White having joined the Court, he now took an important personal step. A few months after his appointment to the bench, White married Mrs. Leita Montgomery Kent, widow of a Washington attorney. The ceremony took place at Saint Francis Xavier Church in New York on November 5, 1894. White had been anxious for James Cardinal Gibbons to solemnize the marriage and had written him, "I dislike to trouble you so much, but so many acts of kindness on your part to myself are fresh in my mind and you are identified with so many endearing recollections in my past that it would be a source of great consolation to have this blessing of my life come to me through your ministry."[26] The cardinal could not comply with White's request,

25. New York *Tribune*, February 19, 1894; Brooklyn *Eagle*, February 21, 1894 (The first ex-Confederate appointed to the Court, Lucius Q. C. Lamar, who served from 1888 to 1893, did not serve a northern circuit); Chattanooga *Times*, February 22, 1894; Chicago *Record*, February 22, 1894; Denver *News*, February 23, 1894; *Catholic Review*, quoted in "Appointment of White," *Public Opinion*, XVI (1894), 522.

26. Edward D. White to James Cardinal Gibbons, undated, in archives of the Archdiocese of Baltimore, 93 L 6.

however, and instead, two of White's longtime Georgetown friends officiated.

Edward White became chief justice during the administration of William Howard Taft. White's membership on the Court necessarily restricted his activities, but it did not prevent a continuing interest in matters that had long held his attention. As associate justice of the Supreme Court, White's influence widened. He drew many to him by the force and charm of a strong personality, and in turn, he made associations of deep influence on his own life. He became particularly close to President Taft, who developed trust in White's judgment on Court personnel. The record shows that as an associate justice from March, 1894, to December, 1910, White was industrious and active. A record of the work of six justices, compiled at President Taft's direction in 1910, showed that White had written 245 opinions in the decade since 1900 with a total of 2,070 pages; this judicial output was exceeded by that of only one member of the bench, Chief Justice Melville W. Fuller.[27] At this time, the president evidently was considering a successor to the elderly chief justice. Within a year Fuller and two associates on the tribunal died: Justice Rufus Peckham on October 14, 1909, Justice David Brewer on March 29, 1910, and Chief Justice Fuller on July 4, 1910.

Never before had a president been compelled to fill so many vacancies in so short a time. The Supreme Court was in poor condition, left with only four experienced members. Taft, of course, did not have to select a new chief justice from this group. In view of the disorganization of the Court's membership, however, such a choice was likely. Justices John Marshall Harlan and Horace H. Lurton were considered probably too old to assume the responsibilities of chief justice, while, conversely, Justice Charles Evans Hughes was judged too young and inexperienced.[28] White would be a logical choice: his economic and political views coincided with those of President Taft; he was acceptable to the progressive wing of the Republican party; and he was personally friendly with Taft.

27. See, for example, George W. Wickersham to William H. Taft, October 13, 1909, in Taft Papers, Library of Congress; Taft Papers, series 1, case 8.
28. Henry F. Pringle, *The Life and Times of Taft: A Biography* (2 vols.; New York: Farrar & Rinehart, 1939), I, 530.

As is the case in such matters, there was no certainty that the appointment would fall to White. Justice Holmes wrote Sir Frederick Pollock sometime before the appointment:

The vacation has been interrupted and saddened by these recurring deaths and I am content to make a new start from Washington. The President said he meant to send for me and talk about the new appointments. . . . As to the Chief Justiceship I am rather at a loss. I should bet he will appoint Hughes, who has given up a chance of being Republican nominee for President. I think White who is next in Seniority to Harlan (too old, etc.) the ablest man likely to be thought of. I don't know whether his being a Catholic would interfere. I have always assumed absolutely that I should not be regarded as possible—they don't appoint side Judges as a rule, it would be embarrassing to skip my Seniors, and I am too old. I think I would be a better administrator than White, but he would be more politic. Also the President's inclination so far as I can judge seems to me towards a type for which I have a limited admiration. I am afraid White has as little chance as I. I really don't care much who is appointed if only he is a man who can dispose of the little daily questions with promptitude and decision. . . . I know of no first rate man except White. His writing leaves much to be desired, but his thinking is profound, especially in the legislative direction which we don't recognize as a judicial requirement but which is so, especially in our Court, nevertheless.[29]

Although President Taft had an outright distaste for many of the political functions of the presidency and sometimes was an uncertain administrator, he firmly believed that he was expert in the selection of judges. Taft had felt little admiration for Fuller as chief justice, for he believed him to be too rigid and too narrow in his interpretation of the Constitution. The president was certainly no Populist in either economic or political beliefs, and he tended to approach most problems, including those of a constitutional nature, with an attitude of organic legalism. White's opinions in the *Insular* cases had, it seemed to him, demonstrated an implicit flexibility that contrasted sharply with the rigid position taken by Chief Justice Fuller in his dissents. Moreover, Taft was at the beginning of his trust-busting campaign, a periodic feature of American national politics. He felt that the government had not presented its pleadings in a way to show that the Sugar Trust violated the Sherman Anti-Trust Act, nor did he like the rebuff to the antitrust legislation de-

29. Oliver Wendell Holmes to Sir Frederick Pollock, September 24, 1910, in Mark De-Wolfe Howe (ed.), *Holmes-Pollock Letters: The Correspondence of Mr. Justice Holmes and Sir Frederick Pollock, 1874–1932* (2 vols.; Cambridge: Harvard University Press, 1941), I, 170.

livered by the Court in 1895. He was well aware of White's dissent in the *Trans-Missouri Freight Association* case, where White began to evolve the line of reasoning that would develop into the "rule of reason" in later cases, and White's line of argument appealed to him. Obviously any kind of contract is restrictive of trade and sets limitations; why then, as White asked, should there not be a distinction between "reasonable restraints" of interstate commerce, which would be permissible, and "unreasonable restraints," which would be illegal? President Taft found this an appealing argument. Finally, there was the simple fact that physically Taft and White were alike, huge men of considerable girth who looked like they ought to be judges even if one of them was not. Sixty-five years old, White was six feet tall, weighed two hundred pounds, and like Taft, gave an appearance of massiveness. Appointments have turned on lesser considerations. Taft's decision was made.[30]

On December 12, 1910, Edward Douglass White's appointment as chief justice was announced. He was the second associate justice of the Court to receive such a promotion (Associate Justice William Cushing of Massachusetts, who was nominated and confirmed as chief justice in 1796, declined the appointment). Although the appointment was initially well received, three years later an ardent progressive would write to Woodrow Wilson to warn him of the Court's conservatism, adding "it was common talk when White was appointed Supreme Justice from Louisiana, that he smelled of coal oil. The rest [of the Court] may be, perhaps, best described as morganheimers." The White appointment may have politically damaged Taft's chances of a second presidential term of office.[31]

White was pleased by the favorable acceptance of his appointment.

30. Taft in Henry P. Dart, Sr., Harry M. Daugherty, William Howard Taft, and others, *Proceedings of the Bar and Officers of the Supreme Court of the United States in Memory of Edward Douglass White*, Washington, December 17, 1921, p. 62, hereinafter cited as *Proceedings*; William H. Taft, *The Anti-Trust Act and the Supreme Court* (New York: Harper, 1914), 59–60; *United States v. E. C. Knight Co.*, 156 U.S. 1 (1895); *United States v. Trans-Missouri Freight Association*, 166 U.S. 290 (1897).

31. Frank A. Mehling to Woodrow Wilson, March 13, 1913, in Wilson Collection, Library of Congress; Charles D. Hilles to Taft, April 19, 1912, in Taft Papers. Among the causes listed are: "(b) the appointment of Chief Justice White; (c) the annual attendance by the President upon the Thanksgiving mass and feast." There is some evidence that aid was sought from prominent Catholics and politicians upon White's behalf. James Cardinal Gibbons to Amasa Thornton, November 14, 1910; Thornton to Taft, November 25, 1910, in Taft Papers.

He was especially affected by the message sent by former president Theodore Roosevelt, writing Roosevelt that "I know nothing that could have touched me more than your message, and I thank you with all my soul for it. I am not vain enough to think that I merit one thousandth part of the kind things that have been said about my appointment, but that I have your kind wishes and feelings gives me the strength to hope that I may not in the discharge of my duties fall too far below the proper standards." [32] Fully aware of its responsibilities, White soberly accepted his new position.

32. Edward D. White to Theodore Roosevelt, December 10, 1910, in Roosevelt Papers, Library of Congress.

V

The Nation and the Court

On March 12, 1894, Edward Douglass White first donned the black robes of a justice of the Supreme Court of the United States. He was becoming a member of a body whose membership was fluctuating at a greater rate than at any previous time in the Court's history. During Chief Justice Fuller's tenure of twenty-two years (1888–1910), no less than eleven new judges, including White, were appointed to the Court: David J. Brewer, Henry B. Brown, George Shiras, Jr., Howell E. Jackson, Rufus W. Peckham, Joseph McKenna, Oliver W. Holmes, William R. Day, William H. Moody, and Horace H. Lurton. The main influences upon the Court and upon White as a new member of that tribunal came from three areas: the state of the nation, the background and judicial philosophies of the justices, and the existing judicial tendencies in deciding the issues of the time.

In early 1893 Frederick J. Turner read before the American Historical Society his seminal paper on "The Significance of the Frontier in American History." With the absorption of free land, Turner argued, the frontier was being closed. Less successful individuals could no longer gather their possessions and move on to new areas that were not so competitive. Despite the passing of the frontier, the usually mobile American would find other ways of meeting his needs. Agriculture was being replaced by industry as the mainstay of American life, and population already tended to concentrate in urban areas where factories and jobs were available.

The concentration of wealth and land ownership implicit in the passing of the frontier attracted the attention of several contemporary writers. One of these was Henry George, who stated the issue clearly in his
Social Problems. Starting from the premise that distribution of wealth un-
derlies political problems, George argued that "the experiment of popular government in the United States is a failure. . . . But speaking generally of the whole country . . . our government by the people has in large
degree become, is in larger degree becoming, government by the strong
and unscrupulous." Although the people continued to vote, George asserted that they were losing their power as "money and organization tell
more and more in elections." Bribery, the pressure exerted by large employers, and the growth of the political machine were so strong in places
"that the ordinary citizen has no more influence than he would have in
China. He is, in reality, not one of the governing classes, but one of the
governed." Finding that his vote means only a change in masters, "he is
beginning to accept the situation, and to leave politics to politicians, as
something with which an honest, self-respecting man cannot afford to
meddle." George was not optimistic in anticipating change, for he found
a lack of "intelligent interest" that would fit political organization to new
conditions. [1]

Another contemporary writer who also saw clearly the political and
economic significance of the closing frontier was Henry D. Lloyd. In his
Wealth Against Commonwealth, Lloyd wrote in the style of Rousseau, "Nature is rich, but everywhere man, the heir of nature, is poor . . . between
this plenty ripening on the boughs of our civilization and the people
hungering for it step the 'cornerers,' the syndicates, trusts, combinations,
with the cry of 'overproduction—too much of everything.'" "Political
government by the self-interest of the individual we call anarchy. It is
one of the paradoxes of public opinion that the people of America, least
tolerant of this theory of anarchy in government, lead in practicing it in
industry. . . . Politically we are civilized; industrially, not yet." Lloyd
foresaw corporate concentration of wealth in which property "was becoming master instead of servant, property in many necessaries of life
becoming monopoly of the necessaries of life." In other words, in 1894
the United States was approaching the culmination of a political revolt

1. Henry George, *Social Problems* (New York: Schalkenbach Foundation, 1939), originally copyrighted by George in 1883, p. 16–17.

against monopoly capitalism and its attending difficulties, a revolt that had been developing in the life of the nation since the Civil War.[2]

After 1865 there had been a virtual economic revolution. Growth in population and wealth were characteristic features of the nation between 1865 and 1900. Population rose at a rate of almost 25 percent for each decade, increasing from 31 million in 1860 to 76 million at the end of the century. Part of this growth was due to the liberal policy on immigration under which 8 million aliens entered the United States between 1870 and 1890. National wealth rose rapidly, increasing from $16 billion in 1858 to $44 billion in 1878 and to $63 billion in 1900. New factories and a swelling agricultural production testified to the general expansion that was taking place. In 1860, 140,433 manufacturing establishments turned out products valued at $1,895,861,000, but in 1900 only 207,514 establishments produced goods valued at $11,406,997,000. Additional farms brought under cultivation totaled over 300 million acres of improved land. As early as 1878 it could be said that the United States was a far different country from that of 1865. "Economically the nation of 1865—a nation which had hardly advanced to the Missouri, which used iron alone, which had a modest railway system and but one and a half billion dollars invested in manufacturing—was a world away from the nation of 1878—a nation which pressed to the Pacific, which was producing large quantities of steel, which had the first railway system in the world and which had invested nearly three billions in manufacturing."[3]

The revolution in industry rested upon a number of factors, many technological, some physical, and a few legal and governmental. The discovery of natural resources and their rapid exploitation provided an obvious base for growth. These resources included iron ore, coal, natural gas, copper, gold, silver, and oil, to which an improved technology derived from science and machine power was applied. Swift utilization converted these resources into usable and valuable products, while a growing domestic population provided an expanded domestic market and foreign commerce was increasing. The development of a huge railroad system and the expansion of, first, telegraph and, then, telephone

2. Henry D. Lloyd, *Wealth Against Commonwealth* (New York: Harper, 1894), I, 496.

3. Charles R. Lingley and Allen P. Foley, *Since the Civil War* (New York: Appleton-Century, 1935), Chapter III, 59; Allan Nevins, *The Emergence of Modern America, 1865–1878* (New York: Macmillan, 1927), 31.

networks supplied an improved communication system. Money begets money; with the increase of national wealth came the capacity to borrow abroad while creating capital at home. Of great significance was a favorable governmental attitude, one not of regulation or of planned development, but of laissez-faire economics, protective tariffs, and especially in the case of the railroads, subsidies. At least equally important to the stand of government on economic matters was the perfection of techniques of corporate organizations, including pools, holding companies, and trusts.[4]

The results of such industrial development over a relatively short period were stunning. With the rising national wealth came a higher standard of living, acceleration of urbanization, population growth including heavy immigration, and the entrance of the nation into world affairs. Cycles of prosperity and depression, periods of unemployment, labor strife, and eventually governmental intervention accompanied this new wealth. Not the least significant among these developments were the concentration of capital and the refinement of that useful legal device, the trust.

The trusts concentrated wealth into large units. From the point of view of those individuals who controlled them, trusts offered substantial advantages: competition was eliminated; unregulated production, which could be economically hazardous, was removed; and economies in manufacturing, transportation, marketing, and funding were made possible. The advantageous use of the corporation, the juristic person, assumed an importance which it had never before held in American life. Equally important, however, was the philosophy developed to buttress concentrated accumulations of wealth.

The basic tenet of this philosophy was simple: the best government was that which governs the least. Private property was inviolable. The acquisition of wealth was a sign of divine favor, and the wealthy were obligated to become still wealthier in order that they might benefit society by their direction. The theoretical foundation of this philosophy lay at hand in social Darwinism, whose leading exponent was Herbert Spencer. In his *Social Statics*, published in 1851, Spencer argued that a struggle for existence between men resulted in the survival of the fittest and that this struggle, continued without government intervention,

4. Samuel Eliot Morison and Henry Steele Commager, *The Growth of the American Republic* (2 vols.; New York: Oxford University Press, 1962), II, 188–89.

would produce human beings who could adapt to their environment so well that they would possess a capacity for highest happiness. "The poverty of the incapable," he wrote, "the distresses that come upon the imprudent, the starvation of the idle, and those shoulderings aside of the weak by the strong, which leave so many 'in shadows and miseries,' are the decrees of a large, far-seeing benevolence." [5] Because social Darwinism identified providence with the "order of nature," individuals, according to this doctrine, have certain rights free from state control. Liberty was the absence of restraints, including those imposed by government.

This congenial philosophy was supported heartily by the bar, which entertained "one simple rule about industry, that it should be free." "The vice of so-called social legislation denying freedom of contract is that it deprives the individual of his 'personal rights' and subjects him to the only tyranny which in this democratic age is possible. . . . The force antagonizing 'personal rights' is not the 'right of property,' but the power of the State exercised in the abridgement of individual liberty." Mr. Justice Holmes declared in vain fourteen years later, in 1905, that "the Constitution does not enact Mr. Herbert Spencer's *Social Statics*." The concentration of money in the hands of a small minority seemed never to have unduly bothered either those who held it or the legal profession. [6]

Even as monopoly capitalism emerged, a steadily increasing discontent spread among farmers and laborers. As early as 1872 a spirit of revolt arose among the western farmers, and they were ready to listen to proposals for reforms of taxation, the currency, and control of corporate interests. Farm problems were acute and had no easy solutions. Farmers were beset with physical hazards peculiar to their occupation: soil exhaustion and erosion, plant and animal disease, too much rain, or not enough rain. They were also helpless in the face of the economic consequences of overproduction and overexpansion of farmland, confronted with declining prices for farm products while costs rose, and burdened with mortgages, exploitation in the domestic market, and competition in

---

5. Herbert Spencer, *Social Statics*, 322, quoted in Alpheus T. Mason, "The Conservative World of Mr. Justice Sutherland, 1883–1910," *American Political Science Review*, XXXII (1938), 453.

6. Frederick N. Judson, "Liberty of Contract Under the Police Power," *Report of the American Bar Association*, XIV (1891), 236, 218–19; dissenting opinion of Holmes in *Lochner* v. *New York*, 198 U.S. 45, 75 (1905).

the world market. Socially they were often frustrated by the isolation of farming and the relative absence of educational, medical, and even religious facilities. Farmers were hostile to state governments as well as to the federal government, for neither level of government was responsive to farm demands in the same sense that they were attentive to industrial, railroad, or financial interests. From 1868 until 1890 the course of farm prices turned downward, and except for occasional periods of rising fortune, the burden of farm debt grew. The American farmer, whether he willed it or not, was becoming "but a tenant at will, or a dependent upon the tender mercies of soulless corporations and absentee landlords."[7]

The farmer's unhappy lot was made more difficult by the protection given to the price of the manufactured commodities he bought. American tariff policy from 1868 onward resulted in increased duties on manufactured goods, this trend peaking for the period in 1890 with the McKinley Tariff Act of that year. The farmer was more than willing to seek redress through the activities of the Grange (the Patrons of Husbandry) and its successor, the Farmers' Alliance, which entered into politics more aggressively than did the Grange. The absorption of the Alliance into the era's movement of political protest, and the movement's early collapse caused the farmers' disenchantment with direct political action.

Labor too was having its difficulties under the rising industrial system. Trouble first began with the railroads, whose rapid overexpansion brought an inevitable day of reckoning. Between 1873 and 1877, wages of railroad employees were reduced 33 percent.[8] Strikes produced by the resulting discontent brought about true industrial violence. President Rutherford B. Hayes sent 250 troops to Maryland, and 10 people were killed in a clash with the troopers. Labor, equally unable either to agree upon objectives or to act as a unit, achieved no lasting adjustment to monopoly capitalism in this period. The Haymarket explosion of May 3, 1887, began a long series of bloody industrial encounters. Strikes and fatalities were common—Homestead, Pullman, the Chicago stockyard

7. Solon J. Buck, *The Agrarian Crusade: A Chronicle of the Farmers in Politics* (New Haven: Yale University Press, 1920), 18; Morison and Commager, *American Republic*, II, 292; Report on Retail Wages and Prices, *Senate Documents*, 52nd Cong., 1st Sess., No. 986, series 2916–918, pts. 1–3; John D. Hicks, *The Populist Revolt: A History of the Farmers' Alliance and the People's Party* (Minneapolis: University of Minnesota Press, 1933), 81.

8. Morris Hillquit, *History of Socialism in the United States* (New York: Funk & Wagnalls, 1910), 200.

strike—and others were to follow. In the meantime, throughout the post–Civil War period, management continued to view labor as a commodity to be bought at the lowest price and used with managerial prerogative. Labor, said management in public announcements, had a rational choice to work or not to work. The loss of jobs, however, in a period of economic scarcity and labor abundance seemed to some observers to be hardly a palatable alternative to long hours and low wages, the more so when there was family hunger to consider.

The doctrine of social Darwinism did not go unchallenged. The early American progressives rejected the major tenets of laissez-faire economics and provided alternative theories of social organization. The progressives did not always agree on specifics, but they accepted basic themes in their anticapitalistic outlook. Society and the state, they argued, have an organic nature in which each individual has an important role to perform for the good of the whole society. For society to operate smoothly and efficiently, the activities of society and state had to be related one to the other in a cooperative fashion, and consequently, laissez-faire thought had to be rejected because its emphasis upon competition disrupts organic unity, destroys cooperation, and retards productive efficiency.

The key injustice brought about by unnecessary capitalistic competition, thought the progressives, was in the unequal distribution of income, creating too great an income disparity and not recognizing the real value of each individual's contribution to society. They wanted "socially useful" labor as the criterion for distribution of income, rather than a labor market acting as a regulator, because they viewed work, not wealth or social position, as the stake in society. This concept required the progressives, in one way or another, to reject the acquisition of wealth and, therefore, to condemn income on the basis of unearned increment. Such a view presented a new theory of distributive justice in which the importance of work, rather than the competition of pecuniary skills, would be the yardstick of the social importance of an individual. Futhermore, the progressives stressed the need for each citizen to share in the responsibilities for the disadvantages of society, because poverty, they reasoned, could never be explained in a society of wealth when all people are expected to contribute socially useful labor.

Finally, progressives, having an unlimited faith in the progress achievable through science and technology, believed that these areas of activity had to be directed to the goal of improving the conditions of society generally. When human productive forces and the benefits of science were unleashed, the progressives contended, an economy of abundance would replace the traditional capitalistic economy and the gains of this society could be equitably distributed throughout to attain greater health, leisure, and moral qualities for all people. Conversely, they held that capitalistic competition would result in inefficiency, with injustice in a bellicose society permitting the good life for only a few.[9]

There was no peace. Instead, movements of political reform appeared in a long series of protests. The Union Labor party, United Labor party, Progressive Labor party, American Reform party, the Grange, the Tax Reformers, the Farmers' Alliance, the Anti-Monopolists, and the Homesteaders arose on the political horizon with programs to remedy real or fancied evils, a trend climaxed by the rise of the Populist party, which made a stirring but unsuccessful drive to bring within its fold all of the elements of dissatisfaction. In 1894 the party was at the peak of its considerable political power.

The rising pressure created a demand for governmental interference to change the rules of the game and to police the more successful participants. Out of the resulting public intervention came many of the constitutional issues of the succeeding decades during which Edward White was on the bench. The role of the Supreme Court, and hence of the individual justices, was important in the developing conflict. Although the Court could not initiate governmental action, it could destroy intervention, or interpret such intervention, and in so doing perhaps revise legislative judgment. In this process the roles of the members of the Court must not be underestimated. By marking out the area within which government could act, the Court could sway, at least temporarily, the course of political action.

A brief review of the Court of 1894 will show something of the background

9. For more complete discussion of these topics, see: Edward Bellamy, *Looking Backward, 2000–1887* (Boston: Houghton Mifflin, 1889), Henry George, *Social Problems* and *Progress and Poverty* (New York: Schalkenbach Foundation, 1936), Simon N. Patten, *The New Basis of Civilization* (Cambridge: Belknap Press of Harvard University Press, 1968), and Thorstein Veblen, *The Theory of Business Enterprise* (New York: Scribner's, 1904) and *The Theory of the Leisure Class* (New York: Macmillan, 1921).

and judicial ideas of the period. More important, it will indicate the judicial tendencies of each justice in relation to the issues of the day.

The chief justice, Melville Weston Fuller, a native of Maine, was an Illinois Democrat appointed to the Court by Cleveland in 1888. He was sixty-one years of age in 1894. Most of his career had been spent in the practice of law in Chicago, a practice in which real property and commercial law had composed the bulk of the cases, but his most noted case was the defense of Charles Cheney, Rector of Christ Church in Chicago, against charges of canonical disobedience before an ecclesiastical tribunal. Fuller's experiences were not such as to give the training needed by a justice who was to be confronted with the social and economic problems coming before the Supreme Court during his tenure. His political activity on behalf of the Democrats in Illinois apparently had had an important influence on his nomination. This activity was partially responsible for the prolonged delay in Fuller's confirmation, which finally came with a vote of forty-one to twenty.[10] On the Court, Fuller gained the reputation of a jurist who favored a strict construction of governmental powers and the defense of federal power as against the rights of the states. Although he took some interest in the improvement of conditions for labor, he was inclined to uphold the rights of person and property against the trend of public regulation. Property and freedom of contract were important legal principles for him.

David Josiah Brewer, born the son of a missionary in Smyrna, Turkey, in 1837, became associate justice of the Court in 1889. When White came to the bench in 1894, Brewer was fifty-seven years of age. In 1858 he had settled in Leavenworth, Kansas, and there pursued a judicial career that culminated in his appointment to the Supreme Court. Justice Brewer was known as a strong defender of property. As a circuit court judge, he had evidenced his regard for the traditional rights of property, and as a justice of the Supreme Court he demonstrated belief in doctrines of freedom of contract and government by injunction. He was a firm believer in social Darwinism, declaring: "It is the unvarying law

10. Cortez A. M. Ewing, *The Judges of the Supreme Court, 1789–1937: A Study of Their Qualifications* (Minneapolis: University of Minnesota Press, 1938), 24; *Journal of the Executive Proceedings of the Senate*, 50th Cong., 1st Sess., 252, 254, 287, 313. Opposition also came from the disappointed adherents of Edward J. Phelps, whom the president had at one time been reported to favor.

that the wealth of the community will be in the hands of the few; and the greater the general wealth, the greater the individual accumulations . . . and hence it always has been, and until human nature is remodeled always will be true, that the wealth of a nation is in the hands of a few, while the many subsist upon the proceeds of their daily toil." That his views were not without influence on the Court is evidenced by the number of opinions he rendered. Justice Brewer delivered the opinion of the Court in 526 cases, of which 70 involved issues of constitutional law. He dissented in 215 cases, of which 18 involved constitutional issues.[11]

Stephen Johnson Field at the age of seventy-eight was the oldest member of the Court, in both years and time of service. Born in 1816 in Haddam, Connecticut, the son of the Reverend David Dudley Field, he became a member of the Supreme Court on March 10, 1863, by nomination of President Abraham Lincoln and confirmation of the Senate. Prior to the Civil War, Field had been a Buchanan Democrat, but when war broke out, he joined the pro-Union group. His experience as a judge of the Supreme Court of California, which state he had adopted as a home after an early association with his brother in New York, largely involved disputes concerning title to land and the mineral deposits of such lands. Field won a reputation as an able judge by helping to bring order out of the chaotic conditions prevailing in California from the Spanish land grants. In his decisions he displayed a tendency to get away from common law notions and to sustain the power of the legislature to act for the "welfare and happiness" of society.[12]

Field, however, became an inflexible constitutional dogmatist as a justice of the Supreme Court. By the time Edward White joined the bench, Field's brand of conservatism was well along its way to maturity as a constitutional dogma. His opinions frequently stated in moral terms the

11. He was successively commissioner of the Federal Circuit Court for the District of Kansas (1861–62), judge of Probate and Criminal Courts of Leavenworth County (1862–64), judge of the First Judicial District of Kansas (1865–69), city attorney of Leavenworth (1869–70), justice of the Supreme Court of Kansas (1870–84), and judge of the Federal Circuit Court, 8th Circuit (1884–89); *Chicago and Northwestern R. R.* v. *Dey*, 35 Fed. 866 (1888), limiting legislative power to fix public utility rates, and *State* v. *Walruff*, 26 Fed. 178 (1886), granting compensation to brewers driven out of business by a prohibition act, and see also *In Re Debs*, 158 U.S. 564 (1895), and "Government by Injunction," *National Corporation Reporter*, XV (1893), 949; *Lochner* v. *New York*, 198 U.S. 45 (1905); *Holden* v. *Hardy*, 169 U.S. 366 (1898), dissent; and *Atkin* v. *Kansas*, 191 U.S. 207 (1903), dissent; David J. Brewer, *The Movement of Coercion*, 5, quoted in Mason, "Conservative World of Mr. Justice Sutherland," 450.

12. *City Slip* cases, 15 Cal. 591 (1860); *Ex Parte Newman*, 9 Cal. 502 (1858).

gospel of wealth and differed little "from the frankly materialistic rationale of William Graham Sumner. There is the same disregard for humane values, the same worship of success, the same standard of individual merit."[13] His opinions were dominated by a dualistic concept of federal and state government, which approximated the theory of Edward Douglass White. This concept placed the two levels of government in neat little categories, surrounded by fixed boundaries with each level sovereign within its own sphere. Strangely, he was also influenced considerably by the doctrine of natural rights. In 1894 Justice Field was already displaying signs of senility, and, in 1897, he resigned after pressure from other members of the Court.

John Marshall Harlan, sixty-one years of age in 1894, was a Kentucky politician turned jurist. In fact, the one year he served as a judge of the Court of Franklin County, Kentucky, was his only judicial experience before appointment to the United States Supreme Court. He was born in Boyle County, Kentucky, in 1833. Before the Civil War he ran for Congress against the Democratic nominee. In 1860 he was a Constitutional Unionist; in 1864 he supported General George B. McClellan for the presidency; and in 1866 he became a Radical Republican. His support of Rutherford B. Hayes in the Republican convention of 1876 led to his appointment in April, 1877, to a presidential commission charged with consolidating rival state legislatures in Louisiana so that some order could be brought into that state. Shortly after a successful completion of this mission, Harlan was nominated to the Court and took his seat December 11, 1877.

As a member of the Court, Justice Harlan wrote the opinion in 705 cases. A sometime owner of slaves and an opponent of abolition, Harlan nevertheless advocated the rights of blacks, especially with his dissent in *Plessy* v. *Ferguson*. His espousal of Republicanism was probably "the most significant political choice he ever made, leading as it did to his eventual appointment to the Supreme Court. Actually, it was a choice that he drifted to rather than made freely."[14] The spirit of his dissent in *Plessy* would make itself felt in the Court's decisions nearly sixty years

13. Robert G. McCloskey, *American Conservatism in the Age of Enterprise: A Study of William Graham Sumner, Stephen J. Field, and Andrew Carnegie* (Cambridge: Harvard University Press, 1951), 124.
14. *Plessy* v. *Ferguson*, 163 U.S. 537 (1896); Alan F. Westin, "John Marshall Harlan and the Constitutional Rights of Negroes: The Transformation of a Southerner," *Yale Law Journal*, LXVI (1957), 654–55.

later, in the 1950s. In his opinions Harlan evidenced judicial belief in the defense of property rights, even contending in one instance that the right to hold public office was a form of property. He upheld civil rights generally and was bitterly opposed in the *Insular* cases to the refusal of the Court to extend all of the Bill of Rights into the unincorporated territories. Harlan sought to protect the police powers of the states and to balance strong nationalism with states' rights. He was scornful of the natural law espoused by Justice Field. A man of strong will, he was aggressive and fought hard in advocating his beliefs.

Horace Gray, now sixty-six years old, had been a member of the Supreme Court since 1881. He was the most scholarly and the best trained in law of any of his colleagues. Born in Massachusetts in 1828, he graduated from the Harvard Law School where he was a contemporary of C. C. Langdell, the father of the case method of legal study. At the age of thirty-six, Gray was the youngest justice of the Massachusetts Supreme Judicial Council, of which he became chief justice in 1873. His chief interest was in the development and history of legal doctrine. Gray's principal asset on the Supreme Court was his knowledge of the growth of the common law.

Henry Billings Brown came to the Court after a long legal career. He was born in 1836 at South Lee, Berkshire County, Massachusetts, and graduated from Yale University in 1856. His legal experience began in 1861 when he was appointed deputy United States marshal in Detroit, where, except for a period of seven years, he continuously held a legal office until his appointment to the Supreme Court in 1890: in 1863 he was an assistant United States district attorney; in 1868, a circuit judge of Wayne County, Michigan; from 1868–1875, engaged in private practice; and from 1875–1890, federal district judge for the eastern district of Michigan. At the time White became a member of the Court, Brown was fifty-eight years of age. During his years of private practice, he had acquired a reputation in the field of admiralty law—he had compiled and published "Reports of Admiralty and Revenue Cases, Argued and Determined in the Circuit and District Courts of the United States for the Western Lake and River Districts." It was in this specialty and in cases involving extradition appeals that he was best known. He upheld the validity of the Income Tax Act of 1894 (*Pollock* v. *Farmers' Loan and Trust Co.*, 158 U.S. 601 [1895]), and believed that the rights of the Constitution did not extend to the territories until so provided by Congress. Brown was a defender of aggregated wealth, arguing that "rich men are essential even to the well-being of the poor. . . . One has but to consider for a moment the immediate consequences of the abolition of large private fortunes to appreciate the danger which lurks in any radical disturbance of the present social system." [15]

George Shiras, sixty-two years old in 1894, had been on the Court since 1892. He was a lawyer with a full background of legal practice, but his career on the Court was not especially distinguished. Born January 26, 1832, in Pittsburgh, Pennsylvania, his career before his appointment to the Court was largely concerned with cases involving the railroad, banking, oil, coal, and iron interests of western Pennsylvania. As a justice he was primarily noted, perhaps unjustly, for supposedly changing his vote on the reargument of the *Pollock* case so as to render the Income Tax Act of 1894 unconstitutional by a five to four decision. He was to retire from the Court in 1903. [16]

The most inconspicuous member of the Court was Howell Edmunds Jackson, who served on the Supreme Court briefly from March 4, 1893, until his death on August 8, 1895. He was born at Paris, Tennessee, on April 8, 1832. He had been a receiver of sequestered property for the Confederacy, a member of the Tennessee Legislature, a United States senator, and a federal circuit court judge. Although nominally a Democrat, he was from an old-line Whig family, and his alliance influenced President Benjamin Harrison, who was faced with a Democratic Senate, in Jackson's appointment to the Court. His failing health prevented Justice Jackson from full-time participation in the work of the Supreme Court after White came to that bench.

Such were the men of the Court that Edward White joined. It was a Court of which only three incumbents had substantial judicial experience on the supreme bench, the other members having been primarily politicians. The constitutional ideas of the group gravitated in the direction of generally accepted concepts of property, freedom of contract, and the relationships between state and federal government. Armed with

15. Henry B. Brown, "The Distribution of Property," *Report of the American Bar Association*, XVI (1894), 218–19.
16. Hampton L. Carson, *The History of the Supreme Court of the United States* (2 vols.; Philadelphia: P. W. Zeigler, 1909), II, 560–64; Charles Warren, *The Supreme Court in United States History* (3 vols.; Boston: Little, Brown, 1922), II, 699.

these weapons the Court was to face an onrush of legal issues brought to the fore by the rising economic and political pressures of their era. These pressures made for a tumultuous period. Given the membership of the Court, any substantial departure from the prevailing ideology of the day was unlikely.

The political and economic developments of the period 1865–1890 gave rise to many constitutional issues involving a delineation of the police power of the states, the relationship of the states to the federal government, and the extent of the authority granted the federal government. None of the cases produced by those issues were more important than those arising from Section 1 of the Fourteenth Amendment to the United States Constitution, which provided: "All persons born or naturalized in the United States, and subject to the jurisdiction thereof, are citizens of the United States and of the State wherein they reside. No State shall make or enforce any law which shall abridge the privileges or immunities of citizens of the United States; nor shall any State deprive any person of life, liberty, or property, without due process of law; nor deny to any person within its jurisdiction the equal protection of the laws."

In the earliest case involving the Fourteenth Amendment, the Supreme Court took the position that its provisions were inapplicable to legislative enactments not involving racial discrimination. This rule was laid down by Mr. Justice Miller in the *Slaughter House* cases with respect to the equal protection clause: "We doubt very much whether any action of a state not directed by way of discrimination against the Negroes as a class, or on account of their race, will ever be held to come within the purview of this provision. It is so clearly a provision for that race and that emergency, that a strong case would be necessary for its application to any other." Justice Field's dissent, in which Chief Justice Salmon P. Chase and Justices Bradley and Noah H. Swayne concurred, was based on his concept of natural law, which bestowed inalienable rights as "the gift of the Creator; which the law does not confer, but only recognizes." Civil liberty is to be found only where each person may pursue his own happiness without constraints except by equal, impartial, and just laws. Miller and his colleagues were not willing to go so far since they perceived the effects of Field's view on the economy of the federal system if the

Fourteenth Amendment were so interpreted. The majority, therefore, favored a more narrow construction of the amendment. [17]

Two years later, in an action that involved the validity of a tax assessment against real property, the Court declared that a person could not be deprived of his property without due process when "as regards the issues affecting it, he has, by the laws of the state, a fair trial in a court of justice." The holding thus emphasized the procedural rather than the substantive aspect of due process. [18]

The legal profession, at this time for the most part champions of laissez-faire and social Darwinism, continued to urge, however, that the due process clause be so construed as to afford protection against arbitrary and unreasonable exercises of the legislative power. Roscoe Conkling, in arguing the case of *San Mateo County v. Southern Pacific Ry. Co.* before the Supreme Court, contended that the Fourteenth Amendment had not been originally intended for the exclusive protection of the Negro. He supported his contention with the previously unrevealed journal of the committee for drafting the amendment, of which he had been a member. This argument was strengthened by the rising demand for the regulation of public utility rates and for protective social and labor legislation. The result was that the Court began to lay the foundations of the modern doctrine of substantive due process. [19]

The dissenting opinion of Justice Field in the *Slaughter House* cases had clearly pointed the way to an extension of the Fourteenth Amendment beyond the limits of the majority opinion. A short time later the author of the opinion in the *Slaughter House* cases indicated that a state statute prohibiting the sale of liquor could violate the due process clause. Finally, in 1887 the Court made plain that the due process clause could act as a restriction upon a state's substantive law regulating property or its use. Thus was "closed the period of groping and uncertainty as to the application of the various phrases of the first section of the Amend-

---

17. *Butchers Benevolent Association of New Orleans v. The Crescent City Live-stock Landing and Slaughter House Corporation*, 16 Wall. 36, 81 (1873); Charles Fairman, *Mr. Justice Miller and the Supreme Court, 1862–1890* (Cambridge: Harvard University Press, 1939), 181–84.

18. *Davidson v. New Orleans*, 96 U.S. 97, 105 (1878).

19. *San Mateo County v. Southern Pacific Ry. Co.*, 116 U.S. 138 (1885); Robert E. Cushman, "The Social and Economic Interpretation of the Fourteenth Amendment," *Michigan Law Review*, XX (1922), 737 et seq; *Bartemeyer v. Iowa*, 18 Wall. 129 (1874).

ment."[20] The principle of the Court's ruling was to be found in those words relating to the limits of police power of the state: "There are, of necessity, limits beyond which the legislation cannot rightfully go. . . . If, therefore, a statute purporting to have been enacted to protect the public health, the public morals, or the public safety, has no real or substantial relation to those objects, or is a palpable invasion of the rights secured by the fundamental law, it is the duty of the courts to so adjudge, and thereby give effect to the Constitution."[21]

The limitations thus far laid down by the Court were in the nature of a warning, for that tribunal had not yet actually declared a state law unconstitutional as a violation of due process of law. This last step was taken in 1890 when the Court held invalid a Minnesota statute that had been interpreted by the courts of that state as rendering final and conclusive a determination of rates by a commission. "The question of the reasonableness of a charge . . . ," said the Court, "is eminently a question for judicial investigation, requiring due process of law for its determination."[22]

Until 1894, in fact, the Court was reluctant to go as far in examining the act of a legislature in fixing rates as it went in the case of an administrative commission. In the year that Edward White became a member of the Supreme Court, however, the doctrine that there were limitations on both the legislature and the administrative commissions in the fixing of rates was clearly announced. Thus, by 1894, the Court had firmly established the Fourteenth Amendment as a limitation upon the power of a state to regulate the economic enterprises of the day through substantive legislation or administrative agency. The Court, as the arbiter of how far this limitation should extend, had "assumed burdensome obligations," which were to be a source of constant agitation during the ensuing decades.[23]

The Court, during the pre-White period, was also confronted with the problem of delineating the power of the state governments under

20. *Butchers Benevolent Association* v. *Crescent City Livestock*, 16 Wall. 36, 122, 127; *Mugler* v. *Kansas*, 123 U.S. 623 (1887); Ray A. Brown, "Due Process of Law, Police Power, and the Supreme Court," *Harvard Law Review*, XL (1927), 947.

21. *Mugler* v. *Kansas*, 123 U.S. 623, 661.

22. *Chicago, Milwaukee, & St. Paul Ry. Co.* v. *Minnesota*, 134 U.S. 418, 458 (1890).

23. *Budd* v. *New York*, 143 U.S. 517 (1892); *Reagan* v. *Farmers' Loan and Trust Co.*, 154 U.S. 362 (1894); Andrew C. McLaughlin, *A Constitutional History of the United States* (New York: Appleton-Century, 1935), 756.

the commerce clause. In 1887 it had begun a trend away from earlier decisions that showed an inclination to extend state power. Nine years earlier the Court refused to permit a state to require separate accommodations for Negroes and subsequently ruled invalid a state tax on the business of an interstate ferry. In another case the Supreme Court held that, even in the absence of discrimination, a state could not levy a tax on drummers engaged in interstate business. It also denied the power of the state, in 1888, to forbid the importation of liquor. Said Justice Stephen J. Field in a concurring opinion: "It is only after the importation is completed, and the property imported is mingled with and becomes a part of the general property of the state, that its regulations can act upon it, except so far as may be necessary to insure safety in the distribution of the import until thus mingled." Two years later the Court extended this protection to articles which were still in their original packages when sold. In this instance, Mr. Chief Justice Fuller completely ignored a line of precedents and went back to a dictum of Marshall's in *Brown* v. *Maryland*, which, in effect, declared that goods imported from one state into another were immune from regulation by the latter before sale in the original package and that the right to sell such goods was incidental to the right to import. Although in 1889 the Court had permitted states to prohibit the importation of infected clothing, unwholesome foods, and similar articles, the result of Fuller's opinion was to handcuff a state when it wished to protect its own standards. Criticism of the decision in *Leisy* v. *Hardin* apparently caused the Court to recede somewhat from its position, for in 1894, the high tribunal held that a state could "exclude from its markets any compound manufactured in another state, which has been artificially colored to cheat the general public."[24]

24. For examples, see *Gilman* v. *Philadelphia*, 3 Wall. 713 (1866), which permitted states to bridge navigable waters, *Osborne* v. *Mobile*, 16 Wall. 479 (1873), upholding a state discriminatory tax, and *Peik* v. *Chicago Ry. Co.*, 94 U.S. 164 (1877), sustaining a state fare regulation when one terminus was within the state; *Hall* v. *DeCuir*, 95 U.S. 485 (1878); *Gloucester Ferry Co.* v. *Pennsylvania*, 114 U.S. 196 (1885); *Robbins* v. *Shelby County Taxing District*, 120 U.S. 489 (1887); *Bowman* v. *Chicago & N.W. R.R. Co.*, 125 U.S. 465, 508 (1888); *Leisy* v. *Hardin*, 135 U.S. 100 (1890); see *Thurlow* v. *Massachusetts*, 5 How. 504 (1849), holding that states may prohibit or regulate by license the sale of an article from outside the state in the original package, *Woodruff* v. *Parham*, 8 Wall. 123 (1869), declaring Marshall's extension of the principle of the "original package" doctrine in *Brown* v. *Maryland*, 12 Wheat. 419 (1827), to commerce between states to be mere dictum, and *Brown* v. *Houston*, 114 U.S. 622 (1885), where the Court refused to apply the "original package" doctrine to interstate commerce; *Kimmish* v. *Ball*, 129 U.S. 217 (1889).

If a state were powerless to protect itself, especially as to shipments of liquor into the state, what could be done under the federal system to make effective its police regulations? Federal legislation of some type was the only way out of the dilemma, but how far could congressional lawmaking reach in this attempt? Following the decision in the *Leisy* case, a wave of severe criticism swept over the Court. One writer later declared: "The doctrines which have been crystallized into the maxims of the law, *salus populi supreme lex* and *sic utere tuo alienum non laeda*, and the early maxim that all rights and all contracts are subject to the police power of the state are annulled." The result of this agitation was the Wilson Act, which provided that intoxicating liquors transported into any state for sale or storage should immediately on arrival be subject to the laws of the state in the same manner as if they had been produced in the state; the liquors should not be exempt from the laws of the importing state because they were introduced in the original packages. The purpose of the legislation was "to give the several states power to deal with all liquors coming from outside their limits upon arrival and before sale, thus rendering the state police authority more complete." [25]

The constitutionality of this act came before the Court in 1891. Daniel Webster argued in *Gibbons* v. *Ogden* that the word *regulate*, definitive of federal power, meant primarily *restrain*. In 1841, the power to prohibit certain branches of trade between the states was questioned but the case was decided on another point. The Court now rejected the proposition that the Constitution guarantees freedom of commerce among the states in all things as well as that the grant to the general government forbids any restraint whatever. "The power to regulate is solely in the general government, and it is an essential part of that regulation to prescribe the regular means for accomplishing the introduction and incorporation of articles into and with the general mass of property in the country or state." The Wilson Act, however, did not entirely remove the protection afforded by the interstate commerce clause, for it modified existing rules only to the extent of causing interstate shipments to come under control at an earlier date than they otherwise would have, that is, after delivery but before sale in the original packages. [26]

25. James D. Andrews, *American Law: A Documentary on the Jurisprudence, Constitution, and Laws of the United States* (2 vols.; Chicago: Callahan, 1908), I, 296; *United States Statutes at Large*, XXVI, 313.

26. Edward S. Corwin, *The Commerce Power Versus States Rights* (Princeton: Princeton

This brief review of leading doctrines of the Court, primarily in the period immediately preceding 1894, has covered the due process and commerce clauses, and provided some clue concerning the trend of Court opinions. A definite tendency to restrict the power of the states in coping with the problems of the day was evident. The Fourteenth Amendment was used to limit substantive legislation in an area where the states could otherwise act, while the commerce power of the federal government was construed in such a fashion as to narrow the field of actual authority. In the future lay the question of how far the Court would go in imposing restrictions on state government and in permitting the federal government to act in areas denied to the states.

The decisions of the Court in this period include a few important civil rights cases arising under limitations upon federal power. In one of these cases the Court answered the question of the validity of an act permitting a demand to be made upon a defendant or claimant, in proceedings other than criminal and arising under the revenue law, for production of papers in his possession. In the event of refusal, the allegations expected to be proved by the papers were to be conceded. The Court held that the application of this statute to criminal proceedings was unconstitutional under the provisions of the Fourth Amendment against unreasonable search and seizure, and also those of the Fifth Amendment establishing that a person cannot be required to be a witness against himself in a criminal case. In another action the Court held invalid a statute dispensing with jury trial in the Police Court of the District of Columbia. The statute was held to violate Article III, section 2 of the Constitution, which provides that the trial of crimes must be by jury. In a third case, the Court ruled that the Fifth Amendment prevented a person from being adjudged in contempt for refusal to testify before a grand jury on the ground that it would incriminate him. In each of these cases the element of personal liberty was an influence on the Court, a fact of some significance because such doctrines as freedom of contract also arise from the same influence.[27]

Two other actions involving national power also merit brief atten-

University Press, 1937), 58–59; *Groves* v. *Slaughter*, 15 Pet. 449 (1841); *In Re Rahrer*, 140 U.S. 545 (1891); *Rosenberger* v. *Pacific Express Co.*, 241 U.S. 48 (1916).

27. *Boyd* v. *United States*, 116 U.S. 616 (1886); *United States Statutes at Large*, XVIII, 187; *Callan* v. *Wilson*, 127 U.S. 540 (1888); *Counselman* v. *Hitchcock*, 142 U.S. 547 (1892). The case arose under *United States Revised Statutes*, Sec. 860 (1875), providing that no evidence obtained from a party by means of a judicial proceeding should be used against him in criminal proceedings in federal courts.

tion. One of these permitted a federal court to order the release of a person held in the custody of a state for the violation of the criminal laws of the state. This case grew out of the shooting, by a deputy United States marshal assigned to Justice Field as a bodyguard, of an alleged assailant of the justice. Since Neagle, the deputy marshal involved, was acting under federal authority, he was held "not liable to answer in the courts of California." The decision provoked a dissent that the rule amounted to an unwarranted invasion of the criminal jurisdiction of a state. In the other case the Court held that the determination of the meaning of "just compensation" within the purport of the Fifth Amendment is a judicial, not a legislative question.[28]

This political and economic climate of the late nineteenth century, the Supreme Court of which Edward Douglass White became a member, and its principal judicial precedents provided the bases from which the Court could move. After 1885 especially, the Court was an exponent of economic individualism and tended to view that tribunal's function as one of protecting the individual against governmental intervention. By the time of White's appointment to the bench, the Court had already rendered novel and significant decisions, and the Constitution had been judicially amended to uphold particular, and somewhat restricted, concepts of liberty and property.

White's appointment seemed unlikely to presage doctrinal and ideological change in the Court. In the *Tardos* case, concerning a riparian owner's liability for levee repairs, he had shown a pragmatic bent of mind when, as an attorney with his first case, he contended successfully for public responsibility of levee maintenance and repair. Neither his education nor his legal and political experience had prepared him, however, to deal with the issues arising from the industrialization of the nation. A wide gap separated opposition to the Louisiana Lottery from trust, pool, and combination problems. Attention to purely legal issues of private law did not provide a dynamic view of Congress' power to regulate interstate commerce, while devotion to common law precedents gave little aid in understanding the American farmer and his concerns. As a Louisiana sugar planter, White understood the economics of sugar, but not

28. *In Re Neagle*, 135 U.S. 1 (1890); *Monongahela Navigation Co.* v. *United States*, 148 U.S. 312 (1893).

the economics of labor. Moreover, he brought with him to the bench a basic acceptance of the precepts found in social Darwinism and joined a tribunal already confident in the truth of those principles. Justices of the Supreme Court have been chosen more frequently because they reflect currently widely held beliefs than because they offer promise of striking and dramatic influence on our public law. In 1894 Edward White was a successful lawyer and state politician who had only recently become one of his state's United States senators. The positions he would take on the issues confronting the Court and what part he would have in development of the conservative world that embraced the Court, the major political parties, and a sizable segment of the nation's population lay ahead. In law, as perhaps in no other field of man's activity, the future is the accretion, on a case-by-case basis, of the past.

VI

Techniques of Judicial Lawmaking

A state without the means of some change," wrote Edmund Burke, "is without the means of its conservation. Without such means it might even risk the loss of that part of the constitution which it wished most religiously to preserve."[1] Certainly the members of the 1787 Constitutional Convention intended to provide ways of constitutional development, although it is doubtful that the direction taken by many permutations in the nearly two centuries since the Constitution was adopted would meet their wholehearted approval.

Formal change in the American system of government is conditioned by the adaptation of the separation of powers doctrine to the Constitution. Although in theory the executive, the judiciary, and the Congress are each representative in the American federal government in one fashion or another, Congress with direct election of representatives and senators is usually considered the most representative in the exercise of the powers allocated to it by Article I, section 8 of the Constitution. The prestige of Congress, however, has been on a gently declining slope during which its policy-making functions have diminished under the impact of both executive growth and the ever-increasing technology of American life. Nevertheless, no federal statute can be enacted without passage by Congress.

Administrative officers and agencies have risen in power, if not in popular affection. Congress' legislative tasks have grown more com-

1. Edmund Burke, *Reflections on the French Revolution and Other Essays* (London: J. M. Dent & Sons, 1910), 19–20.

plex, and the origin of legislation, under which administrative rules and regulations affecting individuals are promulgated, has shifted largely to the executive and the professional bureaucracy. This administrative process has developed chiefly, but not entirely, since the latter part of the nineteenth century and includes administrative determinations by boards, commissions, and officers, either as such determinations actually occur or as it is thought they ought to occur. Some system and order were finally put into the administrative process at the federal level by enactment of the Administrative Procedure Act of 1946.

Courts are the third source of lawmaking, proclaiming case-by-case rules and rendering decisions which impinge upon the action of individuals as well as governments. Courts thus occupy a central function in the American lawmaking process, performing what Benjamin N. Cardozo referred to as the "judicial process," the actual determining of controversies as they come before courts and as such determinations may be ideally conceived to take place.[2] The judicial process overlapped and, to some extent, blotted out the functions of the other lawmaking agencies in the period from 1885 to 1937. Courts can and do make law by three methods: the development of rules during the course of decisions affecting the rights of litigants, the construction and invalidation of legislative enactments both state and federal, and the review of administrative action.

The common law technique of making law has aroused endless discussion on the issue of whether courts are, in fact, "making" law or "discovering" law. Whatever the academic thesis concerning the mysteries of the process, two facts seem evident. The first is that, when federal courts rule on constitutional issues, they are dealing essentially with questions of political power, such matters as the regulation of interstate commerce not being easily comparable, for example, to personal injury actions, suits in real property involving private parties, or felony cases. Second, the courts bring new rules of public law into being to affect the actions, rights, and duties of governments as well as individuals. The judicial

2. Benjamin N. Cardozo, *The Nature of the Judicial Process* (New Haven: Yale University Press, 1921). Compare with Roscoe Pound, *The History and System of the Common Law* (New York: P. F. Collier & Son, 1939), 5.

process has been described by the Judicial Council of Massachusetts in these terms:

> It is one of the great merits and advantages of the common law, that, instead of a series of detailed practical rules, established by positive provisions, and adapted to the precise circumstances of particular cases, which would become obsolete and fail, when the practice and course of business, to which they apply, should cease or change, the common law consists of a few broad and comprehensive principles, founded on reason, natural justice, and enlightened public policy, modified and adapted to the circumstances of all the particular cases which fall within it. These general principles of equity and policy are rendered precise, specific, and adapted to practical use, by usage, which is the proof of their general fitness and common convenience, but still more by judicial exposition; so that, when in a course of judicial proceedings, by tribunals of the highest authority, the general rule has been modified, limited and applied, according to particular cases, such judicial exposition, when well settled and acquiesced in, becomes itself a precedent, and forms a rule of law for future cases under like circumstances. The effect of this expansive and comprehensive character of the common law is, that whilst it has its foundations in the principles of equity, natural justice, and that general convenience which is public policy; although these general considerations would be too vague and uncertain for practical purposes, in the various and complicated cases, of daily occurrence, in the business of an active community; yet the rules of the common law, so far as cases have arisen and practices actually grown up, are rendered, in a good degree, precise and certain, for practical purposes, by usage and judicial precedent. Another consequence of this expansive character of the common law is, that when new practices spring up, new combinations of facts arise, and cases are presented for which there is no precedent in judicial decision, they must be governed by the general principle, applicable to cases most nearly analogous, but modified and adapted to new circumstances, by considerations of fitness and propriety, or reason and justice, which grow out of those circumstances. The consequence of this state of the law is, that when a new practice or new course of business arises, the rights and duties of parties are not without a law to govern them; the general considerations of reason, justice and policy, which underlie the particular rules of the common law, will still apply, modified and adapted, by the same considerations to the new circumstances. If these are such as give rise to controversy and litigation, they soon, like previous cases, come to be settled by judicial exposition, and the principles thus settled soon come to have the effect of precise and practical rules.[3]

The law thus grows by analogical reasoning through which precedents established in one case are extended to somewhat different, yet similar

---

3. *Norway Plains Co.* v. *Boston & Maine R.R.*, 1 Gray 263 (1854).

situations of fact. The process, however, is less automatic than simply laying down the facts of a new case beside those of a leading precedent and mechanically applying *stare decisis*. Cardozo makes it clear that a judge is not free to innovate at will; rather he "is to exercise a discretion informed by tradition, methodized by analogy, disciplined by system, and subordinated to the 'primordial necessity of order in the social life.' Wide enough is the field of discretion that remains."[4]

There is no federal common law, the law which federal courts apply consisting exclusively of the United States Constitution, treaties, statutes enacted by Congress, and the laws, both common and statutory, of the several states of the Union. In applying the rule of common law to a problem or in determining the general law prior to *Erie* v. *Tompkins* in 1938, though, a federal court, and ultimately the Supreme Court, could be an agency for the common law type of judicial lawmaking. Under the principle of *Swift* v. *Tyson* the federal courts often referred to "general law" in deciding cases in which jurisdiction was based on diversity of citizenship. Since *Swift*, in effect, permitted federal judges and state judges to apply different rules of law in deciding the same type of cases, some careful court selection resulted as attorneys sought to try cases in whichever court the law was likely to be more favorable to their cases. With the decision in *Erie Railroad* v. *Tompkins* any assumption of power by the federal courts to create a federal common law was ended. The law now applicable to diversity cases in federal courts is that of the state, whether declared by statute or judicial decision.[5]

In dealing with cases which involved a resort to "general law" or to the interpretation of the law of a state, Edward White employed a technique that piled up precedents to establish the doctrine he was seeking to apply and followed by putting the doctrine into practice with the case at hand. This approach was mixed frequently with an appeal to reason. Using precedents on which to construct his argument, White drew not only on common law cases but upon the writings of the civil law as well. *Singer Manufacturing Co.* v. *June Manufacturing Co.* is almost a casebook illustration of the White methodology. This case concerned a suit by the Singer Company to restrain the June Company from the use of the word *Singer* on sewing machines manufactured by the latter and from other

4. Cardozo, *Judicial Process*, 141.
5. *Swift* v. *Tyson*, 16 Pet. 1 (1842); *Erie Railroad* v. *Tompkins*, 304 U.S. 64 (1938).

practices allegedly designed to mislead the public into thinking that the machines were made by the Singer Company. The action also sought to have the defendant account for profits made on its machines already sold. The case turned largely on the issue of whether the name *Singer* had become a generic term, designating the type of machine to which the Singer Company was no longer entitled after expiration of patent rights. White's opinion made an exhaustive review of the American, English, and French authorities on the principles with which the case was concerned, and on the basis of this review, he concluded that "the result, then, of the American, the English, and the French doctrine universally upheld is this, that where, during the life of a monopoly created by a patent, a name, whether it be arbitrary or be that of the inventor, has become, by his consent, either express or tacit, the identifying and generic name of the thing patented, this name passes to the public with the cessation of the monopoly which the patent created."[6] The justice then added in typical White fashion, "It remains only to apply these legal conclusions to the facts already capitulated." The result of his application in this particular case was the conclusion that the defendant, June Manufacturing Company, though entitled to use the name "Singer," had misused it by not making clear in the advertisements and on the machines themselves that the defendant, not the plaintiff, was the manufacturer.

In *Groves* v. *Sentell*, which involved the issue of the divisibility of a mortgage under Louisiana law, White went back to the principles of the *Code Napoleon*, Laurent's *Principes de Droit Civil Français*, Rodiere's *On Indivisibility*, and the decisions of the French Court on Cassation. As was frequently the case in White's opinions, he found little doubt among the authorities on the principle he was enunciating. It was "sanctioned by a unanimous course" of decisions and authority, or "it was no longer open to controversy."[7]

White was not content to rely on development of principles from precedent alone. He also made frequent appeals to reason. In *Texas and Pa-*

---

6. *Singer Manufacturing Co.* v. *June Manufacturing Co.*, 163 U.S. 199 (1896).

7. *Groves* v. *Sentell*, 153 U.S. 465 (1894); *Missouri Pacific Ry. Co.* v. *George H. McFadden*, 154 U.S. 155 (1894); *Schuyler National Bank of Schuyler, Nebraska* v. *Jane Gadsden, et al.*, 191 U.S. 681 (1903).

cific Ry. Co. v. *Andy Archibald,* he was confronted with the question of the duty of a railroad toward its employees to inspect cars switched from another road, to which they were to be returned after loading. Counsel for the railroad argued that such a duty extended only to the inspection of cars actually to be hauled by the road to which they were switched. White rejected this argument as "unsupported by any authority" and "without foundation in reason. [It wanted] in reason, because as the duty of the company to use reasonable diligence to furnish safe appliances is ever present and applies to its entire business, it is beyond reason to attempt by a purely arbitrary distinction to take a particular part of the business of the company out of the operation of the general rule, and thereby to exempt it, as to the business so separated, from any obligation to observe reasonable precautions to furnish appliances which are in good condition."[8]

Sun Printing and Publishing Association v. *Moore* may be examined with interest as an example of White's method of handling cases other than those involving constitutional issues or the construction of statutes. This case dealt with the liability of the publishing company under an agreement by which its managing editor had chartered a yacht with a provision for stipulated damages if the vessel were not returned. In order to dispose of the case, White consumed twelve double-column printed pages in his opinion, cited or quoted from approximately seventy cases, examined the statutes of William III, the decisions of the Master of the Rolls, and *Story on Equity Jurisprudence.*[9]

The second method of judicial lawmaking available to the courts arises from the review of legislative actions. In the case of the Supreme Court of the United States this function has a two-fold aspect. The Court, in effect, may make law by denying the validity of acts of Congress or of state statutes that create new rules to govern specific situations different from those developed by the common law. The Court may also determine the limits of and point the direction of congressional and state legislative enactments by its construction of statutes in individual cases while upholding the validity of the laws. Its authority with respect to enactments

8. *Texas and Pacific Ry. Co.* v. *Andy Archibald,* 170 U.S. 670 (1898).
9. *Sun Printing and Publishing Association* v. *Moore,* 183 U.S. 642 (1902).

by state legislatures, however, is more limited in this respect because the Court adheres to the rule that, on state statutes, it will follow interpretation by the courts of the state.

For example, Justice White's opinion in *Howard* v. *Illinois Central R. R. Co.* and *Brooks* v. *Southern Pacific Co.* (popularly known as the first *Employers' Liability* cases) denied the validity of a federal statute abrogating the fellow servant doctrine as applied to interstate carriers. They arose from *United States Statutes at Large*, XXXIV, 232. Section 1 made carriers engaged in interstate commerce liable to employees or their personal representatives for damages resulting from the negligence of any of the carrier's "officers, agents, or employees." Section 2 provided that an employee should not be barred from recovery in actions against such carriers where his negligence was slight and that of the employer was gross in comparison. Under the old common law rule, an employer was not liable to his employees for injuries caused by the negligence of a fellow servant, and the defense of contributory negligence, in addition, made recovery by the employee for injuries sustained in the course of employment even more difficult. The act of Congress before the Court in the *Employers' Liability* cases eliminated the fellow-servant rule from application to interstate carriers and greatly modified the defense of contributory negligence. White's opinion for the Court held the statute to be unconstitutional, thus rendering these changes void and placing the law back on the common law basis.[10]

In the area of statutory review devoted to the construction of statutes, White's development of the so-called rule of reason in the *Anti-Trust* cases is a significant illustration of molding the law by judicial interpretation. The antitrust legislation was a by-product of the growth of monopoly capitalism in the United States. As early as the 1870s, monopolies had evoked protests in various third party platforms. In 1884 Benjamin Butler had used the issue to create a brief flurry on the political scene, and four years later both the Republican and Democratic parties adopted planks declaring their opposition to combinations. In the same year the first general bill against trusts was introduced in Congress, loosening a tide of proposed legislation. The Fiftieth Congress dealt with some twenty antitrust measures, while the first session of the Fifty-first Congress was

10. *Howard* v. *Illinois Central R.R. Co.* and *Brooks* v. *Southern Pacific Co.*, 207 U.S. 463 (1908). Chapter VII contains further discussion of these cases.

presented with no less than fifteen such bills. The result of this ferment was the Sherman Anti-Trust Act of July 2, 1890, which the Senate adopted by a vote of 52 to 1 and the House of Representatives by 242 to 0, with eighty-five members not voting.[11]

The unanimity displayed in the passage of the Sherman Act has produced varying hypotheses about its intent and purposes. Some observers have contended that the measure was meant to have enacted into law the usual common law terms that make those restraints of trade that are unreasonable and primary in their effects illegal, the Court being presumably left free to reach this point on its own. In debates on the bill, which was drawn up by Senators George F. Hoar, William M. Evarts, and others, Hoar appeared to believe that the measure would enact the common law rule relating to restraints of trade. Others have maintained that Congress was intimidated by public opinion and made the statute ambiguous in order to pacify the public without injuring business interests.[12] Still others believed that Congress genuinely thought that combinations and trusts were endangering the laissez-faire system and hoped that this measure would put brakes on such a development. Were it not for the fact that those persons who were the most ardent defenders of the system of free competition did not genuinely believe in the implications of the system, this last argument would be convincing. To them, however, laissez-faire did not mean freedom of competition so much as freedom from governmental supervision and restrictive legislation. To visualize the political representatives of such groups as those in oil and sugar passing measures in the name of laissez-faire economics is difficult.

Whatever the motives of Congress in enacting the statute entitled "An Act to Protect Trade and Commerce Against Unlawful Restraint and Monopolies," there can be no doubt that much uncertainty clouded the law's meaning and application.[13] Relevant sections of the Sherman Act read:

Sec. 1. Every contract, combination in the form of trust or otherwise, or con-

---

11. Henry R. Seager and Charles A. Gulick, *Trust and Corporation Problems* (New York: Harper, 1929), 369; *Congressional Record*, 51st Cong., 1st Sess., Index, 690.

12. For Hoar's important comments in the debate on the measure, see *Congressional Record*, 51st Cong., 1st Sess., 2563, 2567, 2589, 2600, 2658, 3147, 3152, 4559; Seager and Gulick, *Trust Problems*, 372.

13. *United States Statutes at Large*, XXVI, 209, C. 647.

spiracy, in restraint of trade or commerce among the several states, or with foreign nations is hereby declared illegal.

Sec. 2. Every person who shall monopolize, or attempt to monopolize, or
combine or conspire with any other person or persons, to monopolize any part
of the trade or commerce among the several states, or with foreign nations, shall
be deemed guilty of a misdemeanor. . . .

Sec. 3. Any person who shall be injured in his business or property by any
other person or corporation, may . . . sue . . . and shall recover threefold the
damages by him sustained.

The critical constitutional question raised by the language of the Anti-
Trust Act was whether Congress could prohibit trusts formed by manu-
facturers that allegedly restrained interstate commerce. Clearly this question would have to be settled first by the lower federal courts and no
doubt ultimately by the Supreme Court, but equally obvious was the
fact that applying the language of Congress to concrete situations would
make interpreting the measure very difficult.

The first interpretation of the Sherman Act by the Supreme Court occurred in 1895. The government had sought dissolution of the American
Sugar Refining Company, which, through contracts with four additional
defendants, controlled the manufacture of more than 90 percent of all
refined sugar in the United States. In *United States* v. *E. C. Knight Co.,*
the Fuller Court, in an opinion by the chief justice, limited the practical
effect of the legislation by refusing to apply it to an almost complete mo-
nopolistic situation. This holding was based upon a sharp distinction between manufacturing and commerce. Since, ran Fuller's argument, commerce follows manufacturing and since the Sherman Act was directed
against trusts engaged in interstate commerce, the statute could not be
held to invalidate trusts engaged in production. The fact that the production might ultimately affect commerce was rejected, and on the face
of the facts, declared Fuller for the Court, the Sugar Trust presented no
violation of the Sherman Act. White was a part of the majority in this decision, which did not bring before the Court the issue of the extent to
which the federal statute restrained monopolies engaged in interstate
commerce, a problem that arose in 1897. It has been argued that the
Knight case virtually halted antitrust prosecutions for a decade and that
the decision itself resulted from the poor preparation and presentation
of the government's case, it being the responsibility of the government

counsel to show that the acts of the Sugar Trust were in interstate commerce.[14]

In March, 1889, a group of railroads entered into an agreement to form a freight association "for the purpose of mutual protection by establishing and maintaining reasonable rates, rules, and regulations on all freight traffic." A series of articles created the association and defined appropriate mechanisms to determine rates, the relation of members to nonmembers, and fines for violations of the code. Three years later a federal district court refused the government's demand for a permanent injunction to prevent its reorganization in the future, but by a vote of five to four, Justice White speaking for the minority, which included Justices Field, Gray, and Shiras, the Supreme Court reversed the judgment of the lower tribunal dismissing the bill.[15]

The briefs for the defendant companies had been drafted and presented by a trio of noted corporation attorneys: John Forest Dillon, James C. Carter, and Edward J. Phelps. Dillon's brief for the Union Pacific and Missouri Pacific Railroads maintained that the Sherman Act was not intended to change the policy declared by the Interstate Commerce Act of 1887 affecting interstate carriers. Ignoring the import of the *Knight* case, that the manufacture of refined sugar did not come within the scope of the commerce power, Dillon argued that the Sherman Act was designed to deal with trusts like the Sugar, Whiskey, Cordage, and Standard Oil trusts.[16] A freight association, he contended, was essential to carrying out the purposes of the Interstate Commerce Act. More significantly, Dillon went back to the common law rules on restraint of trade and argued that the Anti-Trust Act did not prohibit reasonable restraints of trade, the question in each case being whether the contract is in its nature reasonable or unreasonable.

Mr. Justice Peckham, speaking for the majority, rejected Dillon's reasoning. The Court first held that the language of the Sherman Act included railroads. Otherwise, in view of the *Knight* case, "its application is so greatly limited that the whole act might as well be held inoperative."

14. *United States* v. *E. C. Knight Co.*, 156 U.S. 1 (1895); James A. McLaughlin, *Cases on the Federal Anti-Trust Laws of the United States* (New York: The Ad Press, 1930), 23–24.

15. *United States* v. *Trans-Missouri Freight Association*, 166 U.S. 290, 292 (1897).

16. Benjamin R. Twiss, *Lawyers and the Constitution: How Laissez Faire Came to the Supreme Court* (Princeton: Princeton University Press, 1942), 190.

The remaining issue was whether to accept Dillon's assertion that the act applied only to combinations unreasonably restraining trade, and on this point, the majority opinion denied the validity of the contention, adding that the language of the act included all conspiracies in restraint of trade and concluding that the words *contract in restraint of trade* meant all contracts of that nature. Congress, said the majority of the Court, intended to include all combinations within the scope of the act. "We are asked," declared Peckham, "to read into the act by way of judicial legislation an exemption that is not placed there by the law-making branch of the government. . . . This we cannot and ought not to do." [17]

It was not so apparent to Justice White that this was the nature of the dilemma before the Court. In fact, he declared that the Court's decision was tantamount to "an assertion that the act of Congress is itself unreasonable." He traced the development of the common law from the original doctrine holding that all contracts in restraint of trade were illegal, through the distinction between general and partial restraints and to the rise of the rule of reason, [18] concluding that reasonable contracts were excluded from the words "in restraint of trade." He maintained that "the theory . . . that the words restraint of trade define and embrace all such contracts without reference to whether they are reasonable, amounts substantially to saying that, by the common law and the adjudged American cases, certain classes of contracts were carved out and excepted from the general rule, and yet were held to remain embraced within the general rule from which they were removed." The results, in his opinion, would not justify such a doctrine because they would "operate to the undue restraint of the liberties of the citizen," would render labor unions illegal, and destroy the "freedom of contract." [19] By using the latter phrase, Mr. Justice White was employing a concept which was to be much used by the Court in protecting yellow-dog contracts. The apparent solicitude for labor of this planter-jurist, at least in this antitrust case, was unusual.

In addition to this argument, White said that the railroads forming the association agreed to charge certain rates because of the great competition between them. He declared: "To hold then the contract under consideration to be invalid when it simply provides for uniform classifi-

17. *United States* v. *Trans-Missouri*, 166 U.S. 290, 326, 340.
18. *Nordenfeldt* v. *Maxim-Nordenfeldt Gun and Ammunition Co.*, App. Cas. 535 (1894).
19. *United States* v. *Trans-Missouri*, 166 U.S. 290, 350, 352, 354, 356.

cation, and seeks to prevent secret or sudden changes in the published rates, would be to void a contract covered by the law and embodied in its policy. . . . The great complexity of the subject presents difficulties enough without its being advisable to add to them by holding that a contract which is supported by the text of the law is invalid, because, *although it is reasonable and just*, it must be considered a restraint of trade."[20] The majority of the Court was not yet willing to read the rule of reason into the public law, perhaps because the decision in the *Knight* case removed the Sherman Act as a serious threat to monopoly capitalism. Nearly fifteen years were to elapse before White as chief justice was able to translate his dissent into fundamental law.

In the famous case against the Northern Securities Company, he left the defense of the rule of reason to Mr. Justice Holmes, who rendered the first of a long line of dissents in his opinion on the issues. The Court was still unwilling at this time to adopt the White thesis of 1897. Although that tribunal had made a long jump toward acceptance of the development of the due process clause, it had not yet completely made the transition to the new judicial sovereignty. In the majority for once, Justice Harlan reemphasized the position of the Court a decade previously. "The act is not limited," he stated, "to restraints of interstate and international trade and commerce that are unreasonable in their nature, but embraces all direct restraints imposed by any combination, conspiracy, or monopoly upon such trade or commerce."[21] Four years later, White as chief justice was able to announce the rule of reason as a canon of American constitutional interpretation.

William Howard Taft had become president in 1909, by which time the Sherman Act had been already transformed into a reasonably effective restraint of corporate greed. Previous interpretations, to be sure, had drawn its lines clearly so that government and business alike knew what the act meant. Although Taft may have been uncertain at times about his own views, he finally concluded that "the act is too valuable, with its judicial interpretations, to permit [legislative] amendments."[22] He, therefore, proceeded with a vigorous executive program of trust-

20. *Ibid.*, 371, my italics.
21. *Northern Securities Company* v. *United States*, 193 U.S. 197, 331 (1904). Justice White's dissent is important for his views on the commerce clause and is considered in Chapter VII.
22. William H. Taft to R. D. Silliman, December 31, 1909, in Taft Papers, Library of Congress.

busting under the direction of Attorney General George Wickersham.

Meanwhile, in 1906 the Government had brought an action against Standard Oil Company of New Jersey, seventy-one other corporations, and seven individuals charging a conspiracy to violate the Sherman Act. The attorney general, Philander C. Knox, alleged that, over a period extending from 1870 to 1906, the defendants had received rebates, preferences, and benefits or other aids of a discriminatory nature from the railroads; had engaged in price cutting to suppress competition; had operated bogus independent companies; had divided the United States into districts for the purpose of limiting production; and as a result of these illegal operations, had made enormous and excessive profits. The exhaustive presentation of the case by young Frank B. Kellogg, special prosecutor for the government, persuaded the lower court, which on November 20, 1909, delivered a judgment upholding the government's contentions.

Appeal was taken immediately to the Supreme Court, and on May 15, 1911, that tribunal acted. In a twenty thousand–word opinion White, now the chief justice, ordered the dissolution of the Standard Oil Trust. He again reviewed the development of the rule of reason in the common law and concluded that, since the Sherman Act was passed in the light of existing conceptions, it was not intended to apply to contracts that do not unduly restrain trade. White stated: "It was intended that the standard of reason which had been applied at the common law and in this country in dealing with subjects of the character embraced by this statute, . . . be the measure for the purpose of determining whether in a given case a particular act had or had not brought about the wrong against which the statute applied."[23]

From this premise the chief justice found little difficulty in disposing of previous interpretations of the act that had rejected the rule of reason. He admitted that general language used in those decisions indicated that the rule of reason was not the proper test, but he maintained, read in conjunction with the text, such was not the holding of the cases because each action referred to the unreasonable character of the combina-

---

23. *Standard Oil Co.* v. *United States*, 221 U.S. 1, 60 (1911); White's adoption of the rule of reason has been attributed to the barrage of arguments made in its behalf by some of the leading members of the American bar: J. F. Dillon, J. D. Johnson, J. C. Carter, Joseph Choate, and W. D. Guthrie. Twiss, *Lawyers and the Constitution*, 213. Johnson represented Standard Oil in this case and lost out on the theory rather than the doctrine itself.

tion involved. White's argument need not be taken too seriously. It is another indication of his innate reluctance to overrule previous decisions. He was willing to go to that limit this time if necessary, however, and declared that, if previous decisions were in conflict with his present interpretation, they were to that extent qualified.[24] The rule of reason, thus, was embedded firmly in the interpretation of the antitrust actions.

One important note may be added. In his dissent in the *Northern Securities* case, White had maintained that the Sherman Act could not apply to the acquisition and ownership of stock because stock was not commerce, such effect as stock ownership might have on interstate commerce being only indirect. He relied on the *Knight* case to support this contention which limited the application of the Sherman Act in substance to the transportation of goods. In the present case he retreated from this position and recognized that the decisions of the Court had made the position of *Knight* untenable when applied to facts such as those presented by the government in the *Standard Oil* case. He rejected expressly the argument of Johnson, counsel to Standard Oil, that the *Knight* ruling applied in the present case. "The view, however, which the argument takes of that case and the arguments based upon that view have been so repeatedly pressed upon this Court in connection with the interpretation and enforcement of the Anti-Trust Act, and have been so necessarily and expressly decided to be unsound as to cause the contention to be plainly foreclosed."[25] What the chief justice had accomplished was to assert the old argument of common law exemption of reasonable restraints. It was a theory which the caustic Justice Harlan in dissent stated "put words into the anti-trust act which Congress did not place there."

Two weeks later the Tobacco Trust was stricken down by the Court. Four years earlier a suit had been instituted against sixty-five American corporations, two English establishments, and twenty-nine persons for alleged conspiracies to violate the Sherman Act. Formed in 1890, the American Tobacco Company embraced within seven years all branches of tobacco manufacturing and by 1898 was in substantial control of the industry. A continuation of the policy of compelling competitors to merge by threats of ruinous competition, followed by shutting down the plants acquired, had resulted in complete domination of the tobacco industry

24. *Standard Oil Co. v. United States*, 221 U.S. 67–68 (1911).
25. *Ibid.*, 68.

when the suit was filed in 1907. White used this set of facts to reaffirm the rule just announced in the *Standard Oil* case, declaring that "the soundness of the rule that the statute should receive a reasonable construction, after further mature consideration, we see no reason to doubt."[26] His statement, attempting to show legal consistency, that "the doctrine thus stated was in accord with all previous decisions of this court" was too much for the aged Justice Harlan. Again in dissent, Harlan remarked that "this statement surprises me quite as much as would a statement that black was white or white was black."

In a period of fifteen years White was able to rewrite the Sherman Act, with a sum total of two dissents and two majority opinions. Together, they are a strong illustration of his ability to shape the judicial policies of the Court. His influence over his colleagues was great, perhaps to no small extent the result of a personality that recalled the great John Marshall, though this must remain a matter of conjecture. It is not conjecture that two important results flowed from the chief justice's efforts. First, the doctrine of the rule of reason greatly expanded the Court's power, establishing it "in the strategic position as interpreter of the just and the reasonable." Second, in the years following 1911, trust prosecutions were rarely successful because combination after combination built arguments for social respectability and raised the claim of reasonableness. In case after case the Court seemed primarily concerned to establish the facts and then to determine the reasonableness or unreasonableness of a given combination's restraint of trade. In *United States* v. *Winslow*, for example, the company's technological advances and its quality of commercial character neutralized, in the Court's opinion, the company's intent to monopolize, its driving competition from the business, and its near preponderance of the industry. In *United States* v. *United States Steel Corporation*, the economic legitimacy of United States Steel established the reasonableness of the combination. For better or worse, the fate of the Sherman Act and any subsequent antitrust legislation lay in the hands of the Court. White's rule of reason left room for little hope that the future of antitrust measures was bright.[27]

Judicial lawmaking also takes place in the judicial review of administra-

26. *United States* v. *American Tobacco Company*, 221 U.S. 106, 180 (1911).
27. Benjamin F. Wright, *The Growth of American Constitutional Law* (Boston: Houghton

tive action. Such review may take one of two forms. It may be a review of the validity of rules and regulations adopted by an administrative body such as the Interstate Commerce Commission, or it may be a review of administrative adjudications. The first type of review may determine whether there has been an improper delegation of power by the legislative body to adopt rules and regulations for governing the subject matter under the jurisdiction of the administrative body. Such review is a question of constitutional law. It may also determine whether the rules and regulations involved are of such substance that they violate constitutional limitations. These cases are comparatively few and concern the application of the same limitations to legislative rule-making. Finally, judicial review of administrative action may determine whether the rules and regulations involved are within the scope of the authority of the agency. All three types of administrative review are problems of constitutional law or statutory interpretation similar to those found in judicial review of legislation.

Judicial review of administrative action may also take the form of a review of administrative adjudications. This type of oversight is a review of quasi-judicial proceedings of administrative agencies—proceedings held to find facts and make determinations of rights based upon the findings. The extent of the review of administrative proceedings involves one of the most controversial issues in administrative law. Indeed, until the relatively recent past, the whole content of administrative law centered about the availability and extent of judicial review. In 1916 Elihu Root addressed the development of administrative law and recognized that this area of the law was here to stay. "We shall go on," he stated. "We shall expand them whether we approve theoretically or not, because such agencies [administrative] furnish protection to rights and obstacles to wrongdoing which under our new social and industrial conditions cannot be practically accomplished by the old and simple procedures of legislatures and courts as in the last generation." He added a cautionary note: "If we are to continue a government of limited powers, these agencies of regulation must themselves be regulated. . . . The rights of the citizen against them must be made plain. A system of ad-

---

Mifflin, 1942), 118–19; Alfred H. Kelly and Winfred A. Harbison, *The American Constitution: Its Origins and Development* (New York: Norton, 1970), 609–10; *United States v. Winslow*, 227 U.S. 202 (1913); *United States v. United States Steel Corporation*, 251 U.S. 417 (1920).

ministrative law must be developed, and that with us is still in its infancy, crude and imperfect."[28]

The issue is the degree of finality to be accorded to administrative determinations, a problem which has been described as the "recurrent central issue" in administrative law. Upon the extent of judicial review of administrative determinations must ultimately depend the success of the administrative process, which has been summed up by the attorney general's Committee on Administrative Procedure in these terms: "From the beginning, the administrative process has been utilized to limit discretion, to effectuate social legislation, to provide for continuity of attention and clearly allocated responsibility, or to provide for action which because of practical or legal limitations neither the Courts nor Congress could themselves handle." If the courts go too far in reviewing determinations made by administrative bodies, they, in effect, take over this process of lawmaking, a task for which they are not especially well equipped. In recognition of this fact the Supreme Court has generally limited its review to inquiry as to whether the administrative agency has acted within the scope of its authority. This limitation is subject to the restriction that, in matters involving a constitutional right, federal courts will exercise an independent judgment concerning issues of law and fact and, even in such cases, still accord weight to administrative findings.[29]

Justice White's opinions relating to the scope of judicial review of determinations by the Interstate Commerce Commission occupy an important position in the development of the doctrine of noninterference. Early in his career on the Supreme Court, White strongly emphasized the view that the Court should not usurp the functions of an administrative body. In *Interstate Commerce Commission* v. *Clyde Steamship Co.*, he declared:

It is now urged that we should enter into an original investigation of the facts for the purpose of considering a number of questions as to preference, as to reasonableness of rates, as to the relation which the rates at some place bore to those at

28. Elihu Root, "Presidential Address," *American Bar Association Annual Reports*, XLI (1916), 368–69.

29. John Dickinson, "Administrative Law and the Fear of Bureaucracy," *American Bar Association Journal*, XIV (1928), 515; *Administrative Procedure in Government Agencies: Report of the Committee on Administrative Procedure Appointed by the Attorney General*, 26 (This committee was established by a request of President Franklin D. Roosevelt to determine "the need for procedural reform in the field of administrative law"). *St. Joseph Stock Yards Co.* v. *United States*, 298 U.S. 38 (1936).

others, in order to discharge the duty which the statute has expressly in the first instance declared should be performed by the commission . . . we have held that, whether the commission by reason of its erroneous construction of the statute had . . . declined to adequately find the facts, it was the duty of the courts, on application being made to them to enforce the erroneous order of the commission, not to proceed to an original investigation of the facts . . . but to correct the error of law committed by that body and, after doing so, to remand the case to the commission.

Where an administrative body had made a finding, the Court, in White's judgment, should not go behind an administrative action or issue to question its "wisdom or expediency." This issue arose when the Pitcairn Coal Company sought a writ of mandamus against the Baltimore and Ohio Railway Company on the ground that the coal company was a victim of discrimination in the allotment of coal cars to move in interstate commerce. The Court, speaking through White, ordered the petition dismissed and held the power of the Court to be restricted to a review of the questions relating to the substantive power of the Interstate Commerce Commission. "Courts, in determining whether an order of the commission would be suspended or enjoined, were without power to invade the administrative functions vested in the commission, and therefore could not set aside an order duly made on a mere exercise of judgment as to its wisdom or expediency." [30]

Nor was the finality of administrative findings to be applied only to cases in which there was a question of fact to be decided. It also extended to the application of rules laid down in a statute to a particular set of facts whether there was a dispute concerning the facts. This view was expressed by Chief Justice White in *United States* v. *Louisville and Nashville Ry. Co.* In that case the Commerce Court had granted an injunction restraining the enforcement of an order issued by the Interstate Commerce Commission upon a finding that the railroad was giving an "undue and unreasonable" preference in violation of Section 3 of the Interstate Commerce Act by granting certain reshipping privileges and

---

30. *Interstate Commerce Commission* v. *Clyde Steamship Co.*, 181 U.S. 29, 32–33 (1901); *Baltimore & Ohio R.R. Co.* v. *United States ex rel. Pitcairn Coal Co.*, 215 U.S. 481, 494 (1910); the finality of administrative determinations was upheld by White in numerous cases, among them *Texas & Pacific Ry. Co.* v. *Cisco Oil Mill*, 204 U.S. 449 (1907), *Southern Pacific Co.* v. *Interstate Commerce Commission*, 219 U.S. 433 (1911), *Interstate Commerce Commission* v. *Delaware, Lackawanna & Western R.R. Co.*, 220 U.S. 235 (1911), and *United States* v. *Louisville & Nashville Ry. Co.*, 235 U.S. 314 (1914).

denying others. The injunction was granted on the premise that, since there was no dispute about the facts, whether an undue preference existed was a matter of law to be decided by the courts. The Supreme Court held that the lower court exceeded its authority in substituting its judgment for that of the Commission. White's opinion stated:

> The court below, in substituting its judgment for that of the commission, on the ground that where there was no dispute as to the facts it had a right to do so, obviously exerted an authority not conferred . . . by the statute. It is not disputable that from the beginning the very purpose for which the commission was created was to bring into existence a body which, from its peculiar character, would be most fitted to primarily decide whether from facts, disputed or undisputed, in a given case, preference or discrimination existed. . . . If the view of the statute upheld below be sustained, the commission would become but a mere instrument for the purpose of taking testimony to be submitted to the courts for their ultimate action.[31]

In interpreting the Interstate Commerce Act, White insured that the Commission would have the opportunity to perform the functions Congress intended it to have by holding that the common law right to recover damages for unreasonable rates was by implication merged with the act and could not be enforced in court, but must be enforced by an original action before the Commission. As White for once concisely phrased it, "The act cannot be made to destroy itself."[32]

This examination of the techniques of judicial lawmaking with respect to Justice White's Supreme Court opinions yields three conclusions. First, he displayed as a judge an overfondness for common law precedents. Second, he gave the Sherman Anti-Trust Act an interpretation that is open to attack as a flagrant example of judicial legislation and that certainly hindered, if it did not make virtually impossible, effective prosecution of any powerful trust. Third, in the early phase of the development of administrative law in this country, White showed an admirable restraint in leaving to administrative bodies their own lawmaking functions.

---

31. *United States v. Louisville and Nashville Ry. Co.*, 235 U.S. 314, 320, 321 (1914).
32. *Texas & Pacific Ry. Co. v. Abilene Cotton Oil Co.*, 204 U.S. 426, 446 (1907).

Chief Justice White, 1910.
Collection of the Library of Congress

The White family house near Thibodaux, Louisiana.

Photography by Adrian Gauthier
Nicholls State University, Public Relations Office

The Fuller Court, 1898: seated are Justices David J. Brewer, John M. Harlan, Chief Justice Melville W. Fuller, Justices Horace Gray, Henry B. Brown; standing are Justices Rufus W. Peckham, George Shiras, Edward D. White, and Joseph McKenna.

Courtesy United States Supreme Court

The White Court, *ca.* 1914–1916: seated are Justices William R. Day, Joseph McKenna, Chief Justice Edward D. White, Justices Oliver W. Holmes, Charles E. Hughes; standing are Justices Mahlon Pitney, Willis Van Devanter, Joseph R. Lamar, and James C. McReynolds.

Courtesy United States Supreme Court

White administering the oath of office to President Woodrow Wilson, March 4, 1913.
Collection of the Library of Congress

White reviewing a parade, February 12, 1921. On his right are a Mr. Gillette and General John J. Pershing. *Collection of the Library of Congress*

Statue of White, which stands in the plaza of the Louisiana Supreme Court building in New Orleans.

Tony Vidacovich

VII

Dual Federalism of the Commerce Power

"Dual federalism," wrote Edward S. Corwin in 1934, "seemed about to pass into eclipse beneath the waxing orb of the commerce power. That it did not was due to no single cause more evidently than the championship of Justice White." The fundamentals of White's theory of the relationship between national power and state power, that is, the doctrine of dual federalism, were stated in a dissenting opinion.[1]

In 1893 the Great Northern and the Northern Pacific were separate and competing railroad lines across the northern part of the United States. In that year the Northern Pacific became bankrupt, and receivers were appointed. Before the foreclosure sale could be held, a majority of the road's bondholders agreed to consolidate with the Great Northern, giving the latter system control of both railroads. This arrangement, however, was frustrated by the courts of Minnesota, which found the merger illegal under a state statute forbidding the consolidation of parallel lines.[2]

The financial titans who wanted a consolidation of the lines were able to evade this obstacle without difficulty. In 1901 the two roads acquired in a joint purchase the Chicago, Burlington, and Quincy Railroad in order to secure entry into Chicago. On November 13 of the same year, James T. Hill of the Northern Pacific, with his associate of the Great Northern, J. P. Morgan, incorporated the Northern Securities Company,

1. Edward S. Corwin, *The Twilight of the Supreme Court* (New Haven: Yale University Press, 1934), 23; *Northern Securities Company* v. *United States*, 193 U.S. 197 (1904).
2. *Pearsall* v. *Great Northern Ry. Co.*, 161 U.S. 646 (1896).

a holding corporation, under the laws of New Jersey, and the stock of the Burlington line was exchanged at a given ratio for the controlling interest in the holding corporation. The government subsequently brought suit to dissolve the Northern Securities Company, charging that its only purpose was to effect a combination of the lines in order to destroy competition within the territory covered by the Great Northern and the Northern Pacific Railroads in violation of the Sherman Act. Indeed, this result was so apparent to a majority of the Supreme Court that, in upholding a decree of the lower court dissolving the corporation, Mr. Justice John Marshall Harlan was moved to exclaim: "No scheme or device could more certainly come within the words of the act . . . or could more effectively and certainly suppress free competition between the constituent companies. . . . The mere existence of such a combination and the power acquired by the holding company as its trustees constitutes a menace to, and a restraint upon, that freedom of commerce which Congress intended to recognize and protect. . . . The entire commerce of the immense territory in the northern part of the United States will be at the mercy of a single holding corporation." [3]

White filed a long dissent questioning the authority of Congress to legislate against the type of combination represented in this case. Admitting that Congress can regulate the instrumentalities of interstate commerce, he argued that its power did not extend to regulating combinations like the Northern Securities Company because the authority to regulate those instrumentalities "is entirely distinct from the power to regulate the acquisition and ownership of such instrumentalities and the many forms of contracts from which such ownership may arise." He attempted to draw a distinction between the regulation of the power of an individual or a corporation "to do" and the power "to acquire and own." With a style reminiscent of his Senate address on the Anti-Option Bill more than a decade earlier, White contended that acquisition and ownership is not interstate commerce and hence is a proper field for state regulation. Ownership of a state corporation cannot be said "in any sense to be traffic between the states or intercourse between them," so that exercise of federal authority over such ownership would extend the power of Congress to all subjects of an essentially local nature. "If it were judged

3. *Northern Securities Company v. United States*, 193 U.S. 197, 327–28 (1904).

by Congress," said White with some prescience of what was to come with the New Deal of the 1930s, "that the farmer in sowing his crops should be limited to a certain production because overproduction would give power to affect commerce, Congress could regulate that subject."[4]

The consequences of the majority's principle could destroy the American system of government. This principle would "not only destroy the state and federal governments, but by the implication of authority by which the destruction would be brought about, there would be erected upon the ruins of both a government endowed with arbitrary power to disregard the great guaranty of life, liberty and property and every other safeguard upon which organized society depends."[5] At this point White gazed into the future, perceived the outline of the New Deal of Franklin Roosevelt, and sought to combat it with James Madison's conception of dual federalism in *Federalist No. 39*.

To sustain his argument, he returned to the narrow doctrine of commerce announced in the *Knight* case, which limited interstate commerce to transportation between the states. As usual when White was fervently espousing a particular line of thought, no doubt existed in his mind that the circumstances at hand came within his precedent, here the Sugar Trust ruling. That case expressly held that the acquisition of stock in one corporation by another in order to control all other enterprises in the industry was not interstate commerce. The underlying philosophy of White's dissent finally cropped up when he rejected the need for national power and declared flatly that dual power could adequately cope with the situation created by trusts and combines. "With the full power of states over corporations created by them and with their authority in respect to local legislation, and with the power in Congress over commerce carried to its fullest degree, I cannot conceive that if these powers . . . be fully exerted, a remedy cannot be provided fully adequate to suppress evils which may arise from combinations deemed to be injurious."[6]

White's dissent illustrates his concept of national and state power, each operating within its defined sphere. This dual authority, he maintained, can deal adequately with problems such as those presented by the Northern Securities Company, yet this national power, confined to the

4. *Ibid.*, 393, 369.
5. *Ibid.*, 391–96.
6. *Ibid.*, 399.

regulation of transportation, could not reach the situation created by the devices of Hill and Morgan. Under White's thesis the states would be left to cope with the problem. This approach produces a logical, if cumbersome, argument on paper. In practice, the contention was worthless. The state of Minnesota had tried to prevent the combination and had failed. Was New Jersey then to undertake the regulation? It would have been one of the miracles of the age if that monopoly-dominated state had deprived itself of a lucrative income and turned its back upon its benefactors by refusing to incorporate the holding company. Even should the miracle have occurred, eager politicians all over the country would have fought for the privilege of seeing the incorporation made in their respective states. White's long experience in Louisiana politics must have shown him, and no doubt did, that a state cannot face problems that are national in character because corporate finance has interstate ramifications.

When the problem involved was more moral than economic in nature, White, along with the majority of the Court in this period, did not seem to be unduly concerned with the invasion of the national government into the sphere of state authority. He thus voted with the majority to uphold congressional enactments for the exclusion from interstate transportation of lottery tickets, adulterated or misbranded foods, women for immoral purposes, and inferentially, obscene literature and articles for immoral use. Each of these actions involved essentially the exercise of a kind of national police power pegged to the commerce clause. Where, however, the problem was of an economic nature, Justice White did not want to extend the national power over interstate commerce.[7]

This reluctance clearly appeared in cases where Congress attempted to bar from interstate commerce articles that were not inherently antisocial but that were to be excluded because of their association with a

7. *Champion* v. *Ames*, 188 U.S. 321 (1903), upholding Act of March 2, 1895; *Hipolite Egg Co.* v. *United States*, 220 U.S. 45 (1911), upholding Pure Food Act of 1906; *Hoke* v. *United States*, 227 U.S. 308 (1913), upholding the White Slave Act of 1910; in *Hoke* v. *United States*, the Court cited with approval a federal court decision, *United States* v. *Popper*, 98 Fed. 423 (1899), upholding the act of February 8, 1897, that forbade transportation of articles for immoral use; for an exposition of the national police power, see Robert E. Cushman, "The National Police Power Under the Commerce Clause of the Constitution," *Minnesota Law Review*, III (1919), 289, 381, and 452.

practice which Congress wished to control. The first of these cases arose out of the so-called commodities clause of the Hepburn Act.[8] For over fifty years prior to 1906, the state of Pennsylvania had sought to promote the development of natural resources by encouraging railroads to invest funds in coal lands. As a result, some roads owned and worked mines; others leased and operated them; and some roads were merely owners of stock in corporations whose primary activity was mining coal. By 1906 six railroads so engaged in Pennsylvania transported the coal with which they were thus associated. To remedy abuses which arose from this practice, Congress amended the Interstate Commerce Act so that any railroad was prohibited from transporting in interstate commerce "any article or manufactured commodity, other than timber and the manufactured products thereof, manufactured, mined, or produced by it, or under its authority, or which it may own in whole or in part, or in which it may have any interest direct or indirect except such articles or commodities as may be necessary [for use in its own business as a carrier.]"[9]

When the railroads contested this provision and the case came before the Court, government counsel argued that it was the intent of Congress to prohibit railroads doing interstate business from being at the same time both producers and owners of the commodities they carried. The legislation was intended, counsel maintained, to prohibit the railroads from carrying articles they had produced regardless of whether, at the time of transportation, they were still the owners.

Had the Court accepted the government's argument, it would have been forced to decide whether Congress had the authority to prohibit the manufacture, mining, production, or ownership of a commodity because the commodity might become at some future time the subject of interstate commerce. White well recognized this fact. "If the contention of the government as to the meaning of the commodity clause be well founded at least a majority of the court are of the opinion that we may not avoid determining the following grave constitutional questions: (1) Whether the power of Congress to regulate commerce embraces the authority to control or prohibit the mining, manufacture, production, or ownership of an article or commodity, not because of any inherent qual-

8. *United States Statutes at Large*, XXXIV, 584.
9. *United States v. Delaware & Hudson Co.*, 213 U.S. 366, 404 (1909).

ity of the commodity, but simply because it may become the subject of interstate commerce." [10]

The Court, however, avoided this issue by holding that the act did not apply to a case where the carrier had disassociated itself from the ownership of the commodity before its transportation and by ruling that ownership, by a carrier, of stock in a bona fide corporation manufacturing, mining, producing, or owning the commodity carried did not constitute ownership of the commodity covered by the Hepburn Act. By interpretation the Supreme Court thereby denied the power sought by the government. White's feelings, and those of the Court, were indicated by reference in his opinion to the rule that, where there are two possible constructions of a statute, the Court must follow the one that will validate the legislation. [11]

The significance of the decision was evident in the words of Justice White. "Nor do we vest it [*i.e.* the power here] upon the hypothesis that the power conferred embraces the right to absolutely prohibit the movement between states of lawful commodities or to destroy the governmental power of the states as to subjects within their jurisdictions." In 1917 he reiterated this view in a dictum delivered during the course of his opinion on the eight-hour law for railroads. "[The] right to prohibit could not be applied to pig iron, steel rails, or most of the vast body of commodities." [12]

This crusade limiting the power of the federal government to regulate interstate commerce reached its fruition in the decision rendering invalid the efforts of the federal government to abolish child labor by prohibiting the movement of goods manufactured by child labor in the channels of interstate commerce. [13] Although Chief Justice White did not deliver the opinion of the Court in the *First Child Labor* case, he voted with the majority that held the statute unconstitutional.

In the *Employers' Liability* cases White also showed his concern for the invasion of the authority of the states. In those actions he was the author of an opinion invalidating an attempt of Congress to regulate the liability of carriers to injured employees, finding that the statute was not

10. *Ibid.*, 406.
11. *Ibid.*, 407.
12. *Ibid.*, 445; *Wilson* v. *New*, 243 U.S. 332, 347 (1917).
13. *Hammer* v. *Dagenhart*, 247 U.S. 251 (1918).

limited to the mere regulation of interstate commerce. Instead, it directed the relation of employer to employees because the employers were engaged in interstate commerce. Justice White almost defiantly rejected the contention of the government, implicit in the *Northern Securities* case, that the act was valid because one who participated in interstate commerce thereby submitted all of his business concerns to the power of Congress. "To state the proposition is to refute it. It assumes . . . the right to legislate concerning matters of purely state concern. . . . It is apparent that . . . it would extend the power of Congress to every conceivable subject, however inherently local, would obliterate all the limitations imposed by the Constitution and would destroy the authority of the states as to all conceivable matters which from the beginning have been, and must continue to be, under their control so long as the Constitution endures." [14] White used strong words in defense of his concept of dual federalism.

In one of his last important decisions, Chief Justice White departed from his general trend of restricting federal power over commerce and introduced the "emergency" doctrine as applied to carriers with a public interest. [15] The issues of this exceptional opinion arose from the proposals of the railroad brotherhoods in March, 1916, that employers establish the eight-hour day as a basis of work and of a structure around which wages could be built. The employers refused labor's demands. President Wilson thereupon proposed that the dispute be arbitrated; the railroads agreed, but their employees did not. Wilson next called for an eight-hour standard for both work and wages. This time the railroads rejected the proposal, and the railroad brotherhoods reacted by calling a general strike within seventy-two hours. To avert this result President Wilson suggested that the Congress write the eight-hour provision into law. Congress responded to the president's request and on September 3, 1916, passed the Adamson Eight-Hour Act. This statute set the hours standard along with the provision that the existing wage scale was to remain in force six months while a select commission of three members appointed by the president studied the effect of the eight-hour day and the issue of wages.

When the Adamson Act came before the Court, it was upheld by a

14. *Employers' Liability* cases, 207 U.S. 463, 502–503 (1908).
15. *Wilson* v. *New*, 243 U.S. 332 (1917).

five to four vote of the justices. White spoke for three other members of the Court while a fifth justice concurred in the majority ruling in a separate opinion. The hour provisions of the statute caused little difficulty; authority to establish the eight-hour day was not regarded as disputable. The real issue was that of wages. The chief justice stated this question briefly: "Or, in other words," he asked, "did [Congress] have the power in order to prevent the disruption of interstate commerce to exert its will to supply the absence of a wage scale resulting from disagreement as to wages between employers and employees and to make its will on that subject controlling for the limited period provided for?" He declared that the fixing of wages was primarily a private matter between employer and employee, a matter not to be controlled or prevented by an exercise of public authority. Failure to exercise this private right, however, might very well create a situation in which government must act to protect the paramount public interest. "The capacity," White stated, "to exercise the private right free from legislative interference affords no ground for saying that legislative power does not exist to protect the public interest from the injury resulting from a failure to exercise the private right." The imminent danger of the interruption of commerce was sufficient grounds for enactment of the Adamson Act. "The power to regulate," said White, "may be exercised to guard against the cessation of interstate commerce threatened by a failure of employers and employees to agree as to the standard of wages." Therefore, the judgment of the Court justified itself. "Whatever would be the right of an employee engaged in private business to demand such wages as he desires, to leave the employment if he does not get them and by concert of action to agree with others to leave upon the same condition, such rights are necessarily subject to limitation when employment is accepted in a business charged with a public interest and as to which the power to regulate commerce possessed by Congress applied and the resulting right to fix in case of disagreement and dispute a standard of wages as we have seen necessarily obtained." [16]

Justice Mahlon Pitney, speaking for the dissenters, argued that White's opinion deprived the carriers of their liberty to agree with employees concerning terms of employment and added that *Adair* v. *United States*, which invalidated a federal statute banning yellow-dog contracts

16. *Ibid.*, 346, 393, 384, 352.

made by railroads, should be controlling.[17] Three of the dissenters, Pitney, Willis Van Devanter, and James C. McReynolds were of the opinion that the Adamson Act did not involve interstate commerce and that, consequently, its provisions did not fall within the power of Congress to regulate commerce.

The majority opinion of Justice White represented the greatest advance that he made in the extension of federal power under the commerce clause, but even here White was careful to point out the narrow scope of the decision and the fact that it was limited to carriers, a limitation, incidentally, which conformed with decisions already noted.

Several points remain to be observed with regard to White's conception of Congress' power to regulate interstate commerce. First, his point of view has been explained in terms of his theory of constitutional law rather than his social philosophy.[18] The fact is cited that he supported social welfare legislation of the states in their exercise of the police power, notably in his concurrence in Mr. Justice Holmes's dissent when the Court held invalid New York's ten-hour statute.[19] On the other hand, when Oregon's Hours-of-Labor Law came before the Court in 1917, he dissented from the majority opinion sustaining the measure.[20] Since his dissent was without opinion, we can only guess at the reasons behind it. The law in question provided not only for a maximum number of hours of labor, but also contained a clause requiring time and a half of the regular wages for overtime work. For this reason it was attacked as a wage law, although the majority interpreted the act purely as an hours-of-service statute and upheld it on this ground. Because White had sustained the police power of the state in hours legislation, the only apparent ground for his dissent in the *Bunting* case is that the act was, at least partly, a wage law and as such in his opinion was invalid. The sole basis on which this distinction could be made was one of social philosophy. It is merely shadow boxing to attempt to place social philosophy and constitutional theory into separate categories, for they are interrelated terms

17. *Ibid.*, 387; *Adair v. United States*, 208 U.S. 161 (1908).
18. Attorney General Harry M. Daugherty in Henry P. Dart, Sr., Harry M. Daugherty, William Howard Taft, and others, *Proceedings of the Bar and Officers of the Supreme Court of the United States in Memory of Edward Douglass White*, Washington, December 17, 1921, p. 55, hereinafter cited as *Proceedings*.
19. *Lochner v. New York*, 198 U.S. 45 (1905).
20. *Bunting v. Oregon*, 243 U.S. 426 (1917).

which overlap. Constitutional theory is largely the projection into public law of social philosophy whether the judge be termed conservative, liberal, or radical.

Second, other statements of Justice White in cases dealing with interstate commerce indicate that his contraction of the term with respect to federal power was based more on an idea that he did not want the power extended to the particular subject than upon any abstract concept of its limitations. In upholding an act of Congress that made it a crime to forge bills of lading in interstate commerce, he rejected the argument that there was no commerce in these bills, and hence they were beyond the scope of federal authority. "This [the argument of the defendant] mistakenly assumed that the power of Congress is to be necessarily tested by the intrinsic existence of commerce in the particular subject dealt with, instead of by the relation of the subject to interstate commerce and its effect upon it. . . . *That power, if it is to exist, must include the authority to deal with obstructions to interstate commerce and with a host of other acts which, because of their relation to and influence upon interstate commerce, come within the power of Congress to regulate.*"[21] Curiously, this concept, formulated by a conservative southern chief justice, formed the basis of the decision upholding New Deal legislation nearly twenty years later.[22] The idea could apply equally well to all of the commerce clause decisions that White delivered invalidating federal legislation, so that the only conclusion we can reach is that White did not use the concept in these cases because he opposed the particular type of act.

Justice White revived James Madison's distinction between federal power over foreign commerce and Congress' authority over interstate commerce. Madison had argued that the power to regulate foreign commerce is a branch of foreign relations in which area the federal government is supreme. In contrast, the power of Congress to regulate interstate commerce is sovereign only in the area of commercial motive and elsewhere must interface with the state police power. The regulation of interstate commerce, therefore, must operate and be defined in terms of the objectives of the police power of the states. The Tea Inspection Act of

---

21. *United States* v. *Ferger (No. 1)*, 250 U.S. 199, 203 (1919), my italics.
22. For examples, see *N.L.R.B.* v. *Jones & Laughlin Steel Corp.*, 301 U.S. 1 (1937), *N.L.R.B.* v. *Fruehoff Trailer Corp.*, 301 U.S. 49 (1937), *N.L.R.B.* v. *Friedman-Harry Marks Clothing Co.*, 301 U.S. 58 (1937), and *United States* v. *Rock Royal Co-operative*, 307 U.S. 533 (1939).

1902 made it unlawful to import tea of an inferior quality into the United States, with standards of quality being determined by the secretary of the treasury after recommendations by a board of seven examiners. When a test came before the Court, White declared that the power over foreign commerce is complete and that no right is so vested as to prevent Congress from determining what articles may be imported and upon what conditions. "We entertain no doubt that it was competent for Congress, by statute," he said, "to establish standards and provide that no right should exist to import teas from foreign countries into the United States unless teas should be equal to the standards." [23] This language is a far cry from his vote of concurrence in the *Child Labor* case, which denied a similar power to Congress to prohibit transportation of goods that failed to meet the standards imposed. That White supported prohibitory power in the *Champion, Hipolite,* and *Hoke* cases is another indication that it was the subject matter of legislation more than abstract legal principles which affected his views.

In all of his decisions interpreting federal power over commerce, White had consciously restricted the scope of national power lest it involve the destruction of the states' rightful place in the federal system. His tender solicitude for the power of the several states did not appear so obviously in decisions concerning state authority.

In cases involving the authority of a state to require licenses of persons and firms doing business within a state and to impose a license tax, White supported the state's exercise of power. He thus upheld a California statute requiring every insurance agent representing any insurance company not incorporated under the laws of the state to file a bond or to represent a company which had filed a bond. In *American Steel & Wire Co.* v. *Speed,* White wrote the opinion of the Court sustaining the statutory imposition of a merchants' tax upon a nonresident corporation. This tax was applied to such a corporation, which shipped its products to a local transfer company for sorting, storing, and delivery in the original package to customers of the corporation. White based his argument upon the determination that, under the circumstances, the goods, when

23. Madison's views are covered in Edward S. Corwin, "The Power of Congress to Prohibit Commerce," *Cornell Law Quarterly,* XVIII (1933), 477; *Buttfield* v. *Stranahan,* 192 U.S. 470, 493 (1904).

stored in the warehouse, were no longer in transit, but had reached their destination and were held in the state for sale. White was also the author of opinions which recognized a state's power to license and regulate pilots for vessels entering the state, to levy a tax on the sale of cartons of cigarettes that were shipped to the retailer from another state, and to impose an occupation tax on the business of erecting lightning rods as an agent of a nonresident manufacturer from whom the agent had received the rods as shipment from out of the state.[24]

When the problem of state taxation of large corporate enterprises operating within the state arose, however, Justice White was to be found in opposition to the exercise of state power and, incidentally, in opposition to the majority of the Court. As corporations grew in both size and activity, their operations frequently extended into several states and occasionally into every state. A single enterprise might carry on its operations within a number of states, "doing business" in all of them in the sense of the sale of its product or services. Yet, the physical properties of a large corporation in a particular state would bear no relationship to the extent of its operations in that state or the proportion of its business conducted there. How could the state tax such a corporation so that it would carry a just share of the tax loads in return for benefits received within the state? The *United States Reports* give many examples of just such a situation.

In one such case, the attempt of Ohio to tax telephone, telegraph, and express companies resulted in *Adams Express Company* v. *Ohio State Auditor,* and in this action, White wrote a dissent that not only expressed his views on the subject involved in the controversy, but also revealed once more his concept of the federal system.[25] In 1893, Ohio enacted a statute, known as the Nichols Act, for purposes of taxing the classes of interstate business operating within the state. The tax was applied on the basis of fractional parts of "a unit profit-producing plant." The method employed in levying the tax was to determine what proportion of the property of the interstate business, both real and intangible, was used to carry on business within the state. This fraction then was applied to the

---

24. *Hooper* v. *State of California*, 155 U.S. 648 (1895); *American Steel & Wire Co.* v. *Speed,* 192 U.S. 500 (1904); *Olsen* v. *Smith*, 195 U.S. 332 (1904); *Cook* v. *Marshall County*, 196 U.S. 261 (1905); *Browning* v. *City of Waycross*, 233 U.S. 16 (1914).
25. *Adams Express Company* v. *Ohio State Auditor*, 165 U.S. 194 (1897).

supposed value of the whole enterprise, as determined by the value of its capital stock, to reach the assessment base. A board of appraisers and assessors was established to apply the statute.

In a five to four decision, Chief Justice Fuller held that the act was a valid exercise of state power. The Court rejected the argument of the express company that the tax violated the commerce power, no more reason being found for limiting the valuation of the Adams Express Company to horses, wagons, and furniture than that of railroads and sleeping car companies to roadbeds, ties, and rails. For one of the few times in actions involving state power in this period, the Supreme Court recognized the inherent unity of large interstate businesses and the difficulty of reaching them. "The property of an express company," declared Fuller, "distributed through different states is an essential condition of the business united in a single specific use. It constitutes but a single plant, made so by the very character and necessities of the business."[26]

In reply to the majority opinion, White wrote one of his more vigorous dissents, contending that the tax violated the commerce clause. He maintained that "it is clear that the recognition of a right to take an aliquot proportion of the value of property in one state and add it to the intrinsic value of property in another state and there assess it, is in substance an absolute denial and overthrow of all the great principles announced from the beginning . . . on the subject of interstate commerce."[27] He refused to admit the force of Fuller's argument that the unity of interstate business must be recognized and found no strength in the thesis that, unless the Court admitted the power of Ohio to tax as claimed, aggregations of capital would escape just taxation by the states.

Another revealing view of White's concept of the federal system is furnished by this same dissent. He argued that the real difficulty with the Ohio tax was not that it encroached upon federal power, but rather that it invaded the rights of the states themselves. He contended that "The wound which the ruling . . . inflicts on the Constitution, is equally as severe upon the unquestioned rights of the states as it is upon the lawful authority of the United States because whilst submitting the states and their citizens to injustice and wrong committed by another state, it

26. *Ibid.*, 221, 222.
27. *Ibid.*, 242.

at the same time greatly weakens or destroys the efficiency of the inter-state commerce clause of the Constitution." In short, the states must be protected not merely from the federal government, but from each other. This line of thought was reflected in two other decisions handed down by the Court on the same day as the *Lightning Rod* case. White's dissents in these cases concerned the attempts of Kentucky to tax interstate corporations.[28]

In another series of cases dealing with the efforts of states to prohibit importation of liquor from other states, White voiced opinions that went far toward creating areas within which neither the federal nor state governments could act. The Prohibition Crusade, which had been under way since the 1850s, gathered momentum following the Civil War and created pressure for state legislation with respect to the "liquor evil." In Iowa a statute was enacted by the legislature to prevent importation of liquor into the state and its subsequent sale, but the statute had been held invalid before White became a member of the Court.[29] In the Iowa case, the Court's opinion declared that a citizen had a right to import liquor into a state and to sell it in the original package. If such were the law, states were left powerless to protect themselves from articles, commodities, or beverages that they might find objectionable.

A few months later Congress passed the Wilson Act, which provided that all intoxicating liquors imported into any state or territory, and remaining there for storage or use, should be subject to the laws of the state or territory upon arrival within its borders whether in the original package or not. The measure was quickly sustained by the Court as a valid exercise of Congress' power over interstate commerce.[30]

Another Iowa statute subsequently made it an offense to carry liquor from one place to another within the state without a permit. Shortly thereafter a box of liquor was transported from Dallas, Illinois, to Burlington, Iowa, and delivered to the station agent who moved it from the platform to a warehouse a few yards away. The agent was tried and convicted for this act under the state statute, but the Supreme Court,

28. *Ibid.*, 243–44; *Henderson Bridge Co. v. Kentucky*, 166 U.S. 150 (1897); *Adams Express Co. v. Kentucky*, 166 U.S. 171 (1897).
29. *Leisy v. Hardin*, 135 U.S. 100 (1890).
30. *United States Statutes at Large*, XXVI, 313; *In Re Rahrer*, 140 U.S. 545 (1891).

speaking through White, reversed the conviction. The Wilson Act, said White, did not apply until the transportation was completed by delivery to the consignee. The "right to receive" was not affected by the Wilson Act, and receipt with the consequent capacity to use remained protected from state action by the commerce clause.[31]

White maintained that federal law permitted the state act to apply before sale where otherwise it would not apply until after sale of the goods shipped into Iowa in the original package. The Wilson Act, however, could not operate in such a way as to permit the state statute to have effect on the goods the moment they reached the state line and before consummation of the contract of shipment by actual delivery. The Wilson Act had contained the words "arrival in the state" for "use, consumption, or storage." These words, White contended, indicated that Congress intended the liquor to cross the state line and not be stopped at the border. If such were not the case, the act would reach beyond the state's jurisdiction and clearly be void: "If the construction claimed be upheld, it would be in the power of each state to compel every interstate train to stop before crossing its borders."[32]

The fact that the Wilson Act followed *Leisy* v. *Hardin* by a few months appeared to indicate to White that Congress merely intended to restrict the right of sale which had been upheld in that case. He declared: "The purpose of Congress to submit the incidental power to sell [which was declared in *Leisy* v. *Hardin*] to the dominion of state authority should not without the clearest implication be held to imply the purpose of subjecting to state laws a contract which in its very object and nature was not susceptible of such regulation even if the constitutional right to do so existed."[33]

This decision and other similar judicial dentistry removed the teeth of the Wilson Act. In *Vance* v. *Vandercook Co.*, White and the Court held invalid a South Carolina statute requiring nonresidents to obtain a permit from state officers before shipment and also demanding that residents communicate their purpose to the state chemist before ordering liquor from another state. And in *American Express Co.* v. *Iowa*, Justice White

31. *Rhodes* v. *Iowa*, 170 U.S. 412 (1898).
32. *Ibid.*, 422.
33. *Ibid.*, 424.

declared that liquor shipped "collect on delivery" from one state to another could not be subjected to seizure under the laws of the latter state while still in the hands of the express company.[34]

Not until the passage of the Webb-Kenyon Act of 1913, which prohibited the transportation of liquors into any state to be "received, possessed, or in any manner used" in violation of state law, was the liquor traffic subjected to stringent control.[35] The act was sustained by the Supreme Court in an opinion by Chief Justice White.

In determining that the Webb-Kenyon Act was within the authority of Congress, White went back to the line of cases of which *Champion* v. *Ames* and *Hoke* v. *United States* are a part. Since Congress could prohibit completely the transportation of liquors in interstate commerce under the doctrine of these cases, it could enact a less stringent regulation. The only issue in *Clark Distilling Co.* v. *Western Maryland Ry. Co.* was not one of power, but of the methods used. Could Congress permit state prohibition of commerce to apply to movements of liquor from one state to another? White had no difficulty in answering this question affirmatively: It was the will of Congress, not that of the states, which was acting upon commerce. Any other theory, declared the chief justice, would amount to a repudiation of *Leisy* v. *Hardin*.[36]

White never went beyond the holding of the *Clark Distilling* case, which was in essence a reiteration of the principle of *Champion* v. *Ames*. When he left the bench in 1921, there was still no indication that White had come to grips with the economic realities of a modern society, national in both scope and character

White preserved and even strengthened the concept of dual federalism in which denial of authority alike to the federal government and to the states to act under the commerce clause of the Constitution created a zone where neither could effectively legislate. This result would flow naturally from the concept of federalism he expressed in terms of a dual form of government under which the states and the nation had separate spheres of power. White left the door open to joint efforts by his strong belief that the commerce power delegated to the federal government and

34. *Vance* v. *Vandercook Co.*, 170 U.S. 438 (1898); *American Express Co.* v. *Iowa*, 196 U.S. 133 (1905).

35. *United States Statutes at Large*, XXXVII, 699.

36. *Champion* v. *Ames*, 188 U.S. 321 (1903); *Hoke* v. *United States*, 227 U.S. 308 (1913); *Clark Distilling Co.* v. *Western Maryland Ry. Co.*, 242 U.S. 311 (1917).

that reserved to the states were intended to be exercised, either independently or jointly, to promote the general welfare.[37] The Court was thus given a basis upon which national-state cooperation may rest and has employed it often enough over the years. When it came to reviewing a federal statute banning child-made goods from entering interstate commerce, White and the Court found that Congress had attempted to coerce states into compliance by federal regulation of a state concern. This dualism, and the part White played in its development, would last through the Taft Court and well into the period of the Hughes Court. Only when, in the Great Depression of the 1930s, there were millions of workers unemployed, an activist president, and a public not satisfied with the general conservatism of the Court would the twilight zone vanish.

Speculation about motivations is always difficult. The years White spent on the bench were a difficult period for state statutes. Between 1899 and the death of Chief Justice White in 1921, state statutes were declared invalid in 194 cases; of these, 102 were held unconstitutional in terms of federalism.[38] From the view of the federal government the situation was somewhat different. No more than four congressional statutes involving the commerce clause were thrown out by the Court. However, in one of these, White wrote the opinion of the Court and was a silent partner of the majority in another.[39] Certainly White was well respected and generally well supported by other members of the Supreme Court.

That he did not try to lead the Court into a broader interpretation of governmental power under the commerce clause is understandable. Perhaps, as a few writers have observed, education in Jesuit institutions influenced his dual federalism, for he was acquainted with the medieval concept of dual jurisdiction over the same territory by church and state. Of no less importance is the fact that, like all of us, he was a product of his times and subject to the process of socialization in contemporary culture that all of us undergo. White was affected to no small extent during his tenure on the bench by the linkage of Constitution and Supreme

37. White shared this conception of the commerce power with other justices. Compare with Justice Joseph McKenna's opinion in *Hoke* v. *United States*, 227 U.S. 308, 322 (1913).
38. Benjamin F. Wright, *The Growth of American Constitutional Law* (Boston: Houghton Mifflin, 1942), 113.
39. *Employers' Liability* cases (*Howard* v. *Illinois Central* and *Brooks* v. *Southern Pacific*), 207 U.S. 463 (1908), and *Hammer* v. *Dagenhart*, 247 U.S. 251 (1918).

Court as symbols. Max Lerner has appropriately stated, "What enabled the propertied groups, in the last analysis, to make use of the judicial power was the strength and evocative force of the Constitutional tradition."[40] New economic constructions and new symbols would result in new judicial doctrines of American federalism, but these would not come in White's time.

40. Max Lerner, "Constitution and Court as Symbols," *Yale Law Journal*, XLVI (1937), 1307.

VIII
The Power to Tax

T he power to tax," said Mr. Justice Holmes, "is not the power to destroy while this Court sits." [1] Dealing with the realities of taxation, the Court requires some method of changing to meet new situations, but it must also reflect stability. Equilibrium is assured by the doctrine of precedent, an authoritative way of reasoning that has been extended by the Supreme Court to questions of political power necessarily involved in constitutional interpretation. Precedent is simply a device by which the old may be conserved in the new, establishing a point of departure for new principles, which, in turn, become precedents and are themselves subject to almost endless refinement. Precedents may be, and indeed have been, frequently used to assist contending social or economic groups to gain and to maintain a dominant position, or they may on rare occasions be set aside ruthlessly in the favor of a particular interest. They were thus set aside in 1895 when the national taxing power was severely restricted, an instance where, as in other tax cases, Edward White emerged as an apostle of nationalism. The contrast that this position affords with his views on the commerce clause may be accounted for partly by his veneration of common law *stare decisis* and partly by his strong belief that Congress possessed a broad but not unlimited power of taxation.

Among the enumerated powers of Congress is the authority to levy taxes, duties, imposts, and excises. Two limitations restrict this grant:

---

1. *Panhandle Oil Co.* v. *Mississippi ex rel. Knox*, 277 U.S. 218, 223 (1928).

first, all levies must be uniform throughout the United States, and, second, no direct tax may be imposed unless it is in proportion to the decennial census tabulating the population of each state.[2] This latter restriction was included in the Constitution as a compromise when the Convention of 1787 had been sorely vexed with the problem of slavery. Many delegates considered slavery a decadent institution, some thought it would soon disappear, but few dared to risk offending South Carolina and Georgia, special advocates of slavery, in the Constitutional Convention. The southern states naturally desired representation on the basis of both slave and free populations, a position which raised the question whether slaves were persons or property. If persons, why should they not be fully represented? Finally, the Convention agreed that, for purposes of both apportionment and direct taxation, slaves should be counted on a three-fifths basis and that importation of slaves would not be interfered with by Congress for a period of twenty years.

Did the inclusion of the phrase "direct taxes" in this provision signify some restricted meaning? The distinction between direct and indirect taxes was by no means clear in the minds of those who framed the Constitution. Chief Justice Fuller in the *Pollock* case quoted Madison's Journal: "Mr. King asked what was the precise meaning of direct taxation. No one answered." Alexander Hamilton sought in vain "for any antecedent settled legal meaning to the respective terms—there is none." Justice William Paterson stated in the *Hylton* case that

the provision was made in favor of the southern States. They possessed a large number of slaves; they had extensive tracts of territory, thinly settled, and not very productive. A majority of the States had but few slaves, and several of them a limited territory, well settled, and in a high state of cultivation. The southern States, if no provision had been introduced in the Constitution, would have been wholly at the mercy of the other States. Congress, in such cases, might tax slaves, at discretion or arbitrarily, and land in every part of the Union after the same rate or measure. . . . To guard them against imposition in these particulars, was the reason of introducing the clause in the Constitution, which directs that representatives and direct taxes shall be apportioned among the States, according to their respective numbers.

Paterson expressed his belief that the objects falling within the rule of apportionment were a capitation tax and a tax on land. Eighty-five years

2. United States Constitution, Art. I, Sec. 8, Para. 1; Sec. 9, Para. 4.

marriag 94 [handwritten annotations]

11/94 [handwritten]

later, in 1881, the Court held specifically that an income tax was not a direct levy and limited the application of the rule of apportionment to land and capitation levies. History seemed to have settled the issue.[3]

The Revenue Act of August 15, 1894, however, raised the question of constitutionality of the income tax once more. The statute, which had been passed while Edward White was a senator and with his support, imposed a flat tax of 2.0 percent on all incomes above four thousand dollars from any sources whatsoever. The tax was in no sense of the term a destructive levy. The act itself can be understood only in the light of the prevailing political and economic situation, for the income tax legislation was simply one more manifestation of an ever-widening gap between social theory and political action. In the eyes of the Democrats, backed by the Populists, the income tax statute struck at the roots of monopoly capitalism, the great reserves of personal property exempted from other forms of taxation. An income tax was a main feature of the protest politics of minor political parties from 1865 to 1894. The 1890s were a period of reform and rumors of reform. This spirit had emerged on a dozen fronts, and the Income Tax Act of 1894 was consistent with the rising progressive revolt. In that year, even while a conservative member of the Senate, White had evidently applied his doctrine of "subjective" constitutionality to the act and had given the tax measure his support. Almost everywhere, however, "solid men" rallied against this menace to property, and among them threats were rife to revive the spirit of the Boston Tea Party.[4]

A test case presently came before the Court. The action was brought by one Charles Pollock, who, as a shareholder of the Farmers' Loan & Trust Company of New York, sought to restrain the bank from paying the federal government a tax on its net profit, including some income derived from bonds of the city of New York and various parcels of real estate. Since both parties to the action were interested in having the tax declared invalid, the suit was clearly moot. Moreover, it was brought in

---

3. *Pollock v. Farmers' Loan and Trust Company,* 157 U.S. 429, 572 (1895); Alexander Hamilton quoted in Edward S. Corwin, *Court Over Constitution: A Study of Judicial Review as an Instrument of Popular Government* (Princeton: Princeton University Press, 1938), 182–83; *Hylton v. United States,* 3 Dall. 171, 177 (1796); *Springer v. United States,* 102 U.S. 586, 602 (1881).

4. Matthew Josephson, *The Politicos, 1865–1896* (New York: Harcourt, Brace, 1938), 106–110.

obvious violation of Section 3224 of the *Revised Statutes*, which forbade suits in any court "for the purpose of restraining the assessment or collection of any tax." Previous judgments, where it was held that the taxpayer, under Section 3224, could bring suit against the collector only after payment under protest, were flatly overruled in *Miller* v. *Standard Nut Margarine Co.* If the method of testing the income tax statute was somewhat devious as well as dubious, at least it had the advantage of resulting in a quick decision on this vital legislation.[5]

The decision of the Supreme Court would rest, probably inevitably, upon the predilections of the individual justices. Nor did the staff of attorneys representing the plaintiff permit them to forget their duty for a moment. All told, seventeen distinguished attorneys participated in the case. W. D. Guthrie represented the plaintiff. Joseph H. Choate also assisted in the assault on the income tax, and Attorney General Richard Olney and James Coolidge Carter defended it. Choate was assisted by an elderly attorney who, as Choate rather naïvely put it, "had an income of his own which was affected, and had a strong idea on the right of private property being at the foundation of civilized society."[6]

On April 8, 1895, Justice Jackson being absent because of a serious and soon to be fatal lung illness, a divided Court rendered judgment that a tax on rents or incomes from real estate was unconstitutional.[7] The same judgment also declared that a tax on incomes derived from bonds of cities was invalid. On three issues—whether one invalid section of the statute voided the whole act; whether the act was unconstitutional as imposing direct taxes; and whether any part of the statute, if not concerning direct taxes, was invalid from lack of uniformity—the Court was divided four to four and so rendered no judgment on them. This outcome was scarcely a satisfactory answer to the propertied class, which had been chiefly interested in obtaining a clear-cut verdict, and because Jackson had not been present at the hearing, the Court granted a rehearing the same year. Counsel's argument was again marked more by impassioned appeals to the prejudices of the bench than by any impressive constitutional arguments. "Against Mr. Choate's position," later

5. *Miller* v. *Standard Nut Margarine Co.*, 284 U.S. 260 (1932); Louis Boudin, *Government by Judiciary* (2 vols.; New York: Godwin, 1932), I, 208.
6. Edward S. Martin, *The Life of Joseph Hodges Choate* (2 vols.; London: Constable, 1920), II, 16.
7. *Pollock* v. *Farmers' Loan and Trust Company*, 157 U.S. 429 (1895).

wrote Robert H. Jackson,"were historical purpose, judicial precedent, and economic logic. . . . His arguments struck as low a note as any great lawyer ever sounded in the Court."[8]

Chief Justice Fuller read the opinion of the Court, which reaffirmed the result of the first hearing and declared a tax on income from personalty invalid; Field concurred in the result; White, Brown, Harlan, and Jackson dissented. The fact that Justice Jackson, who participated in the rehearing, and Brown, who had been with the majority on all points in the first case, both dissented indicated that one member of the Court who had supported the validity of the tax in the first hearing had changed his vote, at least so far as income from personalty was concerned. The vacillating jurist was long supposed to be Justice George Shiras, but other candidates have since been advanced.[9] White's dissent in both hearings not only upheld the Revenue Act of 1894, but also emphasized adherence to precedent where matters of property and taxation were concerned. Chief Justice Fuller's reasoning was almost a complete break with the past, but White realized what Fuller apparently did not—that when the court stepped into this vital public issue, it was not removing the problem from the political system. Instead, Fuller and his colleagues were projecting the Court into politics.

Chief Justice Fuller plunged at once into the argument that a tax on income from real estate was a direct tax and must be apportioned. He asserted that an examination of the period during and immediately after the Constitutional Convention of 1787 demonstrated that the "distinction between 'direct' and 'indirect' taxation was well understood by the framers of the Constitution and those who adopted it," despite the evidence to the contrary. He further contended that in 1787 "all taxation on real estate or personal property or rentals or incomes thereof were regarded as direct taxes." He was unable to show, however, that any such tax existed at that date, a lack of evidence that subsequent research has confirmed. Fuller's historical review concluded with the assertion that the power to levy direct taxes was granted with the understanding that it would be used only in extraordinary emergencies.[10]

8. Robert H. Jackson, *The Struggle for Judicial Supremacy: A Study of a Crisis in American Power Politics* (New York: Knopf, 1941), 45.
9. Corwin, *Court Over Constitution*, 194–201.
10. *Pollock v. Farmers' Loan*, 157 U.S. 582–83, 158 U.S. 607–13, 157 U.S. 563–64, 158 U.S. 620–21.

When the case had its first hearing the chief justice had attempted to distinguish the *Pollock* case from *Hylton* v. *United States*, where it was conceded that direct taxes were levies on land itself. From this initial premise, Fuller, with a hiatus in his logic, jumped to the doubtful conclusion that the term applied also to rentals. In *Springer* v. *United States*, an income tax had been sustained by the Court, but Fuller pointed out that the income in this instance was derived from personal services and bonds. The Court had made no distinction in that case, and it might be, he argued, that the tax on bonds was direct while that on earnings was indirect. This line of thought was somewhat wide of the mark, for the Revenue Act of 1894 did not tax rentals as such but the net income. Land, as Justice White put it, was reached by a "double indirection." The same argument applied to incomes from personalty.

This "double indirection" also applies to the means by which Chief Justice Fuller shifted the burden of proof from the plaintiff to the government. Specifically, he argued that general principles of taxation—presumably gleaned from the writings of economists—ruled that the category into which a tax falls depends upon the incidence of the tax. A tax which could not be shifted was direct, and since an income tax could not be shifted, it was direct and unconstitutional. This interpretation came back to plague Mr. Justice White. In the litigation over the inheritance tax five years later, White would declare with a bland disregard for facts: "The fallacy is the premise. It is true that in the income tax cases the theory of certain economists by which direct and indirect taxes are classified with reference to the shift of same was adverted to. But this disputable theory was not the basis of the conclusion of the Court. The constitutional meaning of the word direct was the matter decided." White's argument was not entirely candid. In his dissent in the *Pollock* case, he took the Court to task for deciding the meaning of "direct" on the theories of economists, yet five years later he not only denied that these theories were the basis of the income tax decision, but proceeded to adjudge the inheritance tax on similar theories. White thus maintained that an inheritance tax was a levy upon the transmission of legacies rather than upon property itself.[11]

White was technically correct in declaring that the meaning was

11. *Knowlton* v. *Moore*, 178 U.S. 41, 82, 57 (1900).

based on constitutional interpretation, but this interpretation in turn was founded on the prevailing theory of 1787. In the *Knowlton* case, however, it appears that White was trying to limit the effect of Fuller's opinion and to remove the economic theories in it. By 1900 the prima facie case of 1895 had become merely disputable theory, for apparently the majority opinion in *Pollock* had established the invalidity of the income tax before the Court took the trouble to read the Constitution. Where there were two possible interpretations, Chief Justice Fuller invariably chose the one that would render the tax invalid. In discussing *Springer v. United States*, he closed his eyes to the fact that the case expressly limited direct taxes to capitation and real estate levies and drew an artificial distinction between income from labor and income from personal property, Fuller himself putting his distinction in the category of "might be." [12]

The predilection upon which Fuller's reasoning was founded came to light near the end of his opinion in the *Pollock* case. He is quoted as saying that a tax on income from land is the same as a tax on land itself. "If," he said, "by calling a tax indirect when it is essentially direct, the rule of protection could be frittered away, one of the great landmarks defining the boundary between the nation and the states of which it is composed would have disappeared and with it one of the bulwarks of private rights and private property." While professing anxiety about the states, Fuller was disclosing a much different motivation for employing the direct tax clause—one directly concerned with protection of private property. [13]

White's dissent, which incidentally is seven pages longer than Fuller's majority opinion, is that of a scholarly lawyer who spoke with deep respect for long-settled usage. All through the case he had shown keen interest, subjecting the attorneys to much questioning and sometimes disconcerting them with facial contortions as the argument took unexpected turns. His dissent was a series of carefully reasoned arguments, although he expressed a general reluctance to elaborate dissents, "the custom of filing long dissenting opinions being one 'more honored in the breach than in the observance.' " A real acceptance of precedent, however, compelled him to take exception to the denial of a power which the government had possessed for over a century because, at this late date in our history, he said, it would serve no useful purpose to determine the mean-

12. *Springer v. United States*, 102 U.S. 586 (1881).
13. *Pollock v. Farmers' Loan*, 157 U.S. 429, 583; Corwin, *Court Over Constitution*, 192.

ing of "direct" by "resorting to the theoretical opinions found in the writings of some economists prior to the adoption of the Constitution or since." [14]

Emphasis on consequences, precedent, and definitely separated and coordinated spheres of government is reflected in White's dissent. An authoritative construction of direct taxes had long since been adopted, and the Carriage Tax of 1794, which had been reviewed by many members of the Constitutional Convention, had rejected the theory that a direct tax is one that cannot be shifted. The *Hylton* case had established that a tax on personal property without apportionment was not a direct tax, and the ruling had not been questioned since then. In addition, statutes that had been enacted between 1861 and 1876 imposing taxes on income from every source had been upheld by following the *Hylton* precedent. Justice White ruefully added: "And now, after a hundred years, after long continued action by other departments of the government and after repeated adjudications by this court, this interpretation is overthrown." The consequences would be disastrous, for it was too late now to destroy the force of those past opinions of the Court by qualifying them as mere dicta, especially when "they have again and again been expressly approved by this Court." [15]

White took Fuller to task for overthrowing *stare decisis* on the basis of theories of economists and not on the meaning of the word "direct" in the Constitution. Such theories, he argued, could help in no way; a long series of decisions had already settled the meaning.

The facts, then, are briefly these: At the very birth of the government a contention arose over the meaning of the word "direct." The controversy was determined by the legislative and executive departments of the government. This action came to this court for review, and it was approved. Every judge of this court who expressed an opinion made use of language which clearly showed that he thought the word "direct" in the Constitution applied only to capitation taxes and taxes directly on land. Thereafter the construction thus given was accepted everywhere as definitive. The matter came again and again to this court, and in every case the original ruling was adhered to. The suggestions made in the Hylton

---

14. *Pollock v. Farmers' Loan*, 157 U.S. 429, 608, 614.
15. *Ibid.*, 616, 618, 619–20; *Pacific Insurance Co.* v. *Soule*, 7 Wall. 433 (1869), *Veazie Bank* v. *Fenno*, 8 Wall. 533 (1869), and *Scholey* v. *Rew*, 23 Wall. 331 (1875); *Pollock v. Farmers' Loan*, 157 U.S. 429, 637, 652.

case were adopted here, and, in the last case here decided, reviewing all the others, this court said that direct taxes within the meaning of the Constitution were only taxes on land and capitation taxes.[16]

White felt deeply not only the significant results of the case at hand, but also the importance of the judgment for the Court's function. He uncovered his philosophy with respect to the position of that tribunal in the American system of government. Calamitous results are likely to occur when settled policies are upset, but they are much more likely to be intensified when the Court impinges on fundamental questions of power and denies essential authority to government. If the Court were to maintain its authoritative position, White contended, it must act as something like a balance wheel in the nation's life. "The fundamental conception of a judicial body," he declared, "is that of one hedged about by precedents which are binding upon the court. . . . If the permanency of its conclusions is to depend upon the personal opinions of those who, from time to time, make up its membership, it will inevitably become a theatre of political strife." [17] This statement expresses White's belief that the Court represents comparative stability and a certain fixedness of position in relation to a changing political periphery.

By overruling the fundamental principle on which the *Hylton* case was founded, that the direct tax clause was limited to capitation and taxes on land and should not be applied in such a way as to cripple Congress's plenary taxing power, the majority in *Pollock* transformed a definite constitutional limitation on Congress into an uncertain restriction. The majority view, which was a crushing blow to the doctrine of precedents, White took to be simply an unwarranted attempt at judicial amendment of the Constitution. This view was fraught with danger to the Court, every citizen, and the Republic itself because the Court, White contended, had merely preferred its own interpretation to that of the authors of the Constitution and of previous justices. "Let it be felt that on great constitutional questions," he commented, "this court is to . . . determine them all according to the mere opinion of those who temporarily fill its bench, and our Constitution will, in my judgment, be bereft of value and become a most dangerous instrument to the rights and liberties of the peo-

16. *Pollock* v. *Farmers' Loan*, 157 U.S. 429, 615.
17. *Ibid.*, 615, 652.

ple."[18] If precedents could no longer furnish a reliable guide, only a rev-
elation to the justices could answer the issue of any given action.

The evident truth of this position was so apparent in the decades of
the 1920s and 1930s that it finally provoked the greatest crisis in the history of the Court. Even so, White viewed the Constitution as a document to be expanded slowly through the application of the traditional
and authoritative technique of common law to what are essentially problems of political power. His view, in fact, left small room for rapid growth
because analogical reasoning must move by stages from one point to another. White's dissent espoused nationalism in the field of taxation more
to adhere to the doctrine of precedents than because he felt any deep-
rooted conviction of the social justice of the income tax. This conclusion
is patent from his pointed argument that longtime effects of the majority
opinion must produce an unhappy result because the majority took invested wealth and "read it into the Constitution as a favored and protected class of property which cannot be taxed without apportionment,"
leaving other forms of industry essential to the prosperity of community
and nation without such a shelter. The very injustice of the majority rule
pointed to the error of its adoption so plainly that "this system should
not be extended beyond the settled rule which confines it to direct taxes
on real estate." White obviously did not concur with Justice Field's view
that the income tax was the beginning of an "assault upon capital," which
must continue until "our political contests will become a war of the poor
against the rich; a war constantly growing in intensity and bitterness."[19]

Two decades later, as chief justice, White was called upon to interpret the Sixteenth [Income Tax] Amendment in relation to the income
tax provisions of the Tariff Act of 1913. The amendment stipulates that
"the Congress shall have power to lay and collect taxes on incomes from
whatever source derived, without apportionment among the several
States." Literally interpreted, a considerable extension of Congress' tax
power would result, but the spirit of *Pollock*, if not the rule, continued to
live in *Brushaber v. Union Pacific Ry. Co.* A stockholder sued to restrain
the railroad company from paying the tax, a procedure very similar to
Pollock's, the stockholder contending that the tax could not be imposed
on the company since the Sixteenth Amendment applied only when all

18. *Ibid.*, 651–52.
19. *Pollock v. Farmers' Loan*, 158 U.S. 601, 712–13; 157 U.S. 429, 607.

income was taxed. White rejected this argument because it would result in irreconcilable conflicts, with one clause of the Constitution pitted against another. He refused to accept arguments that an income tax violated the uniformity clause and that the Fifth Amendment was a limitation upon the taxing power. Referring to the *Pollock* case, he commented that the Income Tax Amendment was obviously intended to simplify the situation which arose from that judgment and to make clear the taxing power held by Congress. The Sixteenth Amendment "was drawn for the purpose of doing away for the future with the principle upon which the Pollock case was decided, that is, of determining whether a tax on income was direct not by a consideration of the burden placed on the taxed income upon which it directly operated, but by taking into view the burden derived, since in express terms the amendment provides that income taxes from whatever source the income may be derived, shall not be subject to the regulation of apportionment." The tax could not be assailed, because it was directly and specifically authorized.[20]

The Sixteenth Amendment was not intended, nevertheless, so far as White was concerned, to create "radical changes in our constitutional system," that is, to be liberally interpreted. In one of his nonstop sentences, which would have done justice in its length and complexity to the novelist William Faulkner, White went on to explain:

The conclusion reached in the Pollock case did not in any degree involve holding that income taxes generically and necessarily came within the class of direct taxes on property, but on the contrary recognized the fact that taxation on income was in its nature an excise entitled to be enforced as such unless and until it was concluded that to enforce it would amount to accomplishing the result which the requirement as to apportionment of direct taxation was adopted to prevent, in which case the duty would arise to disregard form and consider substance alone and hence subject the tax to the regulation as to apportionment which otherwise as an excise would not apply to it.[21]

The words of the Sixteenth Amendment, "from any source whatever," did not broaden the taxing power in the least, nor did the amendment grant power to levy income taxes. That power was already possessed by Congress. Apparently all the amendment did accomplish, in White's

20. United States Constitution, Amend. XVI; *Brushaber* v. *Union Pacific Ry. Co.*, 240 U.S. 1, 18 (1916).
21. *Brushaber* v. *Union Pacific*, 240 U.S. 16–17.

opinion, was to change the method of taxation by altering *Pollock*'s rule so that income taxes were relieved from the necessity of apportionment. What White and the Court had evidently done here was to look behind the purpose of the amendment and decide that it was limited to erasing the error of 1895.

Income from state and federal securities, as well as that from salaries paid to state or federal employees, could now be taxed no more than before the amendment. If the Court restored the power of Congress to tax to the place it held before 1895, White's interpretation admitted no expansion of power and, in fact, restricted congressional action somewhat along the same lines Fuller had sought. The retreat from this issue would not come until nearly a generation after White left the bench.[22]

After 1895 suits that came before the court were more frequently a challenge to the power of Congress to tax by the rule of uniformity of levies, which hitherto had always been considered to apply to excises. White resisted this attack by falling back on the history of excise taxation. One such case is *Knowlton* v. *Moore*, whose issue was the validity of an act of 1898 by Congress imposing a tax on legacies inherited from estates.[23] In meeting the objections that the levy was direct and also violated the uniformity clause, Justice White stated a number of his basic theories in defining his concept of inheritance taxes.

He began with a detailed history of the tax. His study of death duty statutes enacted by the state and federal governments showed that "they rest upon the same fundamental conception which has caused the adoption of like statutes in other countries." He proposed to define the precise purpose of the tax in order to avoid any possible misunderstanding. The tax, he stated, was placed upon the power to transmit legacies or successions, but it was not a manifestation of the state's power to regulate the "devolution of property upon death"; it was simply a levy upon receipt of property at death.[24] This kind of tax was in no sense a direct tax, since congressional enactments of 1797, 1862, and 1864, as well as various state laws, had treated levies of this nature as duties, not as direct taxes, a view which the Court had upheld.[25]

22. *Graves* v. *New York ex rel. O'Keefe*, 306 U.S. 466 (1939).
23. *Knowlton* v. *Moore*, 178 U.S. 41 (1900).
24. *Ibid.*, 49, 57, 59.
25. *Scholey* v. *Rew*, 23 Wall. 331 (1875).

The inheritance tax was assailed as contrary to the constitutional provision requiring uniformity throughout the United States, but White denied that the uniformity required was intrinsic. "By the result then of an analysis of the history of the adoption of the Constitution," he declared, "it becomes plain that the words 'uniform throughout the United States' do not signify an intrinsic, but simply a geographic uniformity." [26] He admitted the possibilities that an inheritance tax might become excessive without discovering among these possibilities any cause to find the tax invalid. The fact that the state and federal governments, each acting within its own sphere, might both tax the same object did not necessarily mean that the power of the one or the other was to be curtailed. As he did in other cases, White consistently saw the federal system as one with two governments, independent and yet the one acting on the other, reflecting again the same constitutional view that had matured while he was a member of the Senate and that he expressed with different results in actions involving the commerce clause.

Counsel for the plaintiff asserted that the usual train of grave results would flow from the progressive inheritance tax because the effect was to destroy the power to receive or pass property at death. With some asperity White met the charge that the Court was departing from strictly judicial duty.

The grave consequences which it is asserted must arise in the future if the right to levy a progressive tax be recognized, involves in its ultimate aspect the mere assertion that free and representative government is a failure, and that the grossest abuses of power are foreshadowed unless the courts usurp a purely legislative function. If such a case should ever arise, where an arbitrary and confiscatory exaction is imposed bearing the guise of a progressive or any other form of tax, it would be time to consider whether the judicial power can afford a remedy by applying inherent and fundamental principles for the protection of the individual, even though there be no express authority in the Constitution to do so. That the law which we have construed affords no ground for the contention that the tax imposed is arbitrary and confiscatory is obvious. [27]

As a rule, White was inclined to permit the fullest possible exercise of the taxing power, especially when the tax on its face was for revenue, even though regulatory purposes were also accomplished by the tax.

26. *Knowlton v. Moore*, 178 U.S. 106.
27. *Ibid.*, 109.

His decision in the *Oleomargarine* case of 1904 illustrates this tendency.[28] This suit involved an act of Congress, against which White voted as a senator, imposing a tax on oleomargarine with provision for a higher tax if the product were colored to resemble butter. Senator White had deemed this measure "subjectively unconstitutional." The issue to be judged by the Court was quite clear: Could Congress step across state lines and regulate an intrastate business by taxation? The Court had previously upheld state regulatory measures that had proved ineffective against unimpeded economic competition from other states.[29] Could a tax whose obvious intent was to suppress the manufacture of a commodity be sustained? White declared that these questions were irrelevant, that "on its face" the measure was for revenue purposes, and that the task of the Court was not to scrutinize the motives of Congress. By his senatorial test of "objective constitutionality," the act was valid.

White also maintained that the Fifth, Sixth, and Tenth Amendments do not limit the federal taxing powers. "Nothing in these amendments," said the justice, "operates to take away the grant of power conferred by the Constitution." The amendments may well qualify all the provisions of the Constitution, but nothing in them has the effect of diminishing the power of Congress to tax, which, within the limits of the fundamental law, is complete. Congress alone must select the objects upon which to impose a levy, and in the exercise of its lawful powers, no want of due process can arise. As White declared elsewhere, "It is also settled beyond doubt that the Constitution is not self-destructive, that the powers which it confers on one hand it does not immediately take away with the other." The power to tax, granted in express terms, cannot be limited or restricted by subsequent constitutional provisions and amendments, especially the due process clause of the Fifth Amendment.[30]

In *Snyder v. Bettman*, White restated in a minority opinion the doctrine that the federal government cannot tax agencies of state government. An action was brought by the executor of David L. Snyder's estate to recover a succession tax paid on a legacy devised in trust to the city of Springfield, Ohio, to establish a public park. The majority of a closely

28. *McCray v. United States*, 195 U.S. 27 (1904).
29. *Powell v. Pennsylvania*, 127 U.S. 678 (1888), *Capital City Dairy Co. v. Ohio*, 183 U.S. 238 (1902).
30. *McCray v. United States*, 195 U.S. 27, 64; *Billings v. United States*, 232 U.S. 261, 282 (1914).

divided Court determined that, since the states had power extending to bequests to the United States, it followed that Congress had the same power to tax the transmission of property by legacy to the states or to their municipalities. It was, said the Court, not a "tax upon the municipality, though it might operate incidentally to reduce the bequest by the amount of the tax."[31]

Dissenting, with Chief Justice Fuller and Justice Peckham in concurrence, White denied that this power belonged to Congress. His opinion was in no way inconsistent with the *Knowlton* case. Citing *Pollock*, he contended that there was no sounder constitutional doctrine than the immunity of states or agencies of states from national taxation. Ample precedents before 1895 proved the existence of this doctrine, and the *Income Tax* case, however much it further limited the taxing power, did not remove restrictions inherent in our federal system. The *Inheritance Tax* case was distinguished because in *Bettman* the tax was on the estate in the hands of the executor and was not a burden in the hands of the recipient, as it had been in *Knowlton v. Moore*. Justice White went on to argue that the power to levy an inheritance tax did not mean that the United States could apply such a tax, otherwise valid, to an object outside its sphere. Once again, as time after time in White's opinions, there was insistence upon the binding effect of precedents.

To my mind no doctrine more dangerous and subversive of a long line of settled authority in this court could be announced than the statement that, although there is no power whatever to tax a particular object, the courts will nevertheless maintain a tax if only indirectly it puts a burden on the forbidden object or that the tax may be sustained because in the judgment of the court the degree in which the Constitution has been violated is not great. Constitutional restrictions are in my opinion imperative, and ought not to be disregarded because in a particular case it may be the judgment of the court that the violation is not a very grievous one.

A judicial tribunal, White thought, should not ascertain the extent of the burden laid upon the municipality by this tax, the duty of the Court being limited to an examination of the statute or the facts of the case. The Court has no such room for meanderings into "subjective constitutionality" as the Senate might possess.[32]

31. *Snyder v. Bettman*, 190 U.S. 249, 252, 254 (1903).
32. *Ibid.*, 255; precedents included *McCulloch v. Maryland*, 4 Wheat. 316 (1819), *Col-*

In *South Carolina* v. *United States*, White reiterated the doctrine of the immunity of state agencies from federal taxation. By act of its legislature, South Carolina had taken over the business of selling liquor through state stores, and in due course its agents were subjected to federal internal revenue laws. When the case came to the Supreme Court for review, Justice Brewer and the majority thought the liquor subject to federal taxation, even though dispensed by the state. Brewer's reasoning was that the state was engaged in a business enterprise. The line thus drawn seemed fair and reasonable, if somewhat vague. White, supported by Justices McKenna and Peckham, thought differently, declaring that, by the ruling and reasoning supporting Brewer's opinion, "the ancient landmarks are obliterated and the distinct powers belonging to both the national and state governments are reciprocally placed the one at the mercy of the other, so as to give each the potency of destroying the other." [33]

This statement illustrates again that much of his constitutional theory focused upon the protection of the federal and state governments from each other, as if they were determined adversaries. Neither level of government, he thought, should be permitted to expand its power to the point where it might inflict injury upon the other. If a tax burden such as that placed upon the South Carolina liquor dispensaries were permitted, it might eventually lead to other impositions which could effectively cripple the government upon whose agency the tax was levied. [34]

The majority, on the contrary, had used this same argument in reverse form. Why could not the states, Justice Brewer asked, use their powers to bring utilities or other businesses under control if a state engaging in business enterprise were exempted from license taxes? "Indeed," he said, "if all the states should concur in exercising their powers to the full extent, it would be almost impossible for the nation to collect any revenue." This curious clash between White and Brewer occurred because the Court had taken unto itself the function of determining the nature of a governmental instrumentality, free from taxation, on an ad hoc basis. However, White again had followed precedents in this case. Meanwhile, from time to time the Court extended intergovernmental

---

lector v. *Day*, 11 Wall. 113 (1871), *Dobbins* v. *Erie County*, 16 Pet. 435 (1842), and *United States* v. *Railroad Co.*, 17 Wall. 322 (1873); *Snyder* v. *Bettman*, 190 U.S. 249, 258, 259–60.

33. *South Carolina* v. *United States*, 199 U.S. 437, 464 (1905).

34. *Ibid.*, 469.

immunity until eventually such immunity embraced royalties from patent rights and protected them from a state income tax.[35]

No less important for showing White's conception of the position of the Court with respect to tax cases is *Pacific States Telephone & Telegraph Co. v. Oregon*, although the tax aspect of this action has been subordinated to others deemed more important.[36] The case illustrates a weighing of the actual motives for which the suit had been instituted, a determination of the relief that could be granted, and a statement of the principles with which the decision was concerned. By resort to the initiative, the Oregon Legislature had enacted a statute subjecting the company to an annual license tax, an action that was attacked on the ground that the use of the initiative made the state government unlawful in form and not "republican."

Chief Justice White's decision dismissed the suit for want of jurisdiction. He went straight to the point. "It [the controversy] is important, since it calls upon us to decide whether it is the duty of the courts or the province of Congress to determine when a state has ceased to be republican in form and to enforce the guarantees of the Constitution on the subject. It is not novel as that question has been long determined by this court conformably to the practice of the government from the beginning to be political in character, and therefore not cognizable by the judicial power, but solely committed by the Constitution to the judgment of Congress." To hold the case justiciable on this ground would be equal to enunciating the doctrine that any citizen could assail in the courts the existence of a state in order to avoid payment of taxes. *Luther* v. *Borden* was absolutely the "leading and controlling case," the Court having long since determined that the issues presented were not within the reach of the judiciary. This reasoning was in line with that of a series of cases in the early 1900s in which the Court declined to rule on a number of state reforms. The result was to make the issue of a republican form of government noncognizable in almost every matter.[37]

The tax was thus binding upon the company, but if the appellant had challenged the tax on other grounds, relief might have been considered.

---

35. *Ibid.*, 455; Benjamin F. Wright, *The Growth of American Constitutional Law* (Boston: Houghton Mifflin, 1942), 129; *Long* v. *Rockwood*, 277 U.S. 142 (1928).

36. *Pacific States Telephone & Telegraph Co.* v. *Oregon*, 223 U.S. 118 (1912).

37. *Ibid.*, 133; *Luther* v. *Borden*, 7 How. 1 (1849); *Pacific States* v. *Oregon*, 223 U.S. 118, 141–42.

White stated, however, that "the defendant company does not contend here that it would not have been required to pay a license tax. It does not assert that it was denied an opportunity to be heard as to the amount for which it was taxed, or that there was anything inhering in the tax or involved intrinsically in the law which violated any of its constitutional rights. If such questions had been raised they would have been justiciable, and therefore would have required calling into operation of judicial power." Such issues, though, had not been raised, and White therefore proceeded to a statement of the basic motive of the action. Reducing the case to its essence, it was the government of Oregon that had been called to the bar of the Supreme Court.[38]

The last decade during which White sat upon the bench witnessed no great change in his position on tax law and was marked by his extension of the national taxing power to subjects previously within neither state nor federal jurisdiction.[39] In 1919 he dissented from the Court's judgment that upheld the Harrison Narcotics Act of 1914. Section 1 of this measure imposed a registration fee upon opium dealers, and Section 2 forbade the sale of narcotics except by a specific order or form. The defendant, Doremus, was convicted of violating this latter provision, but, on demurrer, the intermediate appellate court ruled that Section 2 was not a revenue matter; rather it invaded the state's police power—a ruling that the Supreme Court reversed, declaring the provision to be one facilitating collection of the fee. White dissented because he viewed the tax structure as too slightly related to Section 2 to justify an attempt on the part of Congress "to exert a power not delegated, that is, the reserved police power of the state."[40] His argument did not differ greatly from his senatorial views on the Anti-Option Bill and indicated that, by his senatorial test of "objective constitutionality," he could find no relationship between the provision and the legitimate authority of Congress. Although consistently a nationalist in taxation, White would not go beyond the precedents marked out to guide him.

38. *Pacific States* v. *Oregon*, 223 U.S. 118, 150.

39. *United States* v. *Bennett*, 232 U.S. 299 (1914), *United States* v. *Bennett (No. 2)*, 232 U.S. 308 (1914), *Billings* v. *United States*, 232 U.S. 261 (1914), *Pierce* v. *United States*, 232 U.S. 290 (1914), *United States* v. *Goelet*, 232 U.S. 293 (1914), *Rainey* v. *United States*, 232 U.S. 310 (1914).

40. *United States* v. *Doremus*, 249 U.S. 86, 95 (1919).

IX
A Union of States:
Virginia v. West Virginia

W e are fain to believe," declared Chief Justice White, "that if we refrain now from passing upon the questions stated, we may be spared in the future the necessity of exerting compulsory power against one of the states of the Union to compel it to discharge a plain duty resting upon it under the Constitution."[1] Suits between states, usually lacking dramatic qualities, have not created the public interest that clings to more controversial social, economic, or political issues. Yet much of the political theory underlying American federalism has developed in this type of case. The concept of a federal system involves the distribution of political power between a national government and several lesser units of government whose status is guaranteed in the fundamental law of the land. That disputes between the states would arise in the American system was foreseen, and the Constitution placed jurisdiction of such action in the Supreme Court as arbiter of the federal system. "The judicial Power shall extend to all Cases, in Law and Equity, arising under this Constitution, the Laws of the United States, and Treaties made, or which shall be made, under their Authority; . . . to Controversies between two or more States."[2] Although established in 1789, not until nearly a half-century had elapsed did the Supreme Court hand down its first judgment in a suit between states.[3]

For the time being, states continued to make rare use of Article III,

1. *Virginia v. West Virginia*, 246 U.S. 565, 604–605 (1918).
2. United States Constitution, Art. III, Sec. 2.
3. *New Jersey v. New York*, 5 Pet. 284 (1831).

Section 2 of the Constitution, and during the first six decades of government under the 1789 document only two additional suits between states were brought, chiefly involving disputes over boundaries.[4] Even so, the Court's handling of these actions produced a number of rulings, among them that the Court may conduct *ex parte* proceedings if a state fails to appear when summoned; that the Constitution does not preclude the use of judicial power in any controversy involving states, although it does not expressly extend the judicial power to all such disputes; and that no prescribed rule of decision is required in such cases.[5] In this line of cases, however, the issue of enforcement of the Court's judgment against a recalcitrant state had not been fully explored. Judgments affecting boundaries were in contrast self-executing, and in other instances, where state officials declined to act, the officials as individuals could be subjected to federal criminal or civil proceedings. None of these instances covered a situation where the Court's decision required "a State in its governmental capacity to perform some positive act. . . . [Such judgments] present the issue of enforcement in more serious form."[6] Not until 1918 would the Supreme Court enunciate the doctrine that judgments against a state in its governmental capacity could be enforced. Edward White was largely responsible for the formulation of this doctrine.

Indeed, Chief Justice White's role in the long and sometimes tedious controversy of the commonwealth of Virginia against the state of West Virginia demonstrated a high degree of judicial statesmanship and a realization that states of the American Union cannot be treated as criminals in the dock. His refusal to go beyond a declaration of the Court's power to enforce its judgment in actions between states recognized that final responsibility for disputes between states may well have to lie with Congress, a more responsive and popular body than the Court. He stressed the fact that the national government can enforce the Court's decree in suits of this sort. Moreover, he developed a theory that placed

---

4. Charles Warren, "The Supreme Court and Disputes Between States," *Bulletin of William and Mary*, XXXIV, 2 (1940), 7–13.

5. *New Jersey v. New York*, 5 Pet. 284 (1831), *Rhode Island v. Massachusetts*, 12 Pet. 657 (1838).

6. Congressional Research Service, Library of Congress, *The Constitution of the United States: Analysis and Interpretation* (Washington: U.S. Government Printing Office, 1973), 726.

the Court as arbiter between contending states, leaving enforcement to the federal government as a whole. As in other areas of constitutional interpretation, White strengthened the Court in these cases as the ultimate umpire of the federal system.[7]

The story of Virginia versus West Virginia reaches far back in the pages of American history. As early as 1793 the Supreme Court exercised power over an action brought by the citizens of one state against another state. The Court declared that only a federal judiciary, created by and responsible to the whole nation, could assure impartiality in such cases and that Article III of the Constitution was applicable to the case at hand. Against this judgment the states raised a hue and cry. Many of the states were heavily indebted and feared prosecution by creditors, this apprehension creating a serious objection to the recently adopted Constitution. Mr. Justice Bradley commented that "the decision . . . in the case of Chisholm v. Georgia, 2 Dall. 419 . . . created such a shock of surprise throughout the country that, at the first meeting of Congress thereafter, the eleventh amendment was almost unanimously proposed, and was in due course adopted by the legislatures of the states." The Eleventh Amendment calmed troubled waters by providing that federal judicial power should not "extend to any suit in law or equity, commenced or prosecuted against one of the United States by Citizens of another State, or by Citizens or Subjects of any Foreign State." Somewhat belatedly the Supreme Court held that the amendment and public law bar a citizen from bringing suit against his own state even though a federal question might be involved.[8]

This conception of sovereignty has a direct bearing upon the problem that faced the Court in 1918. While the Eleventh Amendment, as well as judicial interpretations of it, did not prevent the Court from hearing cases based upon the character of the parties to the suit, it did delay for more than a century settlement of the issue concerning rendition of money judgments. Some evidence exists that, had not parts of Article III been stricken out by the Eleventh Amendment, suits instituted by individuals against states would have determined the question long before White's

7. *Virginia v. West Virginia*, 246 U.S. 565 (1918).
8. *Chisholm v. Georgia*, 2 Dall. 419 (1793); *Hans v. Louisiana*, 134 U.S. 1, 11 (1890).

tenure on the Court.[9] When the West Virginia controversy reached its final stage, however, the issue was still open.

Virginia v. *West Virginia* was a legacy of the Civil War. In 1861 a convention of the commonwealth of Virginia rescinded the act of the Convention of 1788 by which Virginia had ratified the Constitution. Virginia then entered the southern Confederacy and with it was conquered by force of arms. The western part of the state, though, had refused to consent to the act of secession, remaining loyal to the Union, and soon a so-called legislature of Virginia, in rump session at Charleston, met the constitutional requirements of Article IV giving permission for the formation of a new state (*i.e.* "New States may be admitted by the Congress into this Union; but no new State shall be formed or erected within the Jurisdiction of any other State; nor any State be formed by the Junction of two or more States, or Parts of States, without the Consent of the Legislatures of the States concerned as well as of the Congress.").[10]

Delegates from western Virginia were elected to serve as a constitutional convention. A petition was forwarded to Congress for the admission of a proposed new state, West Virginia, and in 1863 the new state entered the Union. Before the Civil War, the area within the boundaries of the new state had benefited by revenues levied in the original commonwealth of Virginia, so that West Virginia subsequently agreed through convention and its constitution to pay an equitable portion of the state debt as it stood before Virginia's act of secession.[11]

There the matter rested. In 1906 the attorney general of Virginia filed a bill before the Supreme Court asking to have West Virginia's share of the debt ascertained and satisfied. The latter state demurred, but the Court overruled its motion and ordered the case tried on its merits. Two years later the suit was sent to a special master for hearings on the issues involved in the action, his report was filed with the Court, and in 1911 the Supreme Court made its first decision in the case. Mr. Justice Holmes, speaking for the Court, approached the case carefully. "The case is to be

9. This conclusion is indicated by a trend of cases, including *Ostwald* v. *New York*, 2 Dall. 401 (1791), 2 Dall. 402 (1792), 2 Dall. 414 (1793), *Vanstopherst* v. *Maryland*, 2 Dall. 401 (1791), *Grayson* v. *Virginia*, 3 Dall. 320 (1796), *Huger* v. *South Carolina*, 3 Dall. 339 (1797), and *Hollingsworth* v. *Virginia*, 3 Dall. 378 (1798).

10. United States Constitution, Art. IV, Sec. 3.

11. James Brown Scott, "The Role of the Supreme Court of the United States in the Settlement of Interstate Disputes," *Georgetown Law Journal*, XV (1927), 146, 157.

considered," he declared, "in the untechnical spirit proper for dealing with a quasi-international controversy, remembering that there is no municipal code governing the matter, and that this Court may be called on to adjust differences that cannot be dealt with by Congress or disposed of by the legislature of either State alone." [12]

Holmes then went on to hold that the ordinances of Virginia, the constitution of West Virginia, and the act of Congress admitting West Virginia to the Union established a contract by which West Virginia would pay her share of the public debt as it existed at the time of West Virginia's separation. The nature of the action and the many factors involved in reaching a just apportionment led the Court to decline to issue a decree for payment until both parties had had full time to adjust it themselves. The master's ratio was taken as a measure for the principal of the debt.

On October 13, 1911, Virginia moved to restore the issue left unsettled by the previous judgment. Its attorney general alleged that West Virginia had taken no steps to end the controversy amicably, but his plea was refused on the ground that no state can be expected to move with the speed of an individual. West Virginia had not yet had time enough. Virginia again renewed the motion after a lapse of two years. Negotiations between the debt commissions of the two states, however, made it doubtful that any hope of voluntary adjustment remained alive, and although Chief Justice White denied Virginia's motion, he assigned the case for hearing the next April, provided no agreement had been reached by then. [13]

When that date was reached, West Virginia requested leave to file a supplemental answer containing items that would substantially reduce the amount set by the Court in 1911. Virginia objected and contended that, since all the items were embraced in the master's report of 1910, they were already determined. The defendant state, however, was granted its request, although the Court pointed out that the application of the ordinary rules of procedure would have made such a grant impossible. This suit was no ordinary action, but rather a basic political controversy,

12. *Virginia v. West Virginia*, 206 U.S. 290 (1907); *Virginia v. West Virginia*, 209 U.S. 514 (1908); *Virginia v. West Virginia*, 220 U.S. 1, 27 (1911).

13. *Virginia v. West Virginia*, 222 U.S. 17 (1911); *Virginia v. West Virginia*, 231 U.S. 89 (1913).

and the Court was reluctant to lay down any definitive rules. Declared Chief Justice White:

> In acting in this case from first to last the fact that the suit was not an ordinary one concerning a difference between individuals, but was a controversy between states involving grave questions of public law determinable by this court under the exceptional grant of power conferred upon it by the Constitution, has been the guide by which every step and every conclusion hitherto expressed has been controlled. And we are of the opinion that this binding principle should not be lost sight of to the end that . . . there may be no room for the slightest inference that the more restrictive rules applicable to individuals have been applied to a great public controversy, or that anything but the largest justice after the amplest opportunity to be heard has in any degree entered into the disposition of this case.[14]

On June 15, 1914, the Court rendered a judgment in favor of Virginia for the sum of $12,393,929.50, which was based upon the determination that West Virginia should assume one-third of Virginia's state debt as it stood on January 1, 1861. Five percent interest would accrue, dating from July 1, 1915.[15] West Virginia was apparently obligated to pay and, if possible, to do so without judicial coercion.

A strong display of power was yet necessary to end the litigation. When June, 1916, came, Virginia applied for a writ of execution because West Virginia had made no move to discharge the obligation, its attorney general claiming that West Virginia could comply only through action by the state legislature which would not meet until 1917. For the first time, in addition, the defendant state challenged the authority of the Supreme Court to enforce a money judgment. White simply ignored this alleged defect of power, denying the writ on the ground that West Virginia had not yet had a "reasonable opportunity" to discharge the judgment.[16] White clearly wanted the Court to be spared from deciding on the issue of power, now impending.

The Court was not to escape so easily from ruling on its power of enforcement. With West Virginia stubbornly displaying no indication of compliance with the judgment, Virginia now asked for a writ of mandamus "directing the levy of a tax by the legislature of West Virginia to pay such judgment" as resulted from the decree of 1915. West Virginia re-

14. *Virginia v. West Virginia*, 234 U.S. 117, 121 (1914).
15. *Virginia v. West Virginia*, 238 U.S. 202 (1915).
16. *Virginia v. West Virginia*, 241 U.S. 531 (1916).

plied by flatly challenging the power of the Court to enforce payment. The issue had at last been bolted out, leaving White determined to make a final disposition in the case. Nearly twelve years had elapsed before this point was reached.

The culminating opinion of this litigation supplied White with the opportunity to elaborate theories basic to American federalism—to patch, as it were, the holes of the federal system with the fabric of his own inclination and bent of mind. There were few guidelines that he could follow. To sustain his position, White would be compelled to move forward without the comforting knowledge that his was a path already indicated by precedents in the *United States Supreme Court Reports*. Nevertheless, his reasoning touched upon several broad fields: the relationship of the states to one another, of the federal judiciary to actions between states, and finally, of Congress to the enforcement of judgments.

The Supreme Court had indeed coerced officers of municipalities to perform specific duties many times, this action always being based on the assumption that their duty was ministerial under the law of the respective states.[17] The decisions applied equally well to existing laws or earlier enactments under which the Court commanded the performance of a specific act, but in no case had any state been compelled to direct municipal officials to perform the actions which the state legislature had imposed upon them. Virginia, however, was asking the Court to issue a writ of mandamus directing the West Virginia Legislature to enact a new statute, so that this line of cases, although cited in West Virginia's brief, offered no solution. Nor was aid and comfort to be found in those cases that had held that the Court can neither levy a tax nor collect one already imposed.[18] Virginia had asked no such thing, but in three years West Virginia had made no effort to discharge the Court's judgment voluntarily. The plaintiff state now requested that the Court command a tax to be levied by the West Virginia Legislature in order to discharge the obligation recognized by the judgment.[19] Virginia simply wanted payment

17. *Supervisors* v. *United States*, 4 Wall. 435 (1867), *Riggs* v. *Johnson County*, 6 Wall. 166 (1868), *Labette County Commissioners* v. *Moulton*, 112 U.S. 217 (1884).
18. *Rees* v. *City of Watertown*, 19 Wall. 107 (1873), *Meriwether* v. *Garrett*, 102 U.S. 472 (1880), *Thompson* v. *Allen County*, 115 U.S. 550 (1885).
19. See Thomas R. Powell, "Coercing a State to Pay a Judgment: Virginia v. West Virginia," *Michigan Law Review*, XVII (1918), 1–18.

and, having failed entirely to reach it by negotiations, was now relying on judicial coercion.

An opinion written by Mr. Justice Brewer in 1904 might be construed to have furnished a precedent by which the Court could well deny the claim of Virginia.[20] In 1866 North Carolina had issued bonds with the provision that they were to be secured, in default of payment, by stocks that the state owned in a railroad company. In 1901 several of the owners of the North Carolina bonds presented ten bonds to South Dakota, which state had then filed a bill before the Supreme Court requesting that the bonds either be redeemed or the security paid in satisfaction of the claim. Brewer delivered the opinion of the Court and found for South Dakota. Speaking for a minority including Chief Justice Fuller, and Justices Day and McKenna as well as himself, White dissented, the essence of his argument contending that the action was not a controversy between states. The majority held otherwise since the plaintiff was a state.

Justice Brewer quoted the *Watertown* case to the effect that "this Court has not the power to direct a tax to be levied for payment of these judgments." From this he reached the significant conclusion of "the absolute inability of a court to compel a levy of taxes by the legislature."[21] This compulsion could be followed only in commanding an inferior municipality to enforce the state law. Brewer's position is sufficiently demonstrated by his out-of-court comment that "if the amount received from the sale of stock had not paid the bonds, the question would have been presented whether we could render a money judgment against a state; and, if so, how it could be enforced. We could not compel the Legislature of North Carolina to meet and pass an act: the marshal could not levy upon the public buildings of the state; what would be the significance of a judgment which the Court was powerless to enforce?"[22] Brewer's reasoning depended a great deal on the *Watertown* case for its force. There the Court was not dealing with a state, but was only declaring that the courts were unable to order a federal marshal to act in the offices of an assessor and collector. Still, it did supply a straw of a precedent, however slender.

20. *South Dakota v. North Carolina*, 192 U.S. 286 (1904).
21. *Ibid.*, 319.
22. *Report of the Thirteenth Annual Meeting of the Lake Mohawk Conference on International Arbitration* (1907), 170–71, quoted in Lawrence B. Evans, *Cases on Constitutional Law* (Chicago: Callaghan, 1937), 891.

For the most part, therefore, White was able to approach the question of coercing a state to pay a judgment singularly free from binding
lines of decision. That Brewer's earlier dictum coincided with his view
was unlikely. White's concept that the states must be protected from the
national government, the states from each other, and the national government from the states did not indicate probable agreement with Brewer.
Everything in the record of his years on the Court since 1894 foreshadowed an enlargement of the power of the Supreme Court as arbiter of
the federal system.

The Court, speaking through Chief Justice White, rendered its opinion on April 22, 1918.[23] White wrote about the questions involved in this
long and difficult litigation, but did not resolve the specific question of
whether the Supreme Court may grant a writ of mandamus to compel
enforcement of the type of judgment made in the Virginia–West Virginia dispute. He simply concluded that somehow a state can be coerced
to discharge its obligation. In this case, he said, compliance could be attained through action on the part of Congress or "appropriate judicial
remedies," without specifying or determining what these remedies were.
Although the opinion delivered by White is thus the expression of a
pious hope that the "wicked" state will meet its obligations to the "good"
state, it still contained an undercurrent that ultimately payment could be
enforced.

White found it convenient for his purposes to erect a sham issue and
then demolish it: can a judgment, he asked, rendered against a state as
such, be enforced against it, including the power of exercising authority
over its governmental powers and agencies? The question received an
affirmative answer when he declared, "Judicial power essentially involves the right to enforce the results of its exercise." He cited three cases
in support of this proposition, two of which held, in effect, that the jurisdiction of federal courts included execution of judgment in conformity
with federal practice not controlled by a state statute, and the third held
that the power to grant an execution of judgment was an inherent part
of the judicial power. Although none of the three cases is concerned
with compelling a state to pay a judgment, White used them as the basis
for stating, "And that this applies to the execution of such power in con-

23. *Virginia v. West Virginia*, 246 U.S. 565 (1918).

troversies between states as a result of the exercise of jurisdiction conferred upon this Court by the Constitution is therefore certain." He regarded the point as established. Granting that the Court, in view of the
power conferred upon it, has authority to hear and to give judgments,
White was not quite correct because hardly anything can be done by the
Court itself to enforce its judgment. Indeed, as far back as 1832 the Court
decided a case against Georgia, only to see its judgment come to naught
when President Andrew Jackson passively supported the state's refusal
to obey.[24]

White stated the truism that sovereignty lay within the sphere of the
national government, and that, when the Constitution granted authority to the Supreme Court to hear actions between states, it modified the
rule that the states were not subject to judicial power. He declared: "As
it is certain that governmental powers reserved to the states by the Constitution—their sovereignty—were the efficient cause of the general rule
by which they were not subject to judicial power, that is, to be impleaded,
it must follow that when the Constitution gave original jurisdiction to
this court to entertain at the instance of one state a suit against another
it must have been intended to modify the general rule, that is, to bring
the states and their governmental authority within the exceptional judicial power which was created." To White, "no other rational explanation
can be given for the provision," because the specific provisions of the
Constitution "that is, the express prohibition which it contains as to the
power of the states to contract with each other except with the consent
of Congress, the limitations as to war and armies, obviously intended to
prevent any of the states from resorting to force for the redress of any
grievance real or imaginary, all harmonize with and give force to this
conception of the operation and effect of the right to exert, at the prayer
of one state, judicial authority over another." What West Virginia asserted, in effect, was that the power to enforce the decree in this particular case encroached upon the power reserved to the states by the Tenth
Amendment. This power was necessarily incompatible with the pur-

24. *Ibid.*, 591; *Wayman v. Southard*, 10 Wheat. 1 (1825), *Bank of the United States v. Hal-
stead*, 10 Wheat. 51 (1825), and *Gordon v. United States*, 2 Wall. 561 (1865); *Virginia v. West
Virginia*, 246 U.S. 565, 591; *Worcester v. Georgia*, 6 Pet. 515 (1832); see also Marquis James,
Andrew Jackson: Portrait of a President (Indianapolis: Bobbs-Merrill, 1938), 304.

pose of the Constitution to create spheres of power in which the national and state governments respectively would be supreme.[25]

White did not, however, regard seriously this appeal to states' rights. "And it is difficult [he said] to understand upon what ground or reason the preservation of the rights of all the states can be predicated upon the assumption that any one state may destroy the rights of another without power to cure or redress the resulting grievance. Nor, further, can it be readily understood why it is assumed that the preservation and perpetuation of the Constitution depend upon the absence of all power to preserve and give effect to the great guarantees which safeguard the authority and preserve the rights of all the states."[26] He thus ripped away from West Virginia any claim of being a sovereign state that it could drape about itself to ward off judicial coercion. When immunities claimed by a state under the Tenth Amendment collide with the claim of another state to the protection of its rights, those immunities are to be pushed aside by the Court, and the right of the injured state to redress remains.

White sought to strengthen this argument with historical support, finding that his conclusions were buttressed by the "history of the institutions from which the provisions of the Constitution under review were derived." He referred to the well-known fact that disputes between the American colonies were adjudicated by the English Privy Council, "the sanctions afforded to the conclusions of that body being the entire power of the realm, whether exerted through a royal decree or legislation by Parliament." This reference satisfied him that, while the power of the English courts at that time fell short of enforcement, the Constitution conferred a greater grant upon the Supreme Court of the United States. Article IV of the Articles of Confederation had provided for the settlement of disputes between states, this article proving to be ineffective because the compact contained inherent defects of power and created "an evil that cried aloud for cure." The Constitution of 1787 was intended to obviate the recurrence of this danger since its provisions "combined to unite the authority to decide with the power to enforce." As a result, declared White: "The state, then, as a governmental entity having been subjected by the Constitution to the judicial power under the conditions

25. *Virginia* v. *West Virginia*, 246 U.S. 565, 595–96.
26. *Ibid.*, 596–97.

stated, and the duty to enforce the judgment by appropriate remedies being certain even though their exertion may operate upon the governmental powers of the state, we are brought to consider the second question."[27]

This second question was, "What are the appropriate remedies for such enforcement?" Up to this point White's opinion had been strong and without qualifications, but it is one thing for a court to proclaim that its judgments may be enforced and another to say how they shall be enforced. It was fairly clear that the Court possessed no power in itself to compel compliance on the part of a state and that the issues involved in an attempt at judicial enforcement would go beyond the ordinary judicial processes and touch basic political questions of the relations of the states within the federal system. Chief Justice White therefore raised the question whether Congress had power to legislate for the enforcement of West Virginia's obligation and concluded that, as incident to its powers to assent to agreements between states, Congress may adopt such legislation as may be necessary to enforce the agreement. The states do not possess a barrier against such acts of Congress, for the latter's power is "plenary and complete, limited of course as we have just said by the general rule that the acts done for its exertion must be relevant and appropriate to the power. . . . The lawful exertion of authority by Congress . . . is not circumscribed by the powers reserved to the states."[28]

Nor is the existence of Congress' power to legislate "incompatible with the grant of original jurisdiction to this court to entertain a suit between states on the same subject." Congress may also establish new remedies in addition to those available under the *Judicial Code*, but such new remedies would not negate any remedies available to the Court, which flow from its power to hear and determine controversies between states. The Court is free to use appropriate judicial remedies to secure compliance. White did no more, though, than to comment on the bare right. Money judgments in suits between states may be carried out by congressional action or some judicial process which White left cloaked in obscurity. Neither congressional action nor the judicial process elimi-

27. *Ibid.*, 597; Powell, "Coercing a State," 16; *Virginia v. West Virginia*, 246 U.S. 565, 599, 600.
28. *Virginia v. West Virginia*, 246 U.S. 600, 602.

nates the other; each cooperates to a common end, the obedience by a state to the Constitution.[29]

This point was as far as White went. He sustained the power of the Court to settle actions involving states and justified its position as umpire between the various units and levels of the federal system, but he recognized wisely that, if quarrels between states reached a point where the rule of the Court itself was spurned, ultimate enforcement of a judicial decree could only come from the federal legislative body. He hoped that his solicitude in this case would avoid the necessity of any exertion of power to compel a state to discharge its constitutional duty. His temperate view prevailed. Shortly after the 1918 decision was handed down, counsel for both Virginia and West Virginia had taken steps to settle the judgment. By his attitude of cautious and reasonable, not hasty and peremptory, action, White had maintained the authority of the Supreme Court. He could do no more and would do no less.

29. *Ibid.*, 604, 603.

X

Keep Out of My Sunlight

A good deal of the history of the United States," wrote Felix Frank-furter, "may be fairly summarized as the process, complicated and confused, of bringing to the masses economic freedom commensurate with their political freedom. But the various interests of human personality are not of equal worth. There is a hierarchy of values." [1] High among these values are the evidences of human spirit embodied in the American Constitution's first ten amendments, the Bill of Rights.

Edward Douglass White's approach to the constitutional issues raised by the Bill of Rights shows that he was not an ardent crusader for individual liberty and that he sincerely believed many restraints had to be placed upon individual freedom. At the same time, White was not as obsessed as many judges in many courts have been with the fanatic fear that freedom of discussion in particular instances would undermine the basis of the American political system. To be sure, a faint undercurrent ran through his decisions indicating a degree of distrust for complete freedom of discussion. He sometimes displayed an allegiance to the common judicial trait of permitting alleged legal principles to outweigh human values, but no doubt White put his faith in those principles on the theory that to consider human values would create a government of men, not of laws.

This kind of rationalization was probably a defense mechanism in a

1. Felix Frankfurter, *Mr. Justice Holmes and the Supreme Court* (Cambridge: Harvard University Press, 1938), 49.

conservative mind that found difficulty in departing from the familiar. Perhaps White's concept of individual liberty can best be described as reflecting the beliefs that conservatism is necessary to preserve representative government and that individuals must be willing to submit to those restrictions on their conduct that are essential to the preservation of the rights of all—in short, to exercise the power of a free people to restrain themselves so that freedom may continue. While exhorting the American lawyer to the defense of liberty, representative government, and the advance of democracy, White commented: "I must confess sometimes, as my thoughts turn to the future and the vast probable increase in our population, to the infinite opportunity afforded those who misguidedly or with intentional wrong preach the destruction of our institutions under the guise of preserving freedom, a great dread comes to me that possibly some day in the future the forces of evil, of anarchy, and of wrong may gather such momentum as to enable them to overthrow . . . the constitutional institutions which the Fathers gave us and deprive us of the blessings which have come from their possession."[2]

Problems raised by governmental interference with the individual's freedom are most acute during periods of national crisis or distress. At other times, except for a few defenders of the democratic faith, people are generally apt to regard utterances to which they are opposed with a complaisant attitude. The offender may be looked upon as a crank, harmless and hardly worth excitement. In times of war, economic distress, or rapid social change, though, these innocuous offenders of community mores take on the aspect of a dangerous malady within the body politic, and when the crisis confronting a people appears great, panic is more likely to take hold of the public and produce a ruthless extermination of all opinions not shared by those wielding power. Growing opposition to the Federalists and their foreign policy, for example, produced the Alien and Sedition Acts of 1798, while at a later date the Civil War brought attempts by the executive to interfere with rights guaranteed by the Constitution. President Lincoln suspended the writ of habeas corpus, but the opposition thus engendered led him to ask and receive congressional

2. "Response of the Late Chief Justice White to Toast at the Annual Banquet of the American Bar Association at Washington, October 22, 1914," *American Bar Association Journal*, VII (1921), 341–42.

authorization for the suspension. Pursuant to congressional action, the writ was suspended in 1871 in nine counties in South Carolina as a result of Ku Klux Klan action and again in 1905 in the Philippines.[3]

When Chief Justice White came to the Supreme Court, the nation was entering a long period of economic strife that inevitably gave rise to many problems closely allied with civil liberties. Indeed, only a short time after White joined the Court, the Chicago Pullman Company strike brought forth from a federal district court one of the most binding injunctions ever issued. In the contempt proceedings that resulted from the defiance of this injunction by Eugene V. Debs, the Supreme Court upheld by unanimous vote the authority of the lower court to limit to the extreme the rights of the individual. Recognizing that the injunction had been given because of the strike's interference with the mails and interstate commerce but without statutory authority, Mr. Justice Brewer had said for the Court that "every government, entrusted, by the very terms of its being, with powers and duties to be exercised and discharged for the general welfare, has a right to appeal to its own courts for any proper assistance in the exercise of the one and the discharge of the other." White concurred silently in this decision.[4]

World War I brought a new assault upon the guarantees of the First Amendment. The Espionage Acts of 1917 and 1918 were the signal for widespread prosecutions involving speeches, newspaper articles, pamphlets, and books: over 1,900 of these proceedings occurred. The case of a German-American who politely refused to subscribe to a Liberty Bond issue on the ground that he did not want either the Allies or the Central Powers to win the war is illustrative of this period. He was promptly arrested and thrown in jail. He was later released by a federal district court, but his misfortune demonstrated the state of the public mind confronting the judiciary.[5]

Chief Justice White's attitude toward restraint of freedom of expression, however, was manifested before the United States entered World War I. One such case, *Toledo Newspaper Co. v. United States*, is important for this

3. *Ex Parte Milligan*, 4 Wall. 2 (1866); *United States Statutes*, XII, 755.
4. *In Re Debs*, 158 U.S. 564, 584 (1895).
5. *United States* v. *Pape*, 253 Fed. 270 (1918).

study.[6] The action, which originally arose from contempt proceedings, grew out of an ordinance enacted by the City of Toledo in 1914. Toledo, Ohio, spurred by the example of Cleveland, adopted an ordinance requiring that a lower streetcar fare should be charged after March 27, 1914, when the franchise of the local street railway company expired. Creditors of the company brought suit in the appropriate federal district court, claiming that, if the company obeyed the order, the property that they held in the company would be destroyed. At this juncture, the Toledo *News-Bee* began publishing articles that attacked the creditors and asserted the city's right to adopt the ordinance. Some time later a man named Quinlivan was arrested for contempt of court for a speech that dealt with the contempt proceedings, which he made at a labor union meeting. The *News-Bee* severely criticized the district court for its action in regard to Quinlivan, and the district court promptly issued an attachment for contempt against the editor of the newspaper for his articles on the Quinlivan case. Two additional charges of contempt were brought: one for the articles dealing with the injunction process and the other concerning the attachment against the editor. The lower court found the defendants guilty on all counts because the published articles manifestly tended to interfere with and obstruct the court in the discharge of its duty.

When the case finally arrived before the Supreme Court, the Court had to determine whether the lower court had applied its contempt powers within the pertinent provisions of the *Judicial Code* outlining those powers: "The said courts [United States] shall have power . . . to punish . . . contempts of their authority: Provided, that such power to punish for contempts shall not be construed to extend to any cases except the behavior of persons in their presence, or so near thereto as to obstruct the administration of justice." White took the point of view that the provisions of the code conferred no new power, but merely marked out the boundaries of the existing authority resulting from grants of the Constitution. The test of whether the courts are acting within the limits of this power, White contended, is the character of the act done and its direct tendency to prevent and obstruct the discharge of judicial duty.

---

6. *Toledo Newspaper Co. v. United States*, 247 U.S. 402 (1918).

Similarly, the test of whether a particular act attempts to influence a court or to intimidate a judge is "the reasonable tendency of acts done to influence or bring about the baleful result . . . and its direct tendency to prevent the discharge of judicial duty, a conclusion which necessarily sustains the view of the statute taken by the courts below."[7]

White had no doubt that the publication of the articles in the Toledo *News-Bee* did indeed have a tendency to obstruct the discharge of judicial duty. This result, he said, was enough. It is not necessary to prove that the articles affected the court, but only that they might have done so. "The wrong," he declared, "depends upon the tendency of the acts to accomplish this result without reference to the consideration of how far they may have been without influence in a particular case."[8]

White rejected the main contention of the appellants that the matters complained of were of public concern and that freedom of the press prevented their being made the basis of contempt proceedings. "This argument," he contended, "involves in its very statement the contention that the freedom of the press is the freedom to do wrong with impunity and implies the right to frustrate and defeat the discharge of those governmental duties upon the performance of which the freedom of all, including that of the press, depends. . . . However complete is the right of the press to state public things and discuss them, that right as every other right, enjoyed in human society, is subject to the restraints which separate right from wrong-doing."[9]

Justice Holmes dissented largely because there was much ado about nothing. In reviewing the publications of the defendant newspaper, he admitted that the articles contained innuendoes not flattering to the personality of the presiding judge, who appropriately enough was named Killits. Holmes wryly remarked that "I confess that I cannot find in all of this . . . anything that would have affected a mind of reasonable fortitude." Apparently Judge Killits was somewhat less strong than his name implied. "Finally," said Holmes, "when there is need for immediate action contempts are like any other breach of the law and should be dealt with as the law deals with other illegal acts. . . . Action like the present

7. *Judicial Code*, sec. 268; *Toledo Newspaper Co. v. United States*, 247 U.S. 402, 418, 419.
8. *Toledo Newspaper Co. v. United States*, 247 U.S. 402, 421.
9. *Ibid.*, 419.

in my opinion is wholly unwarranted by even color of law." Justice Louis D. Brandeis concurred in the dissent. [10]

The *Toledo* case had not followed precedents and was historically in error. In 1941 the Court flatly overruled *Toledo*, holding that the words "in their presence [the Courts] or so near thereto as to obstruct the administration of justice" possessed only a geographical meaning. Contempt thus applies to acts committed "in the vicinity of the court, disrupting the quiet and order or actually interrupting the court in the conduct of its business." [11]

Chief Justice White did not deliver any of the important opinions dealing with the Espionage Acts, but his line of thought can perhaps be drawn from his tacit concurrence in the landmark cases. The first of these affirmed the conviction of one Schenck, the general secretary of the Socialist party, for conspiracy to obstruct the enlistment service. He was found to have sent out a circular that attacked the selective draft statute. In a unanimous decision delivered by Mr. Justice Holmes, the Court held that the right of free speech was not an absolute and unchanging right. "The question in every case," said Holmes, "is whether the words are used in such circumstances and are of such a nature as to create a clear and present danger that they will bring about the substantive evils that Congress has a right to prevent." In March of the same year, an undivided Court, speaking again through Mr. Justice Holmes, reiterated the "clear and present danger" rule in the conviction of Eugene V. Debs for a speech which was found to have obstructed the draft. [12]

In November, 1919, the Court decided one of the most widely known of the *Espionage Act* cases, and a split in its ranks began to appear. The defendant, Abrams, was convicted for issuing pamphlets that opposed the expedition of United States troops to Russia. The majority of the Court, including White, apparently tortured the interpretation of the act to uphold the conviction. The language of the statute prohibited certain acts, which would hinder the prosecution of the war against Germany;

10. *Ibid.*, 402, 425, 426; White had also upheld the power of the House of Representatives to punish for contempt in *Marshall* v. *Gordon*, 243 U.S. 521 (1917), which was reaffirmed in *Toledo*.

11. *Nye* v. *United States*, 313 U.S. 33 (1941).

12. *Schenck* v. *United States*, 249 U.S. 47, 52 (1919); *Debs* v. *United States*, 249 U.S. 211 (1919).

since the United States, however, was not at war with Russia, the Court was confronted with the dilemma of how to sustain the conviction of a defendant whose only intent was to impede a war with Russia. This problem was solved by a broad construction of "intent" under the act to include all actions, the reasonable consequence of which would hamper the war with Germany. The general strike that the defendant advocated would produce such an obstruction, declared the Court. Justices Holmes and Brandeis dissented from this opinion and contended that the statute properly applied to acts the motive of which was to hinder the war with the Central Powers. Holmes's dissent is generally considered to be a judicial classic. "But when men have realized that time has upset many fighting faiths, they may come to believe even more than they believe the very foundations of their own conduct that the ultimate good desired is better reached by free trade in ideas—that the best test of truth is the power of the thought to get itself accepted in the competition of the market, and that truth is the only ground upon which their wishes safely can be carried out. That at any rate is the theory of our Constitution. It is an experiment, as all life is an experiment." [13] These decisions are important in studying the constitutional philosophy of Edward White because they show that he was not disposed to help out civil liberties perhaps unnecessarily curtailed by the spirit engendered in wartime legislation. By the same token, he was unlikely to become a crusader for the Bill of Rights.

Although he delivered no decisions involving the Espionage Act, White was expressing his judicial opinion on civil rights in other matters growing out of the wartime legislation. World War I had given rise to various legislative enactments affecting the individual, and in due time, these measures came before the Supreme Court for its review. Among these wartime statutes was the Selective Draft Law, which subjected all male citizens between twenty-one and thirty years of age to military draft. It was not to be supposed that Chief Justice White, or the members of any federal court, would declare the draft law invalid, for it was fundamental to the prosecution of a successful war. The decision itself was significant, but not surprising. Before the United States declared war against the Central Powers, the Court had anticipated that compul-

13. *Abrams v. United States,* 250 U.S. 616, 630 (1919).

sory military service would be assailed as involuntary servitude under the Thirteenth Amendment. In *Butler* v. *Perry* the Court answered this putative objection: "It [the Thirteenth Amendment] introduced no novel doctrine with respect of services already treated as exceptional, and certainly was not intended to interdict enforcement of those duties which individuals owe to the State, such as services in the army, militia, on the jury, etc. The great purpose in view was liberty under the protection of effective government, not the destruction of the latter by depriving it of essential powers." Accordingly, in the *Selective Draft Law* cases, White dismissed the objection under the amendment as an argument that "was refuted by its mere statement." White expressed in these cases his philosophy of the relationship of the individual to the State. Compulsory military service, he thought, is neither repugnant to a free government nor in conflict with the constitutional guarantees of individual liberty. To him, "the very conception of a just government and its duty to the citizen includes the reciprocal obligation of the citizen to render military service in case of the need and the right to compel." [14]

In a series of cases based upon the draft statute White reaffirmed his original position and applied it to various situations. *Goldman* v. *United States* upheld the law in a case of conspiracy to dissuade persons from registering. This rule was reaffirmed in *Kramer* v. *United States*. In *Cox* v. *Wood* the Court, speaking through White, held that Congress may conscript for duty in a foreign country, and the exercise of this power does not interfere with freedom of religion. *Jones* v. *Perkins* denied a writ of habeus corpus to a defendant arrested for violating the draft statute. [15]

Congress not only undertook the mobilization of manpower and the unification of public opinion, but also attempted to organize private business extensively for the prosecution of the war, an effort which resulted in the passage, among other statutes, of the Food Control Act of 1917. Section 4 of this measure made it unlawful for any person to make "any unjust or unreasonable rate or charges in handling or dealing with any necessaries." In his opinion on litigation growing out of this statute,

14. *Selective Draft Law* cases, 245 U.S. 366 (1918); *Butler* v. *Perry*, 240 U.S. 328, 333 (1916); *Selective Draft Law* cases, 366, 378.
15. *Goldman* v. *United States*, 245 U.S. 474 (1918); *Kramer* v. *United States*, 245 U.S. 478 (1918); *Cox* v. *Wood*, 247 U.S. 3 (1918); *Jones* v. *Perkins*, 245 U.S. 390 (1918).

Chief Justice White held the section invalid on the ground that the mere existence of a state of war could not suspend or change the operation of the guarantees and limitations of the Fifth and Sixth Amendments upon the power of Congress. The statute, he declared, was so vague and uncertain that it did not adequately inform the defendant of the charges against him. "To attempt to enforce the section," said White, "would be the exact equivalent of an effort to carry out a statute which in terms merely penalized and punished all acts detrimental to the public interest when unjust and unreasonable in the estimation of the court and jury." [16]

The war and the spirit it bred did not create all the problems involving the Bill of Rights coming before the Supreme Court of the United States. One of the most important provisions of the Bill of Rights safeguards the right of trial by jury. For many years it had not been clear whether this provision of the Seventh Amendment operated upon state courts when they were trying cases concerning state statutes. White made it plain that the amendment applies only to proceedings in federal courts and is not applicable to every right of a federal character created by Congress. To argue that it is relevant created, he thought, "a confusion by which the true significance of the amendment is obscured, that is, it shuts out of view the fact that the limitations of the amendment are applicable only to the mode in which power or jurisdiction shall be exercised in the tribunals of the United States and therefore that its terms have no relation whatever to the enforcement of rights in other forums merely because the right enforced is one conferred by the law of the United States." [17] This view was simply an orthodox one that might well have been written by any member of the Court.

In a significant case concerning individual liberties, however, White

---

16. *United States Statutes*, XL, 277, Sec. 4, amended by Act of October 22, 1919 (*United States Statutes*, XLI, 298, Sec. 2); *United States* v. *Cohen Grocery Co.*, 255 U.S. 81, 89 (1921). This decision was upheld in various other suits involving different types of business. See *Tedrow* v. *Lewis & Co.*, 255 U.S. 98 (1921), *Kennington* v. *Palmer*, 255 U.S. 100 (1921), *Kinane* v. *Detroit Creamery Co.*, *United States* v. *Swartz*, and *United States* v. *Smith*, 255 U.S. 102 (1921), *Weed* v. *Lockwood*, 255 U.S. 104 (1921), *Willard* v. *Palmer*, 255 U.S. 106 (1921), and *Oglesby Grocery Co.* v. *United States*, 255 U.S. 108 (1921). The same fate befell Section 4 of the Lever Act which made conspiracies to exact "excessive prices" illegal. See *Weeds, Inc.* v. *United States*, 255 U.S. 109, 111 (1921).

17. *Minneapolis & St. Louis R.R. Co.* v. *Bombolis*, 241 U.S. 211, 220 (1916).

departed widely from what would seem to be a logical result. This departure came about in a case arising under the provisions of the Eighth Amendment prohibiting cruel and unusual punishments.[18] Weems, a disbursing officer in the Philippine Islands, was found guilty by the courts of that commonwealth of making false entries in a wage book, a crime that was not serious and, under the criminal codes of our states, would have brought only a light punishment. The criminal code of the Philippines, however, was merely a reenactment of the old Spanish Code, which was severe in its retribution even on minor criminals. Consequently, after conviction Weems was sentenced to fifteen years in prison and was subjected to painful labor, ball and chain, civil interdiction, disqualification to vote, and surveillance through life. He appealed this conviction on the grounds that the sentence violated the cruel and unusual punishment provision of the Philippine bill of rights. Since the Court agreed that this provision had the same meaning as its counterpart in the United States Constitution, the justices were called upon to determine the meaning of the Eighth Amendment.

A majority of the Court held that the sentence in this case violated the Eighth Amendment and therefore reversed the judgment, several points of cleavage appearing between the vigorous dissent of White and the majority opinion of Mr. Justice McKenna. The latter took the point of view that the provision against cruel and unusual punishment could not be interpreted only in the light of what was cruel and unusual at the time the Constitution was adopted, but must be expanded to meet the progress of humane ideas of punishment. Hence, McKenna argued, punishments that would be valid by reason of their character or *type* can transcend the provision of the amendment because of their severity in relation to the crime committed. They thus become cruel and unusual penalties within the prohibition. Examined in this light, Weems's sentence was found invalid by McKenna and the rest of the Court's majority because of its excessive nature.

White, on the other hand, rejected a broad interpretation of the word *cruel*. He limited it to the *character* of the punishment as determined by what was torturous and inhuman at the time of the adoption of the Con-

18. *Weems v. United States*, 217 U.S. 349 (1910).

stitution and argued that McKenna had established a theory of proportionate punishment and set up the courts as judicial bodies to determine whether in particular cases the punishment fits the crime. This Gilbert and Sullivan approach, he thought, was contrary to the intent of the amendment. "The word cruel, as used in the amendment," explained White, "forbids only the lawmaking power in prescribing punishment for crime and the courts in imposing punishment from inflicting unnecessary bodily suffering through a resort to inhuman methods for causing bodily torture . . . which had been made use of prior to the Bill of Rights and against the recurrence of which the word cruel was used in that instrument."[19]

A clear split on the meaning of the word *unusual* in the Eighth Amendment also appeared. Justice McKenna claimed that the courts can look at the punishment to determine whether it is in itself unusual. White, on the contrary, thought that the intent of the term was to limit judicial discretion in applying legal modes of punishment and only prohibited the legislative power from bestowing an illegal discretion upon the judiciary. He would not accept the proposition that "by judicial construction constitutional limitations may be made to progress so as to ultimately include that which they were not intended to embrace." He therefore found the majority opinion in direct conflict with this principle because it accomplished two results:

(a) the clause against cruel punishment which was intended to prohibit inhuman and barbarous bodily punishments is so construed as to limit the discretion of the lawmaking power in determining the mere severity with which punishments not of the prohibited character may be prescribed, and (b) by interpreting the word "unusual" adopted for the sole purpose of limiting judicial discretion in order thereby to maintain the superiority of the lawmaking body so as to bring about the directly contrary result, that is, to expand the judicial power by endowing it with a vast authority to control the legislative department in the exercise of its discretion to define and punish crime.[20]

This reluctance to extend the judicial power was an unusual approach for White because the primary effect of many of his decisions was to create new power in the Supreme Court and to transfer to that tribunal much of the sovereignty of the federal government. In *Weems* his oft repeated

19. *Ibid.*, 349, 409.
20. *Ibid.*, 411.

tendency to regard historical precedent with an unyielding veneration was apparently once more the controlling factor.

In three important race relations cases, Chief Justice White demonstrated that his Deep South background was no bar to a modest, yet significant expansion of civil rights for Negroes. By 1895 several southern state legislatures had enacted statutes or the people of these states had approved constitutional amendments that in effect disenfranchised blacks. Mississippi had participated in depriving Negroes of suffrage rights by a combination of poll taxes and the ability to read and interpret the Mississippi Constitution, and these provisions had been found not inconsistent with the Fifteenth Amendment, which forbade denial of suffrage by any state for reasons of race, color, or previous condition of servitude.[21]

Other states took the route of establishing a so-called grandfather clause.[22] This clause, restrictive in its effects on suffrage generally, combined two features: an educational or literacy test and a provision that the literacy test need not be met by those persons who were qualified voters in 1866 or 1867, dates prior to the Act of Congress of March 2, 1878, requiring Negro suffrage in ten southern states, and to the 1870 ratification of the Fifteenth Amendment, which made suffrage rights of Negroes a part of the Constitution. In addition, this exemption also applied to lineal descendants of legal voters in 1866 or 1867. The practical effect of the grandfather clauses was to bar Negro voting while permitting some illiterate whites to register and vote.

An amendment to the Oklahoma Constitution embodied the grandfather clause with an effective date of January 1, 1866. A federal court convicted certain Oklahoma election officials, charged with the enforcement of election laws, of depriving Negroes of their suffrage rights. When the litigation reached the Supreme Court, Chief Justice White, speaking for a unanimous tribunal, found no difficulty in affirming the conviction. Stating that the Fifteenth Amendment did not take away from the state its power over elections, he commented that "in fact, the very command of the amendment recognizes the possession of the general power by the state, since the amendment seeks to regulate its exercise as to the

21. *Williams* v. *Mississippi*, 170 U.S. 213 (1898).
22. Among these states were Alabama (1901), Georgia (1908), Maryland with restricted applicability to Annapolis (1908), North Carolina (1902), and Virginia (1902).

particular subject with which it deals." After reviewing the effects of the amendment, he asked "how can there be room for serious dispute concerning the repugnancy of the standard based upon January 1, 1866 [a date which preceded the adoption of the amendment]?" He found not the slightest reason for basing the classification upon a period prior to the adoption of the Fifteenth Amendment, concluding that "the 1866 standard never took life, since it was void from the beginning of the operation upon it of the prohibitions of the Fifteenth Amendment." [23] In addition, the literacy test was invalid as a result of its association with the grandfather clause in the Oklahoma Constitution.

In the second case, White dealt with a Maryland statute, applicable to Annapolis, which established in 1908 three classifications for voting, one of which qualified all persons who were legal voters on or prior to January 1, 1868, and the descendants of these voters. White, again speaking for a unanimous Court, affirmed a lower court judgment against the Maryland election officials. The grandfather clause, declared White, was "void because it amounts to a mere device of the operative effect of the Fifteenth amendment, and based upon that conception, proceeds to re-create and re-establish a condition which the amendment prohibits." [24]

In the third case White, as a silent member of the majority, voted to invalidate a municipal ordinance which prevented Negroes from living in a particular district. [25] In this action a white plaintiff, seeking to convey property to a Negro, was permitted to challenge an ordinance preventing the sale of the property to Negroes because the black defendant was using the municipal ordinance as his defense.

Was there a trace of irony in White's position in this series of cases? He was, after all, a conservative chief justice from the Deep South, who, moreover, had sought, years before, to oust Louisiana's Reconstruction government and return control of Louisiana to the white population. He was also a chief justice with fixed views on the nature of American federalism, and *Guinn* and *Myers* certainly imposed a measure of control over the electoral process that traditionally had been the province of the state governments. He had consistently maintained the thesis that the state and federal governments should move cooperatively, yet sepa-

23. *Guinn v. United States*, 238 U.S. 347, 363, 364–65 (1915).
24. *Myers v. Anderson*, 238 U.S. 368, 380 (1915).
25. *Buchanan v. Warley*, 245 U.S. 60 (1917).

rately, but the language of the Fifteenth Amendment was prescriptive and mandatory. He would not, indeed could not, interpret the amendment out of existence. Any personal beliefs he might have had on the subject of black voting and other black rights were subordinated in these cases to the necessities of the law. As the nation's chief justice, it was his responsibility to apply the Constitution, and his lifelong service to law could not allow him to act differently.

Whatever his inner thoughts may have been, the decisions are significant. They mark the beginning of the modern movement for black equality in the United States and its pluralistic society. There would be many cases involving the rights of Negroes in American society in the following decades until, at last, the landmark decisions barring segregation in the public schools and universities of the land would be delivered by the Court.[26]

The protection of civil liberties is the hallmark of democratic political theory. With emphasis upon the rights of the individual, civil liberties are an important feature distinguishing democracy from other forms of politically organized society, and advocates of democratic government unanimously agree that the protection of civil liberties must be continued and expanded. Indeed, much of the Court's history in recent decades has been made by such an expansion, but herein lies the greatest danger to those liberties. Although almost everyone favors them, at least symbolically, many have different ideas as to what civil liberties mean and what steps should be taken to safeguard them. As a result, under the guise of protecting civil liberties, action may be taken which effectively destroys them. In the last analysis the protection of civil liberties is one more manifestation of the never-ending and all-inclusive conflict of freedom versus the authority and power of the state, with the synthesis of this clash taking whatever form is indicated by the particular interpreter's concept of social policy.

Edward White was thus confronted with two main trends of thought concerning the meaning and preservation of civil liberties. The first of these resolved the impasse completely in favor of freedom, holding that the rights of the individual can best be protected by denying the state the

26. *Brown v. Board of Education*, 347 U.S. 483 (1954), 349 U.S. 294 (1955).

power of intervention except in cases of overt action threatening the existence of the state. This view is based ultimately on the assumption that any modification in favor of an immediately desirable objective opens the door to endless modifications that eventually will destroy the very liberties they are allegedly protecting. This position was never fully represented on the Court during White's tenure, but the closest approach was in the opinions of Justices Holmes and Brandeis. The former came nearer to this ideal with his doctrine of "clear and present danger" as the test of validity for state intervention.[27]

The other view rejected the principle of an abstract right and regarded the problem as solely a practical one of immediate public policy, involving the acceptance of concessions and sanctioning inroads upon the abstract right in order to obtain what seemed to be the current needs of the social order. Under this view, civil liberties are an expanding or contracting principle, which may be as variable as the judicial foot. Chief Justice White definitely belonged to this latter group. Attorney General Harry M. Daugherty, in presenting to the Supreme Court the resolutions of the bar of that court following the death of White, gave expression to this view in his summary of the late chief justice's position. "It may be said," remarked Daugherty, "that he was no extreme advocate of absolute liberty, either of person or contract. . . . Chief Justice White was a believer in the Constitution, yet he saw the dangers resulting from an abuse of the Constitution by those who seek to invoke it through the agency of our judiciary for their own purposes and against the legitimate rights of all the people."[28] A plea of American citizens to their government might well be that of Diogenes: "Keep out of my sunlight." To this plea White probably would have replied, "There must be an occasional partial eclipse if that sunlight is to be preserved." To destroy in order to preserve is bad logic, and possibly contains the seeds of bad law.

27. *Schenck v. United States,* 249 U.S. 47, 52 (1919). The doctrine was obiter dictum in this case.

28. Henry P. Dart, Sr., Harry M. Daugherty, William Howard Taft, and others, *Proceedings of the Bar and Officers of the Supreme Court of the United States in Memory of Edward Douglass White,* Washington, December 17, 1921, p. 56.

XI
The New *Jus Gentium*

W
alking along the streets of Washington, White had the habit of stopping when he wanted to emphasize some point, delivering his thought to his companion, and then resuming his stroll. Discussing the Insular Doctrine on one of these walks, he stopped, half-turned to his fellow stroller of the day, and said, "Why, if we hadn't decided them that way, this country would not have been a nation!" [1] Appropriately, he expressed himself strongly, for perhaps the most politic, yet pragmatic constitutional doctrine elaborated by Edward White is that embodied in the *Insular* cases. At the beginning of a new century, when the fruits of a policy of expansion were questioned on many sides, verbal and political battles swirled about the Court as it determined the status of the newly acquired territories. The presidential election of 1900 spelled the defeat of the Anti-Imperialist League, and the next year Finley P. Dunne's Mr. Dooley gave utterance to his epigram, "The Supreme Court follows the election returns."

The problem that confronted the Court in 1901 presented nothing new. All expanding nations have eventually been faced with the task of absorbing and governing alien elements that are gathered into their widening horizons. This process has been accompanied normally by a reluctance to extend to foreign peoples the privileges and laws of the ab-

---

1. Versions of this story were related in newspaper articles and legal periodicals at the time of White's death. It also crops up in several letters concerned with White's role in formulating the doctrine. It is consistent with his reasoning and is probably true rather than apocryphal.

sorbing nation. The reluctance is especially strong when the attached people have a radically different culture, and their community is not as far advanced in what we please to term civilization as that of the conqueror. To meet the problem of dealing with the islands acquired by the Spanish-American War, White was singularly well equipped. His early training in Louisiana gave him knowledge of civil cases and texts, and his understanding increased with study and collection of foreign legal periodicals.[2] He consequently possessed a considerable storehouse of knowledge of the civil law, which was the original law in the acquisitions of the Treaty of Paris (1898) and remained the basis of municipal law in many of them.

The ancient Roman republic stood face-to-face with this problem of assimilation two thousand years ago.[3] Its legions carried out the conquest of Italy, and aliens flocked to the protection of Rome's victorious banners. In the eyes of the republic, the dependent people were not citizens, but rather foreigners to the *jus civile*. They were denied the civil law which extended to citizens of the republic, but political necessity compelled Roman lawyers to deal with them. Those lawyers drew on all the customs of alien groups, creating from the mixture a *jus gentium*, or law of nations. Wherever a usage could be observed in practice among a large number of separate peoples, it was set down as a part of the law which was common to all people and all nations.[4] This code gradually became identified with the *jus naturale* and out of it stemmed the philosophical content of natural law and the more pragmatic Anglo-American legal division of equity.

No modern nation but the United States has been faced with the same type of problem in peacetime, and we have extended the privileges of the Constitution and our fundamental law to all those emigrating to our

2. The chief justice's civil law books are to be found in the Law Library of Loyola University, New Orleans. The remainder of his library was donated by Mrs. White to Tulane University.

3. Leon Homo, *Primitive Italy and the Beginnings of Roman Imperialism* (London: Paul-Trench-Trubner, 1926). B. II, Chap. V, provides a detailed statement of Rome's solution. At an earlier date, Alexander the Great of Macedonia also dealt directly with the problem of assimilation; see William W. Tarn, *Alexander the Great* (Boston: Beacon Press, 1956), Chap. III.

4. Sir Henry Maine, *Ancient Law* (London: Dent & Sons, 1917), 29. See also George W. Keeton, *The Elementary Principles of Jurisprudence* (London: Pitman & Sons, 1930), 171, 281, 283–84, William Seale Carpenter, *Foundations of Modern Jurisprudence* (New York: Appleton-Century-Crofts, 1958), 52–54.

soil. As early as 1828, Chief Justice John Marshall declared that the government might acquire territory by conquest and treaty. Congress had not only the grant of authority under Article IV of the Constitution to "make all needful rules and regulations respecting the territory . . . of the United States," but the right to govern, which is derived from the "inevitable consequences of the right to acquire territory."[5] His judgment that the judicial article does not extend to territorial courts implied that all provisions of the Constitution were not extended to territorial acquisitions. When American imperialistic ambitions subsequently brought under our aegis new lands and peoples distant and alien to us, the question arose "whether the Constitution follows the flag." The relationships of the new territories, acquired by the Treaty of Paris from Spain, came quickly before the bar of the Supreme Court, where, in the resultant series of cases, White formulated the Insular Doctrine, blending his theories with Marshall's opinion that the sovereign United States may annex lands and Congress govern them by making all needful rules.

Admittedly, in 1898 the power of Congress to acquire new lands and the right of the president to control them was beyond doubt. Whether this power was more than transitional remained open to question. Although territorial acquisitions such as the Louisiana Purchase had been made with the distinct understanding that they should immediately or presently be constituted as territories or states, the situation of the Philippine Islands, Guam, and Porto Rico was new.[6] The peace treaty with Spain provided merely that, "the civil rights and political status of the native inhabitants of the territories hereby ceded to the United States shall be determined by the Congress." These words contained no answer to the question of Congress' power to govern the new territories independently of the Constitution and the rights guaranteed by it to the citizens of the United States. That answer was left for the courts to determine.

The difficulties which the Supreme Court was to have in reaching its conclusions became evident with the first of the *Insular* cases. A suit was brought to recover duties on goods imported from Porto Rico to the United States after the cession of the island by the Treaty of Paris but before Congress had acted to settle the status of Porto Rico. Duties had

5. *American Insurance Co.* v. *Canter*, 1 Pet. 511, 543 (1828).
6. The current spelling *Puerto* in place of *Porto* did not become official until 1923.

been paid under the Dingley Act, which laid customs on commodities imported "from foreign countries." Was Porto Rico a foreign country? Five members of the Supreme Court found no authority for the view that a "district ceded to and in the possession of the United States remains for any purposes a foreign country." Therefore, at the time the duties were exacted, Porto Rico was a territory of the United States, and the duties were "illegally exacted." Four members of the Court, including White, dissented, expressing uncertainty concerning the island's status and declaring that there was no clear distinction between foreign and domestic territories.[7]

The Foraker Act of 1900 laid the question of the status of the new acquisitions clearly in the lap of the Court by establishing a civil government for Porto Rico and levying a duty of 15 percent on imports into the United States from that island. The Constitution clearly requires that taxes, duties, and imports levied within the United States shall be uniform, so that, if the island were a part of the United States and not a foreign country, the Foraker Act was invalid. This proposition was the precise form of the legal question raised by the importer, Downes, when he sued Bidwell, collector of the Port of New York, to recover duties paid on commodities imported from Porto Rico.[8]

The "conclusion and judgment" of the Court came from a badly divided bench. Justice Brown delivered the opinion binding upon the action at hand and upheld the act. White concurred in a separate opinion, and Justices Shiras and McKenna went with him. In a dissenting opinion written by Chief Justice Fuller, Brewer and Peckham joined in strong disagreement with the opinion of the Court. Mr. Justice Harlan, that vigorous dissentient, brought up the rear with vitriolic disapproval.

Brown was a modernist by temperament. He regarded the Constitution as a social instrument of limited value and not everywhere apposite.[9] Therefore, declaring that Congress possessed unlimited power over the political relations of the territories, his majority opinion limited

---

7. *De Lima* v. *Bidwell*, 182 U.S. 1, 200ff. (1901); Mr. Justice Brown spoke for the majority. In *Dooley* v. *United States*, 183 U.S. 151 (1901), Brown reiterated the result of *De Lima*. Justice White concurred in the judgment, but added that he saw no distinction from *De Lima* v. *Bidwell*.

8. United States Constitution, Art. I, Sec. 8; *Downes* v. *Bidwell*, 182 U.S. 244 (1901).

9. Frederic R. Coudert, "The Evolution of the Doctrine of Territorial Incorporation," *Columbia Law Review*, XXVI (1926), 826.

the application of the Constitution to the states. As a territory "appurtenant to and belonging to the sovereignty of the United States," Porto Rico was not within the uniform tax provision of the fundamental law unless Congress so deemed. By dictum, Justice Brown inferred that territories have a minimum of rights that Congress cannot abridge: rights protected by prohibitions extending to the root of congressional power and natural rights protected by fundamental law.

Brown attempted to resolve the dilemma of assimilation by his so-called extension theory. Thus, when legislating for new territories to which our flag had been extended before this case, Congress had been limited by the Constitution only because it had previously declared that document applicable. From historical evidence Brown concluded that congressional action proceeded on the assumption of such an extension. "The Constitution," he declared, "was created by the people of the *United States*, as a union of *states*, to be governed solely by representatives of the *states*. [Therefore Congress might] dispose of and make all needful rules and regulations respecting the territories." [10]

While a review of the decisions determining the power of Congress on this point was not entirely harmonious, the majority opinion reduced them to two points of view. One held that the Constitution does not apply to territories without legislative action; the other stated that such legislation is in fact unnecessary because the Constitution possesses force in new acquisitions from the moment of their cession to the United States. Ruling in favor of the first theory, Brown stated that "where the Constitution has once been formally extended by Congress, neither Congress nor the territorial legislature can enact laws inconsistent therewith." Counsel for Downes maintained that the *Dred Scott* case definitely ruled that the provisions of the Constitution, relating to liberty and property, applied by their own force in the territories. New territories, however acquired, were, counsel argued, an integral part of the Union. [11]

Brown denied the finality of the ill-famed Taney judgment to the effect that the Constitution *ex proprio vigore* applied to new territory, because the country had not acquiesced in the opinion and the Civil War had "produced such changes in judicial, as well as public sentiment, as to seriously impair this case." Not entirely convinced, he sought to indi-

10. *Downes* v. *Bidwell*, 182 U.S. 244, 250, 251, 271, italics Justice Brown's.
11. *Ibid.*, 271; *Scott* v. *Sandford*, 19 How. 393 (1857).

cate a possible loophole and discovered it in a distinction between the types of prohibitions on Congress. Some go to the very foundations of congressional power and affect its capacity to act at all by prohibiting absolutely the commission of certain acts irrespective of time and place. Without binding himself, Justice Brown hinted that the first eight amendments might belong to such a category. Some prohibitions permit action; however, they limit its extent. As in the present case, Congress could deny uniform duties because the phrase "throughout the United States" had not been extended to the territory by its legislative action.[12]

A second indication of Brown's reluctance to include the fruits of the new imperialism in the Union cropped out in his distinction between *natural* and *remedial* rights. "We suggest, without intending to decide, that there may be a distinction between certain natural rights, enforced in the Constitution by prohibitions against interference with them, and what might be termed artificial or remedial rights which are peculiar to our own system of jurisprudence. Of the former class are the rights to one's own religious opinions . . . to personal liberty and individual property. . . . Of the latter class are the rights to citizenship, to suffrage . . . and to particular methods of procedure . . . some of which already have been held by the states to be unnecessary for the proper protection of individuals."[13]

The concurring opinion of Mr. Justice White was scholarly and vigorous. As a man with the background of a prosperous planter, he was confronted with the problem of permitting the forceful imperialists of the day to retain their gains and yet, at the same time, protecting vested interests against an influx of duty-free sugar and tobacco from the islands. As an American nationalist, he also felt strongly on the subject and favored no action that might be taken to indicate a weakening of the national will.

Although stated in terms of American public law, his solution of the problem of overseas territorial absorption not unnaturally went beyond our traditional constitutional concepts. He therefore brought forth a new *jus gentium*. Rome, it will be recalled, had dealt with the problem of assimilation by creating the law of nations, that is, a collection of the laws and mores of particular tribes and peoples. White met the problem of

12. *Downes v. Bidwell*, 182 U.S. 244, 273–74, 277.
13. *Ibid.*, 282–83.

new American insular possessions by splitting constitutional law into two categories: fundamental law, similar to the *jus gentium*, applying to "incorporated" and "unincorporated" territories alike; and laws peculiar to American jurisprudence, akin to the *jus civile*, which apply only to the states and such territories as have been "incorporated" by Congress. Although not extending the Constitution in its entirety to the peoples acquired by treaty, White did recognize a body of fundamental principles that reached them.

It is true that Justice Brown had hinted at this solution in his division of constitutional prohibitions and rights. He was apparently confused, however, about the deeper significance of his extension doctrine and did not go as far as White. To the latter went the task of drawing out the application of the principle. As White viewed it, the sole question raised by *Downes* was whether Porto Rico had been incorporated as an integral part of the Union at the time of passage of the Foraker Act. From this beginning he proceeded to review the relationship that new acquisitions had to the union of states and organized territories.

White laid down a number of propositions which he believed were fundamental with respect to the government of the United States. They included:

Second. Every function of the government being derived from the Constitution, it follows that that instrument is everywhere and at all times potential in so far as its provisions are applicable. . . .

Seventh. In the case of the territories, as in every other instance, when a provision of the Constitution is invoked, the question which arises is, not whether the Constitution is operative, for that is self-evident, but whether the provision relied on is applicable.

Eighth. As Congress derives its authority to levy local taxes for local purposes within the territories, not from the general grant of power to tax as expressed in the Constitution, it follows that its right to locally tax is not to be measured by the provision empowering Congress "to lay and collect Taxes, Duties, Imposts, and Excises," and is not restrained by the requirement of uniformity throughout the United States. But the power just referred to, as well as the qualification of uniformity, restrains Congress from imposing an impost duty on goods coming into the United States from a territory which has been incorporated into and forms a part of the United States.

After examining the precedents relating to the applicability of constitutional provisions to territories acquired by the United States, White found that the sole issue was "whether the particular tax in question was levied in such form as to cause it to be repugnant to the Constitution." This is to be resolved by answering the inquiry, "Had Porto Rico, at the time of the passage of the act in question, been incorporated into and become an integral part of the United States?" He discovered no difficulty whatsoever in American acquisition of the island and its people. The United States, exercising authority implicit in sovereignty, may acquire territory.[14]

He thus stated, "The decisions of this court leave no room for question that, under the Constitution, the government of the United States in virtue of its sovereignty supreme within the sphere of its delegated power, had the full right to acquire territory enjoyed by every other sovereign nation."[15] Incidental to such authority is Congress' power to establish a government for acquired territory. New territory, although under the rule of the United States, is not an integral part of the body politic, he contended, subject to all of the constitutional provisions that apply to states and incorporated territories. Acquisition of land by itself does not mean that the Constitution is thereby extended without congressional action. Rejecting counsel's theory of *ex proprio vigore*, White declared that such an argument could rest only on the assumption that the United States "under the Constitution is stripped of those powers which are absolutely inherent in and essential to national existence."[16] A necessary consequence of this inherent power is congressional freedom from restrictions in legislating for newly won lands. The peoples themselves, the location of the territory, and other circumstances may be considered freely without the constitutional restrictions which normally apply in dealing with states.

No power of disposal would exist, furthermore, if all territory upon cession to this nation immediately became a part of the Union under the Constitution. Economic competition and fear of racial conflict were uppermost in White's mind, and like Justice Brown, White was loath to accept any doctrine which might preclude disposition of new lands and

14. *Ibid.*, 289, 292, 299.
15. *Ibid.*, 302–303; in support of this conclusion, White cited *American Insurance Co.* v. *Canter*, 1 Pet. 511 (1828), *Scott* v. *Sandford*, 19 How. 393 (1857), *Stewart* v. *Kahn*, 11 Wall. 493 (1871), *United States* v. *Huckabee*, 16 Wall. 414 (1873), *Jones* v. *United States*, 137 U.S. 202 (1890), and *Shively* v. *Bowlby*, 152 U.S. 1 (1894).
16. *Downes* v. *Bidwell*, 182 U.S. 244, 311.

peoples,[17] or deprive Congress of a free hand in dealing with them. It was at this point that White formulated the doctrine of incorporation. To him it seemed that, while Jefferson had not questioned the power to acquire Louisiana, he did have some doubts about its incorporation. Hence, the treaty with Napoleon read: "The inhabitants of the ceded territory shall be incorporated into the Union of the United States. . . . *as soon as possible according to the principles of the Federal Constitution.*" White read this statement to mean that the Louisiana Territory came eventually as an incorporated territory into a union of states and incorporated territories. "The territory acquired by the Louisiana Purchase [he argued] was governed as a mere dependency, *until* . . . it was by action of Congress incorporated as a territory into the United States and the same rights were conferred in the same mode by which other territories had previously been incorporated, that is, by bestowing the privileges of citizenship and the rights and immunities which pertained to the Northwest Territory." [18] In effect, what White had done was to establish for the United States a distinction parallel to that which the Roman senate maintained between its territory proper and its annexations.

One more step, however, was required to complete the process. A line of demarcation was needed between the new "law of nations" and the law applicable only to our citizens. To meet this need, White advanced the concept that the power of Congress over inhabitants of unincorporated territories is not unrestrained, for constraints exist even though the territories are not subject to the entire Constitution until made so by legislative action. This result flows from the dichotomy Justice Brown had noted, the distinction that he read into the prohibitions of the Constitution. White, too, found that there are certain constitutional rights to life and property affecting the capacity of Congress to act at all. In addition, he contended, "it does not follow that there are not inherent . . . principles which are the basis for all free government which cannot be with impunity transcended." When powers may be exercised, it is necessary in the particular case to examine the status of the territory to discover if it is such an integral part of the United States that it is subject to the specific constitutional provision in question. On the basis of this doctrine, which incidentally reaffirmed the sovereignty of the Supreme

17. Coudert, "Territorial Incorporation," 832.
18. *Downes* v. *Bidwell*, 182 U.S. 244, 326, 244, 333, my italics.

Court, White declared, "The result of what has been said is that whilst in an international sense Porto Rico was not a foreign country, since it was subject to the sovereignty of and was owned by the United States, it was foreign to the United States in a domestic sense, because the island had not been incorporated into the United States, but was merely appurtenant thereto." Without defining the word *incorporate*, White concurred in the judgment that the Foraker Act was valid, and although subject to the dominion of the United States, the people of the island did not possess all of the rights and privileges guaranteed by our Constitution.[19]

The remainder of the Court received White's doctrine with varied attitudes. Justice Gray agreed substantially, but also separately. He would not at this time place undue restrictions on Congress. If the latter were not ready now to construct a complete government for Porto Rico, "it may establish a temporary government, which is not subject to all the restrictions of the Constitution." Chief Justice Fuller delivered a dissenting opinion with which Justices Brewer, Harlan, and Peckham concurred. By bent of mind Fuller was an antiimperialist. He spoke scornfully of the word *incorporation*, deriding it as "possessed by some occult meaning" and went on to decry White's theory in scathing language. "There is nothing in the 'literal construction [of the Constitution] so obviously absurd, or mischievous, or repugnant to the general spirit of the instrument, as to justify those who expound the Constitution' in giving it a construction not warranted by its words." The last word was had by Mr. Justice Harlan, who felt "constrained to say that this idea of 'incorporation' has some occult meaning which my mind does not apprehend. It is enveloped in some mystery I am unable to unravel."[20]

From the point of view of public law, the judgment of the Court in *Downes* was unsatisfactory. Division of opinion among the members of the Court was balanced. Logic and the Constitution had apparently vanished. Within the next decade, however, the situation was clarified by the acceptance of White's theory. He spoke once more as a concurring justice and then in 1905, acting for the Court, converted his Insular Doctrine into the law of the land.

19. *Ibid.*, 244, 291, 341–42.
20. *Ibid.*, 346, 374, 391.

In 1898 the Hawaiian Islands were annexed to the United States by a Joint Resolution of Congress "as 'a part of the territory of the United States . . . subject to the sovereign dominion thereof,' . . . with the following condition: The municipal legislation of the Hawaiian Islands, not exacted for the fulfillment of the treaties so extinguished, and not inconsistent with this joint resolution *nor contrary to the Constitution of the United States, nor to any existing treaty of the United States, shall remain in force until the Congress of the United States shall otherwise determine."* [21] A short time later one Mankichi was convicted of manslaughter, after a trial without grand jury indictment, and in accordance with Hawaiian statutes, was found guilty by a petit jury vote of nine to three. He thereupon petitioned through counsel for a writ of habeas corpus, and the matter found its way to the Supreme Court, where his attorney claimed that the provisions of the Fifth and Sixth Amendments guaranteeing indictment by grand jury and trial by jury were applicable. Once more the Supreme Court had to decide whether the Constitution followed the flag. Reversing the lower court, which had granted the petition, Justice Brown again delivered the judgment of the Court. White filed a separate opinion that concurred with the result of the case. As usual, Chief Justice Fuller and Justices Brewer, Harlan, and Peckham dissented.

Now, if the joint resolution were literally interpreted, Mankichi's contention was strong. However, Brown ruled that Congress intended the original Hawaiian Code to apply. It seemed to him that Congress meant the resolution to stand for only a short time and did not want to disturb the practice "hitherto well known and acquiesced in." The words "contrary to the Constitution of the United States" would operate only upon additional legislation. Finally, though most of the privileges and immunities of the Bill of Rights were applied by the annexation, the rights claimed here were not fundamental. They were merely a method of procedure "well calculated to conserve the rights of their citizens to their lives, their property, and their well-being." [22]

The concurring opinion of Mr. Justice White, in which McKenna joined, elaborated the theory he had enunciated in the *Downes* case. He announced early his view that Hawaii was not an integral part of the

---

21. *United States Statutes*, L, 750, quoted by the Court in *Hawaii* v. *Mankichi*, 190 U.S. 197, 209 (1903), my italics.

22. *Hawaii* v. *Mankichi*, 190 U.S. 217–18 (1903).

United States and that the Fifth and Sixth Amendments were not applicable because "neither the terms of the resolution nor the situation which arose from it served to incorporate the Hawaiian Islands into the United States and make them an integral part thereof . . . [and] the mere annexation not having affected the island . . . it is not open to question that the provisions of the Constitution as to grand and petit juries were not applicable to them. In other words, in my opinion the case is controlled by the decision in Downes v. Bidwell." Fundamental laws, as distinguished from all others, did extend to American insular possessions. "In other words, having by the resolution itself created a condition of things absolutely incompatible with immediate incorporation, Congress, mindful that the Constitution was the supreme law, and that its applicable provisions were operative at all times everywhere and upon every condition and person, declared that nothing in the joint resolution continuing the customs legislation and local law should be considered as perpetuating such laws, where they were inconsistent with those fundamental provisions of the Constitution, which were by their own force applicable to the territory with which Congress was dealing." [23]

The joint resolution, however, stated that only such municipal legislation should continue in force as did not violate the Constitution, no mention being made of fundamental provisions. While the majority opinion refused to apply the Fifth and Sixth Amendments because Congress did not propose such action, White argued that Congress' resolution extended only those provisions that would be ordinarily applicable. Evidently, he did not consider the two amendments fundamental. Justice Brown declined to say what would have been the case had there been no resolution or had the words "contrary to the Constitution" not been in the resolution of annexation. White tackled the problem squarely, holding that the two amendments did not extend to Hawaii without congressional action, but neither here nor anywhere else did he indicate what constitutional provisions were applicable or inapplicable.

Of course, White must have seen the gap in his reasoning: what fundamental rights did apply? The literal-minded Chief Justice Fuller pounced on this hiatus in the logic and dissented. "Nor were we informed what those fundamental rights are. This is not a question of na-

23. *Ibid.*, 219, 221.

tural rights, on the one hand, and artificial rights on the other, but of the fundamental rights of every person living under the sovereignty of the United States in respect to that Government." Justice Harlan remained as disturbed by the *Mankichi* judgment as he had been by *Downes*. "I dissent altogether," he stated, "from any such view. . . . If the principles now announced should become firmly established, . . . Thus will be engrafted upon our republican institutions, controlled by the supreme law of a written Constitution, a *colonial* system entirely foreign to the genius of our Government and abhorrent to the principles that underlie and pervade the Constitution." [24]

White's views were to prevail over those of Brown, Fuller, or Harlan. At last, in 1905, Justice White spoke for a majority of the Court, and his theories bore the imprint of acceptance by that tribunal. Section 171 of the Alaskan Code adopted by Congress provided that six persons should constitute a legal jury for trials for misdemeanors. A resident of the Territory of Alaska was convicted under this section, and his subsequent appeal to the Supreme Court alleged a violation of the Sixth Amendment. The single question to decide was whether Alaska was an integral part of the United States with the status of an incorporated territory. White stated: "This declaration, although somewhat changed in phraseology, is the equivalent, as pointed out in Downes v. Bidwell, of the formula, employed from the beginning to express the purpose to incorporate acquired territory into the United States—especially in the absence of other provisions showing an intention to the contrary." In 1911 Justice Day reiterated the Insular Doctrine. Pitney stated it three years later, and White again relied on it in 1920. Two years later the Supreme Court without dissent accepted his law of territories. [25]

Speaking of this line of cases, one writer dismissed them with the cavalier sentence that "they were of little significance in the history of the Supreme Court." [26] Presumably this opinion was founded on the as-

---

24. *Ibid.*, 226, 236, 237, 240, italics Justice Harlan's.

25. *Rassmussen* v. *United States*, 197 U.S. 516, 522 (1905); Justices Brown and Harlan concurred in separate opinions; *Dowdell* v. *United States*, 221 U.S. 325 (1911); *Ocampo* v. *United States*, 234 U.S. 91 (1914); *Public Utility Commissioners* v. *Ynchausti*, 251 U.S. 401 (1920); *Balzac* v. *Porto Rico*, 258 U.S. 298 (1922).

26. Ernest S. Bates, *The Story of the Supreme Court* (Indianapolis: Bobbs-Merrill, 1936), 228.

sumption that they did not involve issues that were continuously developing in public law since these cases were outside the general trends illustrated by the expansion or contraction of the commerce power or of the due process clause. This view must be rejected. The effect of the Insular Doctrine was significant because it removed from Congress some restrictive provisions of the Constitution in legislating for new territories unless such lands have been incorporated. This fact achieves a heightened importance if considered against the possibility, remote as it may now seem, that Congress once more may be confronted with the task of dealing with newly acquired lands and peoples.

White may or may not have gone beyond the bounds of the Constitution to find a source for his Insular Doctrine, but this issue is not material. Certainly he drew much from John Marshall. The parallel with Roman law is suggestive, although there is no definite evidence which can be cited. Many important doctrines of constitutional law, moreover, have been drawn from other legal systems and fitted into place with more orthodox doctrines. What is significant is that the Insular Doctrine permitted the Court to resolve the dilemma that faced it. It was politically impossible for the Supreme Court to rule that the United States could not retain the islands; it was inexpedient to extend to the new peoples immediately all the provisions of the Constitution, differing as much in cultural and political background as the inhabitants of these islands did from the rest of our people. Still, they could not be suspended indefinitely in a governmental vacuum. White provided an answer to these puzzling questions with his synthesis of legal theory and political reality.

XII

The Final Years

see Pollock

S oon after his appointment as an associate justice, Edward White, at the age of forty-eight, married Leita Montgomery Kent. His late marriage may have resulted partly from the death of his mother with whom he had lived since she had been widowed for the second time; it may also have been a consequence of his appointment to the Supreme Court, the achievement of his highest ambition. At any rate, the White household was a happy one, and Mrs. White was highly praised as a hostess, "that rare combination, a woman of the great world, and a gentle, thoughtful housekeeper." [1] White was both sentimental and tender in his family relationships, as illustrated by a contemporary story. An afternoon walk was a daily event with him, and when he returned from one of these excursions, he always brought Mrs. White a single rose. Vice-President Thomas R. Marshall told how one afternoon he accompanied White, and their route led them by a florist's shop where White purchased two roses, giving one to the vice-president with the suggestion that he present it to Mrs. Marshall. [2]

The home life of the Whites was quiet but not reclusive. In fact, they were happy for their home to become a center for Louisianians who were in Washington for one purpose or another. The meals, prepared and served in the tradition of New Orleans cooking, were famous and doubtless sufficient to help White maintain his large physique. Somewhat curiously, because it left White open to criticism of partiality, the Whites

1. *In Memoriam*, 149 La. vii, xii (1921).
2. Thomas R. Marshall, *Recollections* (Indianapolis: Bobbs-Merrill, 1925), 338.

179

entertained old friends from home who had come to Washington to argue cases before the Supreme Court. Although there is no evidence that anybody objected to this practice, there are indications that White had a highly developed sense of interpersonal relationships.

This sense was demonstrated by a change Chief Justice White made in the Court's conference procedure. He was well aware that conference discussions of some cases aroused hot words and some animosity. The inevitable result was that a few members of the Court, at least temporarily, were not on speaking terms with each other. White decided to try to heal old wounds and avoid new ones by introducing a new practice. Illustrating that commonplace conventionalities often lubricate the rough spots of everyday association, White, as chief justice, insisted on a formal daily greeting when the Court was in session. When all of the justices had donned their black robes, White would greet each one in the order of seniority with, "Good morning, Mr. Justice" and receive the reply, "Good morning, Mr. Chief Justice." [3] Visitors to the Court's robing room were instructed neither to speak to nor to make any recognition of the justices until White had arrived and completed this simple ceremony.

White's membership on the Supreme Court restricted his activities. It did not, however, prevent continuing interest in matters that had long held his attention. When he heard that the Georgetown University debating team would soon speak on the merits of an income tax, he wrote to Father Havens Richards. "Thinking it might aid our young men," he said, "I have directed the record clerk to make a collection of matters on file in the controversy now pending. If you think it best, please place these papers at the disposal of the gentlemen who are to participate in the Boston debate." Despite his interest in education generally and in his alma mater, Georgetown, in particular, the responsibilities of his judicial duties led him to decline the offer of a professorship in the Georgetown School of Law. Regretfully he wrote, "The work which is on me now is just as pressing as it can be and has left no time to do anything else. It is work of the most serious nature, involving the greatest responsibility. As a pure matter of duty, I do not feel that the time should be taken from it for any purpose whatsoever. You know, I hope, that the welfare of Georgetown in all its departments is a matter of concern to

3. Hampton L. Carson, "Memorial Tribute to Edward Douglass White," *Report of the American Bar Association*, XLVI (1921), 25, 28–29.

me, and your request would be complied with were it possible to do so."
In the same spirit he also declined appointment as a commissioner to
negotiate peace terms at the end of the Spanish-American War.[4]

As Associate Justice Edward White's influence widened, many people were attracted to this large and somewhat bearish man from Louisiana. He was particularly close to President William Howard Taft in political and economic attitudes, and Taft came to rely on White's judgment
of Court personnel as well as of some other problems. In 1909 the attorney general wrote the president:

Justice White drew me aside just before the Court opened this morning and told
me in the strictest confidence to be shared only with you that Justice Peckham's
illness is angina pectoris, and that the end may come at any time. He says that
the Justice has no idea that he is seriously ill. But, he said, "the condition of this
Court is such that any vacancy which occurs ought to be filled at the earliest
moment and I want the President to know of this impending event. So that he
may have all the more time to think of a successor." He again asked me not to
bring any important cause before the Court as at present constituted.[5]

Taft also called on White for advice on other appointments. In the summer of 1910 White wrote Charles Norton, Taft's secretary, offering to
consult with the president, then on vacation at Beverly, Massachusetts,
on the qualifications of an office-seeker whose name is not known. "The
President did me the honor [he wrote] to mention a name to me on the
17th day of last June and incidentally to suggest that if I could to obtain
some data throwing some light on the subject. Considerable search has
been made by me in the only way available, that is in respect, etc. [*sic*] I
was going to write my impressions but concluded not to pester the President on his vacation." Within a week White offered again to come to
Boston. From his summer home at Port Hope, Ontario, he wrote Norton
a third time. Alarmed about an associate, he related to the president's
secretary that "through the kindness of Preston [Gibson, a nephew] I was
whirled about rapidly and saw both Justices Holmes and [William H.]
Moody, the latter was heartbreaking." He reassured Taft on the negotia-

    4. Edward D. White to the Reverend J. Havens Richards, S.J., March 11, 1895, White
to Father Richards, May 18, 1895, both in the archives of Georgetown University; Edward D.
White to James Cardinal Gibbons, September 7, 1898, in the archives of the Archdiocese of
Baltimore, 96 N 2.
    5. George W. Wickersham to William H. Taft, October 13, 1909, in Taft Papers, Li-
brary of Congress.

tions for Canadian reciprocity, adding, "The more I think of the Iowa business, the less significant it seems. The President has the country back of him and will grow stronger and stronger as the days go by."[6]

White was not as close to President Woodrow Wilson, apparently, as he had been to Taft. When rumors began to circulate that President Wilson and the chief justice had viewed a certain moving picture privately and expressed approval of it, White wrote Joseph P. Tumulty, Wilson's secretary about it.

After talking with you the other day on the subject of the picture show, I wrote to the gentleman in New York and had an answer from him. In writing him I told him that I was so situated that if the rumors about my having sanctioned the show were continued that I might be under the obligation of denying them publicly and say, it might be, that I do not approve of the show and, therefore, if the owners were wise, they would stop the rumors. Incidentally in the letter I said: "I have reason to know—although not authoritatively so—that the name of the President also has been used and that he might be obliged to take the same course that I have indicated if the rumors were not stopped" . . . I don't send this letter to put upon the files, but only for your information.[7]

White's letter was evidently referring to Thomas Dixon's promotional activities on behalf of D. W. Griffith's motion picture *The Birth of a Nation*.

Griffith had based his film on Dixon's novel *The Clansman*, which was essentially racist in its view of the Ku Klux Klan's role in the Reconstruction South. A young organization, the National Association for the Advancement of Colored People, founded in 1910, was seeking to ban showings of Griffith's film. Dixon, who had an obvious financial interest at stake, went to President Wilson and, according to Dixon's unpublished autobiography, persuaded the president and his cabinet to view the picture in the East Room of the White House.[8] Dixon, who later recalled that Wilson offered fervent praise, then went to see White. He remembered telling the chief justice that he wanted the Supreme Court to see a movie which Wilson had seen and approved. White warmed to the conversation and said:

6. Edward D. White to Charles D. Norton, July 16, July 23, August 8, 1910, all in Taft Papers.

7. Edward D. White to Joseph P. Tumulty, April 5, 1915, in Woodrow Wilson Collection, Library of Congress, VI, Box 1051.

8. Eric F. Goldman, *Rendezvous with Destiny: A History of Modern American Reform* (New York: Knopf, 1952), 228. Goldman cites his source as Thomas Dixon, "Southern Horizons" (MS in the possession of Mrs. Madelyn Dixon), 432–35.

"You tell the true story of the Klan?"

"Yes—for the first time—" Dixon replied.

He removed his glasses, pushed his book aside and leaned back in his big swivel chair. His strong lips contracted and then relaxed into a curious smile. He leaned toward me and said in low tense tones:

"I was a member of the Klan, sir. . . . Through many a dark night, I walked my sentinel's beat through the ugliest streets of New Orleans with a rifle on my shoulder. . . . You've told the true story of that uprising of outraged manhood?"

"In a way I'm sure you'll approve."

"I'll be there!" he [White] firmly announced.[9]

Dixon then proceeded to counter the NAACP's attack on *The Birth of a Nation* with statements of alleged approval of the film by the president and the chief justice of the Supreme Court of the United States. Neither Wilson nor White subsequently made public any denial despite White's threat, and the NAACP continued its fight against the film.[10] A careful reading of White's letter of April 5, 1915, to Tumulty reveals only White's feeling that his position as chief justice might oblige him to deny publicly his approval of the film and to say, "it might be," that he did not approve of it. In the absence of any firm statement from White, evidence of his Klan membership must rest upon Dixon's credibility.

In a memorandum in 1916, Chief Justice White replied to an inquiry from President Wilson requesting information on the religious affiliations of the justices of the Court, the number of that tribunal's membership appointed by President Taft, and the breakdown of justices appointed from southern states. White replied and enclosed a letter from Postmaster General Albert Burleson to Joseph Tumulty that threw more light on the geographical distribution of Court appointments in the South as well as the appointments from the populous states of Illinois, New York, Ohio, and Pennsylvania. In March, 1917, President Wilson wrote White that "I hope it will be possible for you without personal inconvenience to administer the oath of office to me in the President's Room at the Capitol on Sunday noon next." Wilson added, "I am taking it for granted that I shall be there attending to the necessary last signatures, etc., of the ses-

---

9. Thomas Dixon, "Southern Horizons," 432–35, quoted in Goldman, *Rendezvous*, 228–29 (quoted by permission of Alfred A. Knopf, Inc.).

10. Goldman points out that within a year or so Griffith made "another technically brilliant movie and its name was *Intolerance*." *Rendezvous*, 229.

sion, and I would be very much complimented if you could yourself be there and do me this service."[11]

From 1910 until his death, discharge of the administrative duties of the Court deeply concerned White. The administrative function of the chief justice was no small task because of the continued increase in the Court's work, especially marked under Chief Justices Waite and Fuller. Some relief was found with the enactment of the Circuit Courts of Appeal Act in 1891. This act created a new level of intermediate courts of appeal for each of the districts and the District of Columbia, and lower court decisions were routed to the new courts of appeal, though "as a gesture to tradition, the Circuit Court duty of Supreme Court justices was not eliminated but little was expected of them."[12] The old circuit courts, retained under the 1891 legislation, were abolished in 1911 when their jurisdiction was merged with that of the district courts. This legislation, however, did not eliminate a statutory right of appeal from lower federal courts and state supreme courts to the Supreme Court. The discretionary principle was not extended until the Judiciary Act of 1925, which was a measure generated by the Taft Court. White did not seek additional reform in federal court procedure, but he did resolve to hear cases coming before the Court as quickly as possible and to refuse to hear actions which were plainly outside of the Court's jurisdiction.

As time passed new members came to the Court until at last only Harlan and White were left of the old-guard judges, the tobacco chewing justices. White remained the same and continued to send a page boy out to buy a few cheap cigars for his use.[13] At first the added work involved in the administration of the Court went well, so that, writing a few years after his accession to the chief justiceship, White could declare, "I am glad to say, so far as administrative progress is concerned, we are getting along fairly well in the Court and are at this time a good many numbers on the calendar ahead of the term last year. I hope before we

11. Woodrow Wilson to Edward D. White, March 2, 1917, in Woodrow Wilson Collection, VI, 76, Box 105.

12. C. Herman Pritchett, *The American Constitution* (New York: McGraw-Hill, 1977), 90.

13. The story was told by Thomas Cropley, a page boy at the time. Francis Biddle to Robert B. Highsaw, January 23, 1943.

reach the termination of this session the blockade on the docket may be relieved." [14]

The chief justice continued his practice of declining to speak publicly. On few occasions did he depart from this self-imposed rule. When asked by the president to attend and speak at the Columbus celebration of 1912, he replied, "I did [decline] because it seemed to me I would subject myself to much criticism if a departure was made as to that celebration from the rule which has caused me to refuse so many invitations of a like nature. . . . Whether the tradition as to the duty of the Chief Justice to abstain from public speaking is in all cases abstractly wise may be doubted, that as a personal rule, it is so, would seem not open to question." Taft was sympathetic to this declaration not to speak anywhere. Work came first, Taft said, but he must ask White. "That is what I am paid for." [15]

At this time White discovered that more and more of the cases that confronted the Court were administrative rather than legal in nature. The Sixteenth Amendment brought with it a host of actions. War claims between contractors and foreign governments were increasingly frequent, and the Court expended much of its time upon them. In the background the war in Europe disturbed White's peace of mind. While early in 1914 he could boast twenty-five more cases were off the docket than the year before, he later the same year exclaimed, "It is difficult for me to do any work, for I have constantly ringing in my ears the noise of the awful conflict along the Belgian and French border and the appalling thought of the splendid men who are there giving up their lives haunts me day and night. . . . I trust in God when the end comes it will come right." [16]

When, on the rainy but dramatic evening of April 2, 1917, President Wilson appeared before Congress and called for a declaration of war on imperial Germany, Chief Justice White "at those electric words . . . dropped his wide-brimmed hat as he clapped his hands together and rose to his feet. He stood there, tears running down his cheeks, while

14. Edward D. White to George W. Wickersham, November 14, 1914, in White Memorial, Thibodaux, Louisiana.
15. Edward D. White to William H. Taft, July 19, 1912, Taft to White, July 21, 1912, both in Taft Papers.
16. White to Wickersham, November 14, 1914, in White Memorial.

everyone else stood up as if at his signal." [17] With American entry into World War I came a flood of actions involving the validity of war measures. All in all, the burden was too heavy for the aging White, whose eyes had developed cataracts and who had "trained himself to recognize voices, and that if he heard a voice once he would recognize it and the speaker again." [18] The Court began to function badly, and in July, 1918, White wrote despairingly, "We pulled through the term and I'm trying to pack up and get away. God help us across the waters. It grows very dark to me, but . . . we will lick them yet."

Meanwhile, the chief justice, plodding away at the cases created by war statutes, remained an obstacle to the fulfillment of Taft's most cherished ambition, the position of chief justice. On March 26, 1921, Taft called on White. "He said nothing about retiring," Taft wrote to Gus J. Karger, a longtime political associate. "He spoke of his illness. He said he could still read, though he had a cataract, and he complained of the burden of work he had . . . and he bemoaned the critical nature of that work and the dangers that might arise from wrong decisions." [19]

Taft had not long to wait. The shadows were darkening. All members of the 1894 Court were gone, and only Justice Joseph McKenna, the senior associate justice, had been on the bench as far back as 1898. Gone also was Justice William H. Moody, who may have carried White's Insular Doctrine to adoption in the conference room, when with some hyperbole he reportedly drew a graphic picture of twelve savage chieftains, all good and true men, filing into the jury room, leaning their spears against the wall, and solemnly reviewing the evidence in a jury trial. The Court was different: some members like Oliver Wendell Holmes of fairly long tenure in 1921, others such as Louis D. Brandeis, John H. Clarke, and James C. McReynolds of more recent appointment. The economic predilections characteristic of the White Court would persist with the majority for a decade and a half, and then they too would go.

17. Francis Russell, *The Shadow of Blooming Grove: Warren G. Harding and His Times* (New York: McGraw-Hill, 1968), 282. It is a small matter, but several contemporary observers have commented on White's fondness for "funny little round hats."

18. Henry P. Dart, Sr., in Henry P. Dart, Sr., Harry M. Daugherty, William Howard Taft, and others, *Proceedings of the Bar and Officers of the Supreme Court of the United States in Memory of Edward Douglass White*, Washington, December 17, 1921, p. 31.

19. Quoted in Henry F. Pringle, *The Life and Times of Taft: A Biography* (2 vols.; New York: Farrar & Rinehart, 1939), II, 956.

On May 5, 1921, in a faltering voice, Edward White delivered his last opinion of the Court. As early as the winter of 1920–1921, physicians had advised the chief justice that an operation on his bladder was necessary. White postponed it because "he felt his presence at the court was imperative."[20] After his dissent in *Newberry* v. *United States*, he could no longer delay surgery and entered Garfield Hospital. On May 18 Justice Holmes wrote Frederick Pollock:

You speak of the last phase of *Virginia* v. *West Virginia*. I have never greatly admired the Chief's mode of writing—for various reasons that I won't go into—but the poor old boy is the object of nothing but sympathy just now. He has stuck to his work (I think unwisely) in the face of illness—cataracts on his eyes that have blinded one of them, and very great deafness. But he has gone to the hospital and was to have an operation performed at 11:30 a.m. today, I was told (not on his eyes). I hope that it is not serious but feel no assurance till I hear the result. His infirmities have made the work harder for others, and I imagine that he has suffered much more than he has told.[21]

The operation was not a success, and he did not rally from it.[22] On May 19, 1921, the ninth chief justice of the Supreme Court of the United States, Edward Douglass White, died.

20. New York *Times*, May 19, 1921.
21. Oliver Wendell Holmes to Sir Frederick Pollock, May 18, 1921, in Mark DeWolfe Howe (ed.), *Holmes-Pollock Letters: The Correspondence of Mr. Justice Holmes and Sir Frederick Pollock 1874–1932* (2 vols.; Cambridge: Harvard University Press, 1941), II, 68.
22. New York *Times*, May 19, 20, 1921, Washington *Evening Star*, May 19, 1921, Chicago *Daily Tribune*, May 19, 1921.

EPILOGUE

Soon after the death of Edward Douglass White in 1921, William Howard Taft at last ascended to the office of chief justice, President Warren G. Harding's nomination of Taft on June 30, 1921, receiving confirmation the same day. The next year Harding appointed George Sutherland of Utah and Pierce Butler of Minnesota to serve as associate justices. Together with two of White's colleagues, Justices Willis Van Devanter and James C. McReynolds, Sutherland and Butler comprised a staunchly conservative wing of the Court. They would express such a strong view of the political and economic world as they perceived it that later, when joined on occasion by Justice Owen J. Roberts or Chief Justice Charles Evans Hughes, they would negate much of the Great Depression-inspired New Deal and precipitate the constitutional revolution of 1937.

Edward Douglass White provided a much more effective defense of the conservative faith than did his successors on the bench. True, White espoused a basically static conception of federalism, championing the development of dual federalism of the commerce and taxing powers. True, White was more interested in the preservation of the economic freedoms implicit in social Darwinism than in human freedoms. True, his rule of reason in the *Anti-Trust* cases did much to undercut the effectiveness of antimonopoly legislation. True, his near veneration for precedent produced an approach in which there was no emotional concern for the impact of his decisions.

He possessed, however, qualities of mind and character and training that, by moderating his own conservatism, made conservatism more meaningful. Although Justice Oliver Wendell Holmes found that his writing "left much to be desired," Holmes believed that his thinking was profound, especially in judicial legislation and concluded that he was "a first rate man." White was both politic and pragmatic, traits evident in his patient handling of the West Virginia–Virginia controversy, his opinion in the *Adamson Act* case, which avoided a crippling nationwide strike of railroad workers under approaching wartime conditions, and his Insular Doctrine. Unlike the majority of the Court in the 1920s and 1930s, White realized the perilousness of always construing the Constitution as an obstacle to social progress. His perception of the Supreme Court's role helped to remove that tribunal, at least temporarily, from the vortex of partisan politics.

White was conservative in his constitutional philosophy, but more wisely so than many of his successors on the bench. He did not seek always to cast the Constitution in a rigidly conservative mold and, indeed, would have opposed such an effort. Instead, perceiving the order and stability inherent in the Anglo-American system of law over the centuries, he sought to preserve it. His domination of the Court was great and his contributions to American public law significant. His approach to his positions as associate justice and then chief justice, as well as his devotion to the Constitution as he understood it, marks him as a jurist to be long remembered in the history of the Supreme Court of the United States.

APPENDIX A
The Strange Case of Tulane University

C hapter III of this study makes reference to White's role in the disposition of the gift of Paul Tulane for higher education in Louisiana. There is more to this study both before and after the
gift than the chronology of historical narration conveniently permits.

The University of Louisiana was established as a public institution in
New Orleans in 1847. In 1881 Mr. Tulane announced that he would make
a gift of a then substantial sum of money for higher education. After
Tulane rejected the first recommendation of his board of administrators,
of whom Edward Douglass White was one, that the donations be made
to the University of Louisiana, the Louisiana Legislature through Act
43 of 1884 established the Tulane University of Louisiana with a self-
perpetuating board and granted tax exemptions to the institution. This
institution then received the Tulane gift. In 1886 the Supreme Court of
Louisiana stated in a unanimous opinion, "It is conceded that Act 43 did
not, of itself, create a new institution, or convert the old state university
into a private school. The University of Louisiana continued, operating
in the same buildings, on state land, enjoying the same rights and fran-
chises. Neither the substantial private support it now received nor its
new governing body changed the character of the institution as a public
college." [1] Two years later a constitutional amendment ratifying Act 43
was adopted which purportedly converted the institution into a private
university. There the matter rested for nearly three-quarters of a century.

1. Quoted in *Guillory* v. *Administrators of Tulane University of Louisiana*, 203 Fed. Supp.
855, 861 (1962).

In 1962 a suit was brought against Tulane University officials charging racial discrimination in the administration of admission policies. Tulane University argued that the university was a private institution. Federal District Judge J. Skelly Wright rejected this argument. Of it Judge Wright said, "This is patent nonsense. Tulane was no different after the electors had recorded their vote. . . . The fact is that as late as 1906, after the university had entirely vacated the old buildings, the Tulane Board, without dissent, so far as appears, considered their school a state institution." Moreover, the then president of the university's governing board, a former member of the Supreme Court of Louisiana, indicated that Tulane University was the University of Louisiana as created in 1847. Judge Wright noted also that as late as 1944 the Louisiana Legislature instructed Tulane to grant scholarships without distinction as to sex.[2]

Judge Wright stated that Tulane University could claim to be private only on the basis of local law and private enterprise, but that "indeed, the University still operated under a special legislative franchise; it continues to enjoy a very substantial state subsidy in the form of unique tax exemptions for commercially leased property; it still receives considerable revenues from lands which the state has not altogether relinquished; and three public officials remain on the governing board."[3] On the basis of these facts Judge Wright ordered the university to admit blacks.

The story does not end at that point. Later in 1962 Judge Frank B. Ellis, who had succeeded Judge Wright on the district court bench, issued a clarification order which set aside the judgment of Judge Wright.[4] He found the Tulane Educational Fund to be a private corporation. "In summary," he stated, "it is the conclusion of this court that the state action or involvement in the affairs of the Tulane Board is not so significant that it may fairly be said that the actions of the Tulane Board are the actions of the State of Louisiana."[5] Tulane University thus retained the private status which it claimed.

2. *Ibid.*, 855–64, 862, 863.
3. *Ibid.*, 863–64.
4. *Guillory* v. *Administrators of Tulane Educational Fund*, 207 Fed. Supp. 554–56 (1962).
5. *Guillory* v. *Administrators of Tulane University of Louisiana*, 212 Fed. Supp. 674, 687 (1962).

APPENDIX B
Cases in Which White Rendered Opinions in the Supreme Court of Louisiana

Louisiana Annotated Reports: 1879–1880

APPENDIX C
Cases Involving Constitutional Issues in Which White Rendered Opinions in the Supreme Court of the United States

---

CIVIL RIGHTS

Carlesi v. New York, 233 U.S. 51 (1914)
Glickstein v. United States, 222 U.S. 139 (1911)
Hawaii v. Mankichi, 190 U.S. 197 (1903)
Hendricks v. United States, 223 U.S. 178 (1912)
Iowa Central Ry. Co. v. Iowa, 160 U.S. 389 (1896)
Kahn v. Anderson, 255 U.S. 1 (1921)
Lewis Publishing Co. v. Morgan, 229 U.S. 288 (1913)
Lovato v. New Mexico, 242 U.S. 199 (1916)
Minneapolis & St. Louis R.R. Co. v. Bombolis, 241 U.S. 211 (1916)
Nobles v. Georgia, 168 U.S. 398 (1897)
Rassmussen v. United States, 197 U.S. 516 (1905)
Rosen v. United States, 161 U.S. 29 (1896)
St. Louis & San Francisco R.R. Co. v. Brown, 241 U.S. 223 (1916)
Talton v. Mayes, 163 U.S. 376 (1896)
Toledo Newspaper Co. v. United States, 247 U.S. 402 (1918)
United States v. Cohen Grocery Co., 255 U.S. 81 (1921), and subsequent cases on the
    Lever Act
Weems v. United States, 217 U.S. 349 (1910)

COMMERCE CLAUSE

Adams Express Co. v. Kentucky, 166 U.S. 171 (1897)
Adams Express Co. v. Ohio State Auditor, 165 U.S. 194 (1897), rehearing at 166 U.S.
    185 (1897)
American Express Co. v. Iowa, 196 U.S. 133 (1905)
American Steel & Wire Co. v. Speed, 192 U.S. 500 (1904)
Armour & Co. v. Virginia, 246 U.S. 1 (1918)
Austin v. Tennessee, 179 U.S. 343 (1900)

Ayer & Lord Tie Co. v. *Kentucky,* 202 U.S. 409 (1906)

Baltimore and Ohio R.R. Co. v. *United States ex rel. Pitcairn Coal Co.,* 215 U.S. 481 (1910)

Browning v. *City of Waycross,* 233 U.S. 16 (1914)

Buttfield v. *Stranahan,* 192 U.S. 470 (1904)

Capital City Dairy Co. v. *Ohio,* 183 U.S. 238 (1902)

Chicago, Rock Island & Pacific Ry. Co. v. *Hardwick Elevator,* 226 U.S. 426 (1913)

Cincinnati, Hamilton & Dayton Ry. Co. v. *Interstate Commerce Commission,* 206 U.S. 142 (1907)

Clark Distilling Co. v. *Western Maryland Ry. Co.,* 242 U.S. 311 (1917)

Compagnie Francaise, etc. v. *Louisiana Board of Health,* 186 U.S. 380 (1902)

Cook v. *Marshall County,* 196 U.S. 261 (1905)

Crossman v. *Lurman,* 192 U.S. 189 (1904)

Darnell & Son v. *Memphis,* 208 U.S. 113 (1908)

DeBary & Co. v. *Louisiana,* 227 U.S. 108 (1913)

Delamater v. *South Dakota,* 205 U.S. 93 (1907)

East Tennessee, Virginia, & Georgia Ry. Co. v. *Interstate Commerce Commission,* 181 U.S. 1 (1901)

Employers' Liability cases, 207 U.S. 463 (1908)

Florida East Coast Ry. Co. v. *United States,* 234 U.S. 167 (1914)

Geer v. *Connecticut,* 161 U.S. 519 (1896)

Henderson Bridge Co. v. *Kentucky,* 166 U.S. 150 (1897)

Hennington v. *Georgia,* 163 U.S. 299 (1896)

Heyman v. *Hays,* 236 U.S. 178 (1915)

Heyman v. *Southern Ry. Co.,* 203 U.S. 270 (1906)

Hooper v. *State of California,* 155 U.S. 648 (1895)

Intermountain Rate cases, 234 U.S. 476 (1914)

Interstate Commerce Commission v. *Clyde Steamship Co.,* 181 U.S. 29 (1901)

Interstate Commerce Commission v. *Delaware, Lackawanna & Western R.R. Co.,* 220 U.S. 235 (1911)

Lake Shore & Michigan Southern Ry. Co. v. *Ohio,* 173 U.S. 285 (1899)

Looney v. *Crane Co.,* 245 U.S. 178 (1917)

Louisville & Nashville Ry. Co. v. *Behlmer,* 175 U.S. 648 (1900)

McNeill v. *Southern Ry. Co.,* 202 U.S. 543 (1906)

Missouri Pacific Ry. Co. v. *Castle,* 224 U.S. 541 (1912)

Missouri Pacific Ry. Co. v. *Kansas Railroad Commissioners,* 216 U.S. 262 (1910)

New York Central & Hudson River Co. v. *Board etc. of County of Hudson,* 227 U.S. 248 (1913)

New York Life Insurance Co. v. *Head,* 234 U.S. 149 (1914)

New York, New Haven & Hartford Ry. Co. v. *Interstate Commerce Commission,* 200 U.S. 361 (1906)

Northern Pacific Ry. Co. v. *Washington ex rel. Atkinson,* 222 U.S. 370 (1912)

Northern Securities Co. v. *United States,* 193 U.S. 197 (1904)

Olsen v. *Smith,* 195 U.S. 332 (1904)

Pabst Brewing Co. v. *Crenshaw*, 198 U.S. 17 (1905)
Pipe Line cases, 234 U.S. 548 (1914)
Postal Telegraph Cable Co. v. *Warren-Godwin Lumber Co.*, 251 U.S. 27 (1919)
Pullman Co. v. *Kansas*, 216 U.S. 56 (1910)
Rhodes v. *Iowa*, 170 U.S. 412 (1898)
Rosenburger v. *Pacific Express Co.*, 241 U.S. 48 (1916)
St. Clair County v. *Interstate Sand & Car Transfer Co.*, 192 U.S. 454 (1904)
St. Louis, Iron Mountain & Southern Ry. Co. v. *Edwards*, 227 U.S. 265 (1913)
St. Louis Southeastern Ry. Co. v. *Arkansas*, 217 U.S. 136 (1910)
Southern Pacific Co. v. *Interstate Commerce Commission*, 219 U.S. 433 (1911)
Standard Oil Company v. *United States*, 221 U.S. 1 (1911)
Stewart v. *Michigan*, 232 U.S. 665 (1914)
Texas & Pacific Ry. Co. v. *Abilene Cotton Oil Co.*, 204 U.S. 426 (1907)
Texas & Pacific Ry. Co. v. *American Tie and Lumber Co.*, 234 U.S. 138 (1914)
Texas and Pacific Ry. Co. v. *Cisco Oil Mill*, 204 U.S. 449 (1907)
Thompson v. *Darden*, 198 U.S. 310 (1905)
United States v. *American Tobacco Company*, 221 U.S. 106 (1911)
United States v. *Delaware & Hudson Co.*, 213 U.S. 366 (1909)
United States v. *Ferger (No. 1)*, 250 U.S. 199 (1919) *(No. 2)*, 250 U.S. 207 (1919)
United States v. *Gudger*, 249 U.S. 373 (1919)
United States v. *Hamburg-American Co.*, 239 U.S. 466 (1916)
United States v. *Louisville & Nashville Ry. Co.*, 235 U.S. 314 (1914)
United States v. *Trans-Missouri Freight Association*, 166 U.S. 290 (1897)
Vance v. *Vandercook Co.*, 170 U.S. 438 (1898)
Western Union Telegraph Co. v. *Boegli*, 251 U.S. 315 (1920)
Western Union Telegraph Co. v. *Kansas ex rel. Coleman*, 216 U.S. 1 (1910)
Wilder Manufacturing Co. v. *Corn Products Co.*, 236 U.S. 165 (1915)
Wilson v. *New*, 243 U.S. 332 (1917)
Yazoo & Mississippi Valley Ry. Co. v. *Greenwood Grocery Co.*, 227 U.S. 1 (1913)
York Manufacturing Co. v. *Colley*, 247 U.S. 21 (1918)

DUE PROCESS—FIFTH AMENDMENT

Billings v. *United States*, 232 U.S. 261 (1914), 232 U.S. 289 (1914)
Buttfield v. *Stranahan*, 192 U.S. 470 (1904)
Clark Distilling Co. v. *Western Maryland Ry. Co.*, 242 U.S. 311 (1917)
Glickstein v. *United States*, 222 U.S. 139 (1911)
Hawaii v. *Mankichi*, 190 U.S. 197 (1903)
Hovey v. *Elliott*, 167 U.S. 409 (1897)
Pierce v. *United States*, 232 U.S. 290 (1914), *(No. 2)* at 232 U.S. 292 (1914)
Pipe Line cases, 234 U.S. 548 (1914)
Portsmouth Harbor Land and Hotel Co. v. *United States*, 250 U.S. 1 (1919)
Rassmussen v. *United States*, 197 U.S. 516 (1905)
Rosen v. *United States*, 161 U.S. 29 (1896)
Sui v. *McCoy*, 239 U.S. 139 (1915)

Talton v. *Mayes*, 163 U.S. 376 (1896)
United States v. *Bennett*, 232 U.S. 299 (1914)
United States v. *Cohen Grocery Co.*, 255 U.S. 81 (1921)
United States v. *Delaware & Hudson Co.*, 213 U.S. 366 (1909)
United States v. *Goelet*, 232 U.S. 293 (1914)
United States v. *Lynah*, 188 U.S. 445 (1903)
Wilson v. *New*, 243 U.S. 332 (1917)

DUE PROCESS AND EQUAL PROTECTION—FOURTEENTH AMENDMENT

Adams Express Co. v. *Kentucky*, 166 U.S. 171 (1897)
Adams Express Co. v. *Ohio State Auditor*, 165 U.S. 194 (1897), rehearing at 166 U.S.
    185 (1897)
Aikens v. *Wisconsin*, 195 U.S. 194 (1904)
American Land Co. v. *Zeiss*, 219 U.S. 47 (1911)
Armour & Co. v. *Virginia*, 246 U.S. 1 (1918)
Atlantic Coast Line R.R. Co. v. *Glenn*, 239 U.S. 388 (1915)
Atlantic Coast Line R.R. Co. v. *North Carolina Corporation Commission*, 206 U.S. 1
    (1907)
Baccus v. *Louisiana*, 232 U.S. 334 (1914)
Bowersock v. *Smith*, 243 U.S. 29 (1917)
Campbell v. *California*, 200 U.S. 87 (1906)
Castillo v. *McConnico*, 168 U.S. 674 (1898)
Central Loan & Trust Co. v. *Campbell Commission Co.*, 173 U.S. 84 (1899)
Chicago, Milwaukee & St. Paul Ry. Co. v. *Kennedy*, 232 U.S. 626 (1914)
Cincinnati Street Ry. Co. v. *Snell*, 193 U.S. 30 (1904)
Corry v. *Baltimore*, 196 U.S. 466 (1905)
Cunnius v. *Reading School District*, 198 U.S. 458 (1905)
Davis v. *Massachusetts*, 167 U.S. 43 (1897)
Delmar Jockey Club v. *Missouri*, 210 U.S. 324 (1908)
Easterling Lumber Co. v. *Pierce*, 235 U.S. 380 (1914)
Farmers & Merchants Insurance Co. v. *Dobney*, 189 U.S. 301 (1903)
Gatewood v. *North Carolina*, 203 U.S. 531 (1906)
Great Northern Ry. Co. v. *Cahill*, 253 U.S. 71 (1920)
Griffith v. *Connecticut*, 218 U.S. 563 (1910)
Hammond Packing Co. v. *Arkansas*, 212 U.S. 322 (1909)
Home Telephone & Telegraph Co. v. *Los Angeles*, 227 U.S. 278 (1913)
Jones v. *Brim*, 165 U.S. 180 (1897)
Kidd, Dater & Price Co. v. *Musselman Grocery Co.*, 217 U.S. 461 (1910)
King v. *Cross*, 175 U.S. 396 (1899)
Lombard v. *West Chicago Park Commission*, 181 U.S. 33 (1901)
Lemieux v. *Young*, 211 U.S. 489 (1909)
Looney v. *Crane Co.*, 245 U.S. 178 (1917)
Louisville & Nashville R.R. Co. v. *Melton*, 218 U.S. 36 (1910)
Louisville & Nashville R.R. Co. v. *Schmidt*, 177 U.S. 230 (1900)

McDonald v. *Oregon Railroad & Navigation Co.*, 233 U.S. 665 (1914)
Mason v. *Missouri*, 179 U.S. 328 (1900)
Missouri Pacific Ry. Co. v. *Castle*, 224 U.S. 541 (1912)
Missouri Pacific Ry. Co. v. *Larabee*, 234 U.S. 459 (1914)
Moffitt v. *Kelly*, 218 U.S. 400 (1910)
O'Callahan v. *O'Brien*, 199 U.S. 89 (1905)
Ohio Oil Co. v. *Indiana (No. 1)*, 177 U.S. 190 (1900)
Pacific Gas & E. Co. v. *Police Court*, 251 U.S. 22 (1919)
Red "C" Oil Co. v. *North Carolina*, 222 U.S. 380 (1912)
Riverside Cotton Mills v. *Menefee*, 237 U.S. 189 (1915)
San Antonio v. *San Antonio Public Service Corp.*, 255 U.S. 547 (1921)
Simon v. *Craft*, 182 U.S. 427 (1901)
Southern Iowa Electric Co. v. *Chariton, Iowa*, 255 U.S. 539 (1921)
Wyandotte County Gas Co. v. *Kansas*, 231 U.S. 622 (1914)
Zayas v. *Lathrop, Luce & Co.*, 231 U.S. 171 (1913)

OTHER POWERS OF THE FEDERAL GOVERNMENT

Power with respect to territories

De Lima v. *Bidwell*, 182 U.S. 1 (1901)
Dooley v. *United States*, 182 U.S. 222 (1901)
Dooley v. *United States*, 183 U.S. 151 (1901)
Downes v. *Bidwell*, 182 U.S. 244 (1901)
Hawaii v. *Mankichi*, 190 U.S. 197 (1903)
Maricopa & Phoenix Ry. Co. v. *Territory of Arizona*, 156 U.S. 347 (1895)
Public Utility Commissioners v. *Ynchausti*, 251 U.S. 401 (1920)
Rassmussen v. *United States*, 197 U.S. 516 (1905)

War power

American Express Co. v. *Michigan*, 177 U.S. 404 (1900)
Crawford v. *Hubbell*, 177 U.S. 419 (1900)
Dakota Central Telephone Co. v. *South Dakota* and following cases beginning at 250 U.S. 163 (1919)
Northern Pacific Ry. Co. v. *North Dakota ex rel Langer*, 250 U.S. 135 (1919)
Selective Draft Law cases, 245 U.S. 366 (1918)

Power of Congress over primary elections

Newberry v. *United States*, 256 U.S. 232 (1921)

Power of federal courts

Ex Parte Hudgings, 249 U.S. 378 (1919)
Marshall v. *Gordon*, 243 U.S. 521 (1917)
Missouri Pacific Ry. Co. v. *Kansas*, 248 U.S. 276 (1919)
National Prohibition cases, 253 U.S. 350 (1920)
Pacific Telephone and Telegraph Co. v. *Oregon*, 223 U.S. 118 (1912)
Pearcy v. *Stranahan*, 205 U.S. 257 (1907)

Virginia v. *West Virginia*, 206 U.S. 290 (1907), 209 U.S. 514 (1908), 220 U.S. 1 (1911),
    222 U.S. 17 (1911), 231 U.S. 89 (1913), 234 U.S. 117 (1914), 238 U.S. 202 (1915),
    241 U.S. 531 (1916), 246 U.S. 565 (1918)
United States v. *Wheeler*, 254 U.S. 281 (1920)
Williamson v. *United States*, 207 U.S. 425 (1908)

OTHER POWERS OF STATE GOVERNMENTS

Abby Dodge, The, 223 U.S. 166 (1912)
Baltzer v. *North Carolina*, 161 U.S. 240 (1896)
Board of Liquidation of City Debt v. *Louisiana*, 179 U.S. 622 (1901)
Chicago Theological Seminary v. *Illinois*, 188 U.S. 602 (1903)
City of Cleveland v. *Cleveland City Ry. Co.*, 194 U.S. 517 (1904)
Consumers' Coal Co. v. *Hatch*, 224 U.S. 148 (1912)
Duluth & Iron Range R.R. Co. v. *St. Louis County*, 179 U.S. 302 (1900)
Grand Rapids & Indiana R. Co. v. *Osborn*, 193 U.S. 17 (1904)
Griffith v. *Connecticut*, 218 U.S. 563 (1910)
Guinn v. *United States*, 238 U.S. 347 (1915)
Gunter v. *Atlantic Coast R.R. Co.*, 200 U.S. 273 (1906)
Innes v. *Tobin*, 240 U.S. 127 (1916)
Kentucky Bank cases, 173 U.S. 636, 662, 663, 664 (1899), 174 U.S. 409, 412, 429, 432,
    435, 436, 438, 439, 799, 799, 800, 800, (1899)
Myers v. *Anderson*, 238 U.S. 368 (1915)
Orr v. *Allen*, 248 U.S. 35 (1918)
Pennsylvania Hospital v. *Philadelphia*, 245 U.S. 20 (1917)
St. Paul Gaslight Co. v. *St. Paul*, 181 U.S. 142 (1901)
Stearns v. *Minnesota*, 179 U.S. 223 (1900)
United States v. *Wheeler*, 254 U.S. 281 (1920)
Weber v. *Freed*, 239 U.S. 325 (1915)

FEDERAL TAXING POWER

Billings v. *United States*, 232 U.S. 261 (1914)
Brushaber v. *Union Pacific R.R. Co.*, 240 U.S. 1 (1916)
Dodge v. *Osborn*, 240 U.S. 118 (1916)
Downes v. *Bidwell*, 182 U.S. 244 (1901)
Knowlton v. *Moore*, 178 U.S. 41 (1900)
McCray v. *United States*, 195 U.S. 27 (1904)
Pollock v. *Farmers' Loan and Trust Co.*, 157 U.S. 429 (1895), rehearing at 158 U.S.
    601 (1895)
Rainey v. *United States*, 232 U.S. 310 (1914)
Snyder v. *Bettman*, 190 U.S. 249 (1903)
South Carolina v. *United States*, 199 U.S. 437 (1905)
Stanton v. *Baltic Mining Co.*, 240 U.S. 103 (1916)
United States v. *Bennett*, 232 U.S. 299 (1914)
United States v. *Doremus*, 249 U.S. 86 (1919)

SELECTED BIBLIOGRAPHY

OFFICIAL DOCUMENTS AND PUBLICATIONS

Dart, Henry P., Sr., Harry M. Daugherty, William Howard Taft, and others, *Proceedings of the Bar and Officers of the Supreme Court of the United States in Memory of Edward Douglass White*. Washington, December 17, 1921.

Louisiana Annual Reports (La. Ann.), Vols. 31–32, 1879–80.

Louisiana Reports (La.), Vol. 141, 1921.

United States Congress. *Congressional Record*

51st Congress, 1st Session, 1890, XXI, 8698–8721, 19150, 10085.

52nd Congress, 2nd Session, 1892, XXIII–XXIV, 5788, 6513–6582.

53rd Congress, 2nd Session, 1894, XXVI, 1773.

―――. *Senate Miscellaneous Documents*, 52nd Congress, 2nd Session, 1893, 40.

United States Supreme Court Reports (U.S.), Vols. 154–256, 1894–1921.

LETTERS AND PUBLISHED CORRESPONDENCE

Archives of the Archdiocese of Baltimore

White, Edward D., to James Cardinal Gibbons, June 25, 1888, April 17, 1889, October 18, 1893, March 10, 1894, September 7, 1898.

Archives of Georgetown University

White, Edward D., to Havens Richards, March 20, April 19, 1893, March 9, 1894, May 18, 1895.

Howe, Mark DeWolfe (ed.), *Holmes-Pollock Letters: The Correspondence of Mr. Justice Holmes and Sir Frederick Pollock, 1874–1932*. 2 vols.; Cambridge: Harvard University Press, 1941. Holmes, Oliver W., to Sir Frederick Pollock, September 24, 1910, May 18, 1921.

Library of Congress, Theodore Roosevelt Papers

White, Edward D., to Theodore Roosevelt, May 10, December 20, 1910.

White, Edward D., to Elihu Root, June 24, 1912.

―――, William H. Taft Papers

White, Edward D., to Charles D. Norton, July 16, 23, August 8, 1910.
White, Edward D., to William H. Taft, November 28, December 12, 1910, February 21, 1911, July 12, 21, 1912, October 13, 14, 1914.
Wickersham, George W., to William H. Taft, October 13, 1910.
———, Woodrow Wilson Collection
White, Edward D., to Joseph P. Tumulty, April 5, August 3, 1915.
Wilson, Woodrow, to Edward D. White, June 17, 1916, March 2, 1917.
Other Correspondence
Biddle, Francis, to the author, January 23, 1943.
Davis, John W., to the author, August 27, 1942.
McKenney, Frederick D., to the author, July 3, 1942.

SECONDARY SOURCES
Books

Abernethy, Thomas P. *From Frontier to Plantation in Tennessee: A Study in Frontier Democracy*. Chapel Hill: University of North Carolina Press, 1932.
Bates, Ernest S. *The Story of the Supreme Court*. Indianapolis: Bobbs-Merrill, 1936.
Boorstin, Daniel J. *The Americans: The Democratic Experience*. New York: Random House, 1973.
Buck, Solon J. *The Agrarian Crusade: A Chronicle of the Farmers in Politics*. New Haven: Yale University Press, 1920.
Cardozo, Benjamin N. *The Nature of the Judicial Process*. New Haven: Yale University Press, 1921.
Corwin, Edward S. *The Commerce Power Versus States Rights*. Princeton: Princeton University Press, 1937.
———. *Court over Constitution: A Study of Judicial Review as an Instrument of Popular Government*. Princeton: Princeton University Press, 1938.
———. *The Twilight of the Supreme Court*. New Haven: Yale University Press, 1934.
Dabney, Thomas Ewing. *One Hundred Great Years: The Story of the Times-Picayune from Its Founding to 1940*. Baton Rouge: Louisiana State University Press, 1944.
Ewing, Cortez A. M. *The Judges of the Supreme Court, 1789–1937: A Study of Their Qualifications*. Minneapolis: University of Minnesota Press, 1938.
Ezell, John Samuel. *Fortune's Merry Wheel: The Lottery in America*. Cambridge: Harvard University Press, 1960.
Fortier, Alcée. *A History of Louisiana*. 4 vols.; New York: Goupil, 1904.
Frankfurter, Felix. *Mr. Justice Holmes and the Supreme Court*. Cambridge: Harvard University Press, 1938.
George, Henry. *Social Problems*. New York: Schalkenbach Foundation, 1939.
Goldman, Eric F. *Rendezvous with Destiny: A History of Modern American Reform*. New York: Knopf, 1952.
Hicks, John D. *The Populist Revolt: A History of the Farmers' Alliance and the People's Party*. Minneapolis: University of Minnesota Press, 1933.

Homo, Leon. *Primitive Italy and the Beginnings of Roman Imperialism*. London: Paul-Trench-Trubner, 1926.

Jackson, Robert H. *The Struggle for Judicial Supremacy: A Study of a Crisis in American Power Politics*. New York: Knopf, 1941.

Lerner, Max. *America as a Civilization: Life and Thought in the United States*. New York: Simon & Schuster, 1957.

Lloyd, Henry D. *Wealth Against Commonwealth*. New York: Harper, 1894.

Lonn, Ella. *Reconstruction in Louisiana After 1868*. New York: Putnam, 1918.

McCloskey, Robert G. *American Conservatism in the Age of Enterprise: A Study of William Graham Sumner, Stephen J. Field, and Andrew Carnegie*. Cambridge: Harvard University Press, 1951.

McElroy, Robert. *Grover Cleveland: The Man and the Statesman*. 2 vols.; New York: Harper, 1923. (An authorized biography.)

Mott, Rodney L. *Due Process of Law: A Historical and Analytical Treatise of the Principles and Methods Followed by the Courts in the Application of the Concept of the "Law of the Land."* Indianapolis: Bobbs-Merrill, 1926.

Nevins, Allan. *Grover Cleveland: A Study in Courage*. New York: Dodd, Mead, 1932.

Perry, Bliss. *And Gladly Teach: Reminiscences*. Boston: Houghton Mifflin, 1935.

Powell, Thomas R. *Essays on the Law and Practice of Governmental Administration*. Baltimore: Johns Hopkins Press, 1935.

Pringle, Henry F. *The Life and Times of Taft: A Biography*. 2 vols.; New York: Farrar & Rinehart, 1939.

Russell, Francis. *The Shadow of Blooming Grove: Warren G. Harding and His Times*. New York: McGraw-Hill, 1968.

Taylor, Joe Gray. *Louisiana Reconstructed, 1863–1877*. Baton Rouge: Louisiana State University Press, 1974.

Twiss, Benjamin R. *Lawyers and the Constitution: How Laissez Faire Came to the Supreme Court*. Princeton: Princeton University Press, 1942.

Warmoth, Henry C. *War, Politics and Reconstruction: Stormy Days in Louisiana*. New York: Macmillan, 1930.

Warren, Charles. *The Supreme Court in United States History*. 3 vols.; Boston: Little, Brown, 1922.

Wright, Benjamin F. *The Growth of American Constitutional Law*. Boston: Houghton Mifflin, 1942.

Articles

Legal Articles

Carson, Hampton L. "Memorial Tribute to Edward Douglass White." *Reports of the American Bar Association*, XLVI (1921), 25–30.

Cassidy, Lewis C. "An Evaluation of Chief Justice White." *Mississippi Law Journal*, X (1938), 136–53.

Chafee, Zechariah, Jr., "Freedom of Speech in Wartime." *Harvard Law Review*, XXXII (1919), 932–68.

"Chief Justice White and His Decisions." *Reports of Louisiana Bar Association*, XXIV (1923), 151–65.

Corwin, Edward S. "Due Process of Law Before the Civil War." *Harvard Law Review*, XXIV (1911), 460–79.

Coudert, Frederic R. "The Evolution of the Doctrine of Territorial Incorporation." *Columbia Law Review*, XXVI (1926), 823–50.

Cushman, Robert E. "The National Police Power Under the Commerce Clause of the Constitution." *Minnesota Law Review*, III (1919), 289–319, 381–412, 452–83.

———. "The Social and Economic Interpretation of the Fourteenth Amendment." *Michigan Law Review*, XX (1922), 737–64.

Dart, Henry P. "The Tribute of a Friend." *Loyola Law Journal*, VII (1926), 74–87.

"Edward Douglass White Memorial Issue." *Loyola Law Journal*, VII (1926).

Fegin, Hugh E. "Edward Douglass White, Jurist and Statesman." *Georgetown Law Journal*, XIV (1925), 1–21, and XV (1926), 148–68.

Frankfurter, Felix. "The Supreme Court in the Mirror of Justices." *University of Pennsylvania Law Review*, CV (1957), 781–96.

Graham, Howard D. "The Conspiracy Theory of the Fourteenth Amendment." *Yale Law Journal*, XLVII (1938), 371–403.

Jesse, Ralph H. "Chief Justice White." *American Law Review*, XLV (1911), 321–26.

Lerner, Max. "The Supreme Court and American Capitalism." *Yale Law Journal*, XLII (1933), 668–700.

Mann, Samuel H. "Chief Justice White." *American Law Review*, LX (1926), 620–37.

Mason, Alpheus T. "Politics and the Supreme Court: President Roosevelt's Proposal." *University of Pennsylvania Law Review*, LXXXV (1937), 659–77.

Powell, Thomas R. "Coercing a State to Pay a Judgment: Virginia v. West Virginia." *Michigan Law Review*, XVII (1918), 1–18.

Ransdell, Joseph E. "Reminiscences of Edward Douglass White." *Loyola Law Journal*, VII (1926), 69–73.

"Response of the Late Chief Justice White to Toast at the Annual Banquet of the American Bar Association, at Washington, October 22, 1914." *American Bar Association Journal*, VII (1921), 341–43.

Scott, James Brown. "The Role of the Supreme Court of the United States in the Settlement of Interstate Disputes." *Georgetown Law Journal*, XV (1927), 146–63.

Other Articles

Alwes, Berthold C. "The History of the Louisiana State Lottery Company." *Louisiana Historical Quarterly*, XXVII (October, 1944), 964–1118.

Beard, Charles A. "The Constitution and States' Rights." *Virginia Quarterly Review*, XI (October, 1935), 481–95.

Buel, Clarence C. "The Degradation of a State; or, The Charitable Career of the Louisiana Lottery." *Century*, XLIII (new series XXI) (February, 1892), 618–32.

"Chief Justice White," *Nation*, CXII (June 1, 1921), 781.

Dart, Henry P. "Chief Justice White." *Louisiana Historical Quarterly*, V (April, 1922), 141–51.

Gannon, Frank S., Jr. "Edward D. White, Chief Justice, 1845–1921." *American Irish Historical Society Journal*, XIX (1920), 235–57.

Hamilton, Walton H. "The Constitution as an Instrument of Public Welfare." *American Labor Legislation Review*, XXVI (January, 1938), 103–107.

Lundberg, Ferdinand. "The Legal Profession." *Harper's Magazine*, CLXXVIII (December, 1938), 1–14.

McGloin, Frank. "Shall the Lottery's Charter Be Renewed?" *Forum*, XII (January, 1892), 555–68.

Mason, Alpheus T. "The Conservative World of Mr. Justice Sutherland, 1883–1910," *American Political Science Review*, XXXII (1938), 443–77.

"Our New Chief Justice." *Review of Reviews*, XLIII (January, 1911), 2–4.

"Passing of Two Great Americans." *Independent*, CV (June, 1911), 589–90.

"Spirit of Chief Justice White." *New Republic*, XXVII (June 1, 1921), 6–7.

Spring, Samuel. "Two Chief Justices." *Review of Reviews*, LXIV (August, 1921), 161–70.

"The New Chief Justice." *Outlook*, XCVI (December, 1910), 894–95.

Walker, A. H. "Unreasonable as Applied to Trusts: A Review of Chief Justice White's Famous Dictum." *Moody's Magazine*, XI (June, 1911), 395–400.

Wickliffe, John. "The Louisiana Lottery: A History of the Company." *Forum*, XII (January, 1892), 569–76.

Wilson, Woodrow. "The Law and the Facts." *American Political Science Review*, V (1911), 1–11.

Newspapers

Baton Rouge (La.) *Gazette*, April 24, 1847.

Brooklyn *Eagle*, February 21, 1894.

Chicago *Herald*, January 9, 1892.

Chicago *Legal News*, March 6, 1894.

Denver *News*, February 23, 1894.

Knoxville (Tenn.) *Sunday Journal*, July 7, 1929.

New Orleans *Bee*, June 6, 1843.

New Orleans *Bulletin*, September 14, 1874.

New Orleans *New-Delta*, May 12, 1892.

New Orleans *Times-Democrat*, January 9, July 18, 22, 27, 1890, January 9, 1892.

New York *Herald*, January 16, 1894.

New York *Times*, January 17, February 17, February 20, 1894, December 13, 1910, May 18, 19, 1921.

Washington (D.C.) *Evening Star*, May 19, 1921.

INDEX